D1266297

Designing Successful Target-Date Strategies for Defined Contribution Plans

Founded in 1807, John Wiley & Sons is the oldest independent publishing company in the United States. With offices in North America, Europe, Australia, and Asia, Wiley is globally committed to developing and marketing print and electronic products and services for our customers' professional and personal knowledge and understanding.

The Wiley Finance series contains books written specifically for finance and investment professionals as well as sophisticated individual investors and their financial advisors. Book topics range from portfolio management to e-commerce, risk management, financial engineering, valuation, and financial instrument analysis, as well as much more.

For a list of available titles, visit our Web site at www.WileyFinance.com.

Designing Successful Target-Date Strategies for Defined Contribution Plans

Putting Participants on the Optimal Glide Path

STACY L. SCHAUS, CFP®

WILEY

John Wiley & Sons, Inc.

Copyright © 2010 by Pacific Investment Management Company LLC. Authored by Stacy L. Schaus, CFP®. All rights reserved.

Published by John Wiley & Sons, Inc., Hoboken, New Jersey.
Published simultaneously in Canada.

No part of this publication may be reproduced, stored in a retrieval system, or transmitted in any form or by any means, electronic, mechanical, photocopying, recording, scanning, or otherwise, except as permitted under Section 107 or 108 of the 1976 United States Copyright Act, without either the prior written permission of the Publisher, or authorization through payment of the appropriate per-copy fee to the Copyright Clearance Center, Inc., 222 Rosewood Drive, Danvers, MA 01923, (978) 750-8400, fax (978) 750-4470, or on the web at www.copyright.com. Requests to the Publisher for permission should be addressed to the Permissions Department, John Wiley & Sons, Inc., 111 River Street, Hoboken, NJ 07030, (201) 748-6011, fax (201) 748-6008, or online at www.wiley.com/go/permissions.

Limit of Liability/Disclaimer of Warranty: While the publisher and author have used their best efforts in preparing this book, they make no representations or warranties with respect to the accuracy or completeness of the contents of this book and specifically disclaim any implied warranties of merchantability or fitness for a particular purpose. No warranty may be created or extended by sales representatives or written sales materials. The advice and strategies contained herein may not be suitable for your situation. You should consult with a professional where appropriate. Neither the publisher nor author shall be liable for any loss of profit or any other commercial damages, including but not limited to special, incidental, consequential, or other damages.

For general information on our other products and services or for technical support, please contact our Customer Care Department within the United States at (800) 762-2974, outside the United States at (317) 572-3993 or fax (317) 572-4002.

Wiley also publishes its books in a variety of electronic formats. Some content that appears in print may not be available in electronic books. For more information about Wiley products, visit our web site at www.wiley.com.

This publication contains information obtained from sources believed to be authentic and highly regarded. Reprinted material is used with permission, and sources are indicated. Reasonable effort has been made to publish reliable data and information, but the author and publisher cannot assume responsibility for the validity of all materials or for the consequences of their use. Certain information contained herein may be dated and no longer applicable; information was obtained from sources believed to be reliable at time of original publication, but not guaranteed. The views contained herein are the authors but not necessarily those of PIMCO. Such opinions are subject to change without notice. This publication has been distributed for educational purposes only and should not be considered as investment advice or a recommendation of any particular security, strategy or investment product.

References to specific securities and their issuers are for illustrative purposes only and are not intended and should not be interpreted as recommendations to purchase or sell such securities. The author or PIMCO may or may not own or have owned the securities referenced and, if such securities are owned, no representation is being made that such securities will continue to be held.

This material contains hypothetical illustrations and no part of this material is representative of any PIMCO product or service. Nothing contained herein is intended to constitute accounting, legal, tax, securities, or investment advice, nor an opinion regarding the appropriateness of any investment, nor a solicitation of any type. Readers should be aware that all investments carry risk and may lose value. The information contained herein should not be acted upon without obtaining specific accounting, legal, tax, and investment advice from a licensed professional.

Library of Congress Cataloging-in-Publication Data

Schaus, Stacy L., 1975–
  Designing successful target-date strategies for defined contribution plans : putting participants on the optimal glide path / Stacy L. Schaus.
      p. cm.
  Includes bibliographical references and index.
  ISBN 978-0-470-59631-9 (cloth)
  1. Defined contribution pension plans–United States.   2. Retirement income–United States–Planning.   I. Title.
  HD7105.45.U6S355 2010
  658.3'253–dc22

                                                                    2009052169

Printed in the United States of America
10 9 8 7 6 5 4 3 2 1

To John, Robert, and Julia

Contents

Foreword

So often when we talk about investing, what we really mean is trading. But providing for one's retirement is investing indeed, and awfully important investing at that, now that most Americans (and, increasingly, people elsewhere in the world) no longer receive traditional defined benefit pensions from their employers. Yet given the solemn duty most of us have to ourselves to ensure we will be able to pay our bills in our golden years, it is alarming how poorly armed we are when it comes to creating a retirement savings plan. Sure, we know that we have to "save." Most folks also probably know they are supposed to generate something like 75 percent or so of their final years' income from their retirement savings once they quit the working world. But how to go about creating that nest egg can stump even the most astute among us. The likelihood of many years of lower U.S. gross domestic product rates, a greater percentage of global growth coming from elsewhere, and more volatility everywhere in the post–financial crisis "New Normal"—and, therefore, lower portfolio returns—is not making that goal any easier to reach. And so employees must look to those they trust—defined contribution (DC) plan sponsors in particular—to put them on the path to reaching their retirement goals. Indeed, plan sponsors today have more control than ever as more of them craft custom target-date strategies for their participants.

This book is an essential resource for these important decision makers as well as their consultants, advisors, and service providers. Stacy Schaus, leader of PIMCO's DC practice, not only provides a definitive overview of trends in the American retirement system, but she also expertly guides pension plan sponsors on how to establish, refine, and maintain the most effective DC plans. Stacy's pension-industry leadership, based on nearly three decades of experience, is particularly on display in her discussion of how to design best-in-class target-date strategies that allow sponsors to effectively manage the DC assets for a diverse employee base, from the young factory employee to the near-retirement executive officer. Other issues critical to the building of custom strategies—costs, fiduciary duty, benchmarking, communication—enjoy an equally authoritative discussion. Underlying all of this is a commitment to a principle that has always motivated everything we do at PIMCO: investing for the long term and managing risk along the way.

If your job involves helping people create and sustain an acceptable standard of living in retirement, you play a role in one of this country's most important long-term goals: dignity and respect. And so I urge you to invest in the ideas and expertise found in this book.

William H. Gross
PIMCO Founder and Co-Chief Investment Officer

Introduction

Defined contribution (DC) plans have rapidly become the primary source of retirement income for the majority of workers in the United States. For most workers to meet their retirement-income goals, two key requirements must be met: They need to participate in DC plans at the appropriate savings level, and the plans must be managed well. Since the inception of the 401(k) plan in 1981, plan design has continually evolved to improve the success of these plans. Fueled in large part by the Pension Protection Act (PPA) of 2006, which supports automatic or default plan features to increase participation, contribution rates, and asset diversification, advancements in DC plan design have accelerated. Among the greatest advancements in DC plan design is the development of custom target-date strategies.

Importantly, the PPA helped drive the growth of an innovative investment strategy that automatically modifies plan participants' asset allocation as they age, an investment approach referred to as "target retirement-date" or "life cycle" strategies. Target retirement-date strategies were blessed by the Department of Labor (DOL) as a Qualified Default Investment Alternative (QDIA), supporting plan sponsor decisions to automatically invest DC savings into this type of investment without explicit permission from participants. Today, target retirement-date strategies have become the primary investment default for DC plans. As a result, they have been growing rapidly in both prevalence and assets.

In many ways, target-date strategies have revolutionized DC plan investing. Rather than offer a lineup of investment choices from which plan sponsors hope participants will select wisely, sponsors can instead hire investment professionals to manage the asset mix for the participants, thus opening the door for more complex and sophisticated investment management. Target-date strategies not only offer the surface-level simplicity that participants desire but also the behind-the-scenes complexity to manage money using the most advanced institutional techniques and asset classes. Even though the first generation of these types of strategies has been criticized by the government and the marketplace, particularly for investment losses experienced by those nearing retirement in 2008, there is no doubt that this investment approach will continue to grow as a mainstay in DC plans. What is more, given the failure of many participants to actively modify their asset allocations as they approach retirement, some DC experts predict that over the next decade, investment in target-date strategies may capture upward of 60 percent of total DC plan assets.

The structure and management of these types of strategies warrant careful consideration. Most plan sponsors are no longer considering whether target retirement-date strategies make sense for their plans but rather how they can gain more control over what has rapidly become the most critical investment option in their plan. In essence, the target-date strategy choice will largely determine a plan participant's ability to retire successfully. Plan sponsors know they need to make the right choice. Given the weight of this decision, more plan sponsors are looking to acquire increased control over the target-date investment options. They are seeking the ability to design an asset-allocation structure that fits their demographics as well as a way to control the lineup of underlying best-in-class investment managers and to drive down fees over time. Their desire for more control over this critical investment choice has driven the evolution of open architecture or custom target-date strategies.

This book is designed to help plan sponsors and their consultants as they consider how to create their own custom target retirement-date strategies. It is divided into four parts that take a close look at the ways in which DC plans are evolving and the relevant trends in plan design. Part 1: DC Plan Evolution and Design Trends begins with a look at how DC fits into the American retirement system, offering insights from individuals who represent our nation's retirement leaders, such as Dallas Salisbury of the Employee Benefit Research Institute, David Wray of the Profit Sharing/401(k) Council of America, and Anna Rappaport, President of Anna Rappaport Consulting and Chairperson of the Society of Actuaries Committee on Post-Retirement Needs and Risks, whose valuable research highlights the increasing role of DC plans. This part then turns to DC plan investment structures, sharing how the range of investments has been modified over time. It also provides research and insights from record keepers and investment consultants, such as Pamela Hess of Hewitt Associates and Ross Bremen of NEPC. It concludes with a discussion of why plan sponsors are showing an interest in using a custom approach and an examination of the pros and cons of an open architecture approach versus buying an off-the-shelf target-date product.

Part 2: Development of Custom Target-Date Retirement Strategies outlines how to set up these custom strategies, starting with a discussion of legal and fiduciary issues with Marla Kreindler and Julie Stapel of Winston & Strawn LLP. It then shares in-depth alternatives to setting up custom strategies with plan record keepers and trustees, presenting insights from consultants such as Matt Rice of DiMeo Schneider & Associates, LLC and plan setup details from Tom Eichenberger of State Street Corporation and Marianne Sullivan of ING Retirement Services. This part also presents solutions for communication issues that arise when sponsors are trying to help plan participants understand target-date strategies. Mary Beth Glotzbach of Morningstar, Inc. and Barb Hogg of Hewitt Associates discuss how to approach these communication issues, including how to apply behavioral finance for better outcomes as well as the basics of designing fund fact sheets and positioning of the strategies on the Web. This part also includes a discussion with Lori Lucas of Callan Associates and others on the costs associated with the setup and ongoing operation of custom target strategies.

Part 3: Designing and Benchmarking Custom Target-Date Strategies delves into the heart of this topic, sharing the many philosophies of asset allocation and glide-path design. It provides insights on glide-path structure from Mark Ruloff of Towers Watson and Thomas Idzorek of Ibbotson Associates as well as from a range of plan sponsors, including Georgette Gestely of the New York City Deferred Compensation Program, Barbara Kontje of American Express, Dan Holupchinski of Deluxe Corporation, and others. This part also features an in-depth examination of the range of asset classes, including traditional assets, such as stocks and bonds, as well as nontraditional assets, such as real estate and commodities. Most importantly, Part 3 shares strategies that show plan sponsors how better to protect DC assets in various economic environments, including market shocks and periods of significant inflation. Stuart Odell of Intel Corporation, Michael Riak of Verizon, and David Fisser of Southwest Airlines Pilots' Association, among others, discuss this important topic. Finally, this part lays out the many approaches to benchmarking target date strategies, at both the glide-path and the asset level. Experts such as Mike Henkel of Envestnet Asset Management and Phil Suess of Mercer Investment Consulting consider market indices, peer group ranking, and other benchmarking approaches.

Plan sponsors who prefer to offer other custom strategies, such as target-risk, will still find this book valuable, as many of these issues are the same as target-date options. Further, even plan sponsors who choose to offer packaged off-the-shelf target-date strategies will undoubtedly find this book helpful as they evaluate products in the market or benchmark the selection they have already made for their plan.

SPEARHEADING THE NEED FOR MORE INFORMATION

For years, we at PIMCO have been dedicated to helping our clients and the consulting community build more successful DC plans, including examining the questions and issues facing plan sponsors regarding custom target retirement-date strategies. In our monthly *PIMCO DC Dialogue*™ series, we have interviewed dozens of retirement leaders and innovators including consultants, academics, lawyers, financial advisors, not-for-profit chief executives, and, most important, plan sponsors from both the private and the public sectors. Working together with this community of dedicated professionals, we aim to improve retirement security for American workers. These individuals have generously allowed their comments and observations garnered in the *PIMCO DC Dialogue*s to be a part of this book.

In the spring of 2008 and 2009, PIMCO joined Pensions and Investments in hosting a series of custom target retirement-date strategy summits where keynote speakers and panelists addressed plan sponsors, consultants, and the investment management community across the country in San Francisco, Dallas, Chicago, and New York City. In this book, we share insights and leading-edge research as well as investment strategies from a wide variety of individuals who generously participated in these summits. We also owe a debt of gratitude to the professionals at AllianceBernstein Investments, BlackRock, Inc., Capital Guardian Trust Company, Wellington Management, and UBS Global Asset Management, who also joined us in hosting this important summit series.

At PIMCO, we also have conducted several DC Consultant Surveys as well as a DC Recordkeeping Survey, all of which aim to help our clients select consultants and record keepers who can support their desired plan design. In 2008 we were delighted to have 32 consulting firms representing over $1.5 trillion in DC assets participate in our consulting survey. In addition, 30 record-keeping organizations administering combined assets of $1.6 trillion shared details about the support they offered. The data and observations from these surveys are cited in several parts of this book.

In addition, we write extensive retirement and investment papers, including our *PIMCO DC Research*, *DC Analytics*, and *Viewpoint* series. Research and observations from these series is also woven into the various parts of this book. Yet it is important to emphasize that this book does not focus only on the philosophies or investment suggestions of those at PIMCO. Rather, it provides an overview of various perspectives from across the industry. To provide objectivity and balance, each chapter of the book has been reviewed and edited by professionals across the country.

WHY ARE COMPANIES TURNING TO CUSTOM TARGET-DATE STRATEGIES?

Four key reasons have been cited for why companies are creating their own custom target-date for their DC lineup:

> **Reason 1. Control of asset management.** Custom target-date strategies enable companies to design their asset allocation or glide path (i.e., how the asset allocation changes as a participant approaches

retirement age, generally becoming more conservative over time) and select their asset classes, leverage the core investment options offered within the plan, and retain the ability to modify their strategies over time. Custom strategies also give them the ability to hire and fire the underlying plan managers, just as they always have been able to do, within both their DC and defined benefit plans.

Reason 2. Fee reduction is another driver toward customization. Fees often are driven down by leveraging both core DC investment offerings and defined-benefit assets, as well as by using lower-cost investment structures (i.e., separately managed accounts, collective investment trusts, and institutionally priced mutual funds).

Reason 3. Companies want greater ease of communication with plan participants, which custom strategies help facilitate. Since the strategies are comprised of allocations to the core investment offerings in the plan, communication of the strategies to plan participants is relatively straightforward.

Reason 4. Companies want fiduciary oversight and transparency. Often plan sponsors think, "Well, if I'm outside of a prepackaged product and I create my own custom mix, I may be subjecting my firm to greater liability." With target-date strategies, you can not only protect your firm but also achieve the greatest level of transparency into the investments and more.

Many consulting firms are already supporting companies interested in creating custom strategies. In fact, in a recent PIMCO survey we found that the majority of firms are willing to provide this type of support. Over three-quarters of them provide glide-path creation. The majority will act as a fiduciary while nearly half will assume responsibility as a discretionary investment manager. The decision to hire a consultant or someone else in the capacity of the fiduciary and investment manager of its target-date strategies can place an organization on equal if not stronger footing with companies that are using packaged target-date mutual funds. This is especially the case when the overall package is simply a better investment product, offering greater control, lower fees, best-in-class managers, and transparency.

In terms of creating custom strategies, 27 percent of consulting clients are offering custom asset-allocation strategies. While many of the largest organizations in the world offer custom strategies, an organization is not required to have large plan assets to enjoy the advantages of this type of strategy. In fact, even plans as small as $1 million are using custom target-date strategies. For the most part, whether an organization can set up target dates depends largely on the support provided by the plan's record keeper.

KEY ISSUES INVOLVED IN OFFERING CUSTOM STRATEGIES

There are certain reasons why organizations may hesitate as they consider whether they should offer a custom strategy. According to the consultants we queried, here are the six key concerns expressed by plan sponsors.

1. **Operational setup.** Many companies are concerned about how difficult it may be to set up custom strategies. How much time it will take? Who is responsible for what?
2. **Asset allocation and oversight.** Another key issue involves the question of who is going to create the glide path and who will be responsible for overseeing it over time.
3. **Asset size.** Some plan sponsors may question whether their plan is large enough to make custom strategies viable.
4. **Liability.** Others may worry who will be liable for the investment structure if the target-date strategies do not perform well.
5. **Time.** Many are concerned with how much time it will take to implement the strategies and whether they have the resources to dedicate to this project.
6. **Communication issues.** Plan sponsors may have many questions about how to communicate the new strategies to participants.

This book addresses all of these issues and more by drawing on recent research as well as the expertise of experienced retirement leaders and innovators across the country.

Custom target retirement-date strategies make sense for many plan sponsors, especially from the standpoint of plan cost and investment management control. As assets grow in these strategies, the approach becomes even more critical. While custom strategies are new in some ways, the methods of supporting both operational needs and communications between plan sponsor and participant are not. For decades DC plans have created blended manager options and ably communicated these investment blends to participants. If you are interested in this investment approach, this book should be of great assistance to you. Its goal is not only to help you understand the value of custom strategies but also to provide expert guidance through the setup and ongoing monitoring of these important strategies. This book provides the support you need and suggests resources to help make custom strategies a reality in your plan. Most important, the support provided will help you create a more optimal DC plan with a greater promise of delivering retirement security for your workers.

Acknowledgments

The inspiration for this book came from the plan sponsor community, including those who have established custom target-date strategies as well as the many who are considering setting them up and wanted all of the in-depth details. In 2006, we wrote a research paper entitled "A Sensible Approach to Custom Target Retirement-Date Strategies," which was our first attempt to bring together experts to answer the many questions raised about establishing these types of strategies. Since that time, we have also written numerous *PIMCO DC Dialogue* pieces that have addressed a broad range of defined-contribution plan design topics, including custom target strategies. This book brings together the ideas of the many experts who contributed to the initial research paper, the *Dialogue*s and summits, as well as others who have written independently on DC design or related issues.

Many people have contributed significantly to the creation of this book. Joy Parker, my collaborator and editor, encouraged the pursuit of this project and then worked with me tirelessly over the last year to make it a reality. Joy has done an outstanding job as the editor of our *Dialogue*s for years, so her understanding of the issues and concerns shared in those pieces helped tremendously as she helped bring each chapter of this book to life. Summer intern Charlie Leisure, a bright student attending Georgetown University, helped lay out the chapters and identified the relevant content from three years of *Dialogue*s and research papers.

My deepest appreciation is extended to the plan sponsors who have pioneered and led the way for others in creating custom strategies and have spent many, many hours of their time sharing the details via *Dialogue*s, summits, and other forums. These plan sponsors include Karen Barnes at McDonald's® Corporation, Charles Claudio at Ahold USA, Inc., David Fisser with Southwest Airlines Pilots' Association, Georgette Gestely with New York City Deferred Compensation Program, Dan Holupchinski at Deluxe Corporation, Barbara Kontje with American Express, John LaCara (formerly the director of the Commonwealth of Massachusetts Deferred Compensation Program), Charlene Mims at Dole Foods Company, Stuart Odell with Intel Corporation, and Michael Riak with Verizon.

In addition, each chapter of this book brought together many experts, including a few who provided an in-depth review of the content. Special appreciation goes to David Wray, president of the Profit Sharing/401(k) Council of America, for endless data, review of material, and passionate support of DC plans; Dallas Salisbury, president and chief executive of the Employee Benefit Research Institute for research and insights; and Pamela Hess, director of retirement research at Hewitt Associates. I also wish to thank the many others at Hewitt who provided invaluable input: Director of Retirement Communication Barb Hogg; DC Leadership Director Curt Young; and Mike Dubois, Jim McGhee (retired target-date operations expert), and Lisa Horuczi Markus (formerly of Hewitt) for providing survey data and careful review of the plan design, communication, operations, and advice chapters. I am also grateful to Matthew Rice, principal and chief research officer of DiMeo Schneider & Associates, LLC, as well as Thomas Eichenberger of State Street Corporation and Marianne Sullivan of ING Retirement Services for providing a foundation for and review of the record-keeping and trust chapter; Mary Beth Glotzbach at Morningstar, Inc. for review and content support of the communication chapter; Marla Kreindler and Julie Stapel at Winston & Strawn LLP for the review of the legal chapter and their input on several other parts of the book; Lori Lucas, DC practice leader at Callan Associates, for many helpful studies, suggestions, and chapter reviews, in particular, of the chapter on evaluating costs; Thomas Idzorek, chief investment officer at Ibbotson Associates, Mark Ruloff, director of asset allocation at Towers Watson, Joseph Simonian, DC analytics leader at PIMCO, and Somnath Basu, professor at California Lutheran University, for contributing to content, analytics and review of the glide-path chapter; Ross Bremen and Rob Fishman, partners at NEPC, Rob Arnott, chairman of Research Affiliates, LLC, and Deena Katz, associate professor at Texas Tech University, for their help with asset classes and alternatives.

Additionally, I wish to thank Zvi Bodie, professor at Boston University, and Anna Rappaport, chairperson of the Society of Actuaries Committee on Post-Retirement Needs and Risks (among many other roles), for their wisdom, counsel, and insights on helping to protect participant assets. Thanks also to Mike Henkel, managing director at Envestnet Asset Management; Matt Ketchum, director at UBS Global Asset Management; Josh Cohen, senior consultant at Russell Investment Group; and Kamila Kowalke, formerly at Dow Jones Indexes, for their addition to content as well as their review of the benchmarking chapter; to Marv Tuttle, CEO , along with Lauren Schadle and Lance Richlin of the Financial Planning Association, for their inspiration, addition to content, and review of the advice and retirement planning material. Finally, I wish to thank Chris Raham, senior actuarial advisor at Ernst &Young, Jody Strakosch, national director at MetLife, Kelli Hueler,

CEO of Hueler Companies, and Tom Streiff, retirement income leader at PIMCO, for their contributions and review of the final chapter on retirement income and guarantees.

Others to whom I am grateful for their contribution to this book include James Delaplane, Jr., partner at Davis & Harman, LLP, for his insights on the legislative landscape; Kurt Walten, senior vice president at the National Association of Real Estate Investment Trusts, Inc., for contributions to the real estate content; economic thought leaders and professors Richard Thaler at the University of Chicago, Shlomo Benartzi at UCLA, Sheena Iyengar at Columbia University, Jodi DiCenzo at Behavior Research Associates, LLC, Olivia S. Mitchell at the Wharton School of the University of Pennsylvania, and Paul Solman at the PBS NewsHour and Yale University, for their writings, research, and insights. I also wish to express my thanks to many in the consulting and advisory community for their contribution to content and thought leadership, including Kevin Vandolder, principal at Ennis, Knupp & Associates; Norman Boone, president of Mosaic Financial Partners, Inc.; Peter Grant, consultant at Towers Watson; Phil Enochs at Russell Investment Group; Phil Suess at Mercer Investment Consulting; Roger Williams, managing director at Rogerscasey; Steve Charlton, partner at NEPC; Charles Stunkard and Matt Radgowski at Wilshire Associates; and Susan Bradley, CEO of Sudden Money Institute.

I also extend a debt of gratitude to PIMCO leadership, including Tom Otterbein and John Miller, for their support of this project. As well as to others on our excellent professional team at PIMCO who individually invested time and energy, including adding to content, editing, designing, and listening to me talk endlessly about this project:

Chistopher Abram
Candi Barbour
Greg Bishop
John Cavalieri
Audrey Cheng
Eugene Colter
Bret Estep
Steve Ferber
Kevin Forhane
Jana Fox
Ying Gao
Zoya Graves

Bob Greer

Jessie Lombardi

Erika Magaña

Suzanne Oden

Mark Olsen

Mark Porterfield

Marianne Shaver

Doug Schwab

Christina Stauffer

Tom Streiff

Joseph Yeon

Den Pestarino

While I cannot name every person, I would like to thank all of the professionals who participated in the Pensions & Investments Target Date Summits as well as those at P&I, including publisher Chris Battaglia, for their support of these important programs. Chris's encouragement of this project led to my introduction to literary agent Cynthia Manson and the interest in the book by John Wiley & Sons. Further, a large thank-you to David Pugh, Natasha Andrews-Noel, Emilie Herman, Tiffany Charbonier and others at John Wiley & Sons for editing and publishing this book.

Finally, my heartfelt thanks go to my family for the patience and support of this project, especially the many late nights and weekend hours that could have been spent with them.

PART One

DC Plan Evolution and Design Trends

CHAPTER 1

DC Plans in the American Retirement System

S omeone once called defined contribution (DC) plans one of the "great social experiments of our time." For many people, a DC plan is the *only* company-sponsored retirement plan they have, and for this reason, plan effectiveness needs to be more than merely an "experiment." People need these plans to function because most will depend on them to provide adequate retirement income. The plans should also be designed to realistically take into account factors such as inflation.

When we refer to DC as a social "experiment," we should recognize that "scientists" in the retirement-plan field have made significant contributions to the status of DC plans today. Two behavioral economists who have done so are Professor Richard Thaler from the University of Chicago and Professor Shlomo Benartzi of the University of California at Los Angeles. Perhaps their greatest DC contribution has been to support automatic programs within the Pension Protection Act (PPA). Working from the premise that inertia is one of the most powerful forces of nature, employee auto-enrollment, auto-contribution escalation, and auto-asset allocation all work together to help put Americans in a better position to retire more successfully.

We need to find better ways to make these retirement plans succeed. What is more, *each* participant must succeed in a retirement plan *individually*. In other words, it is not good enough for a group of employees to reach their retirement-income goals *on average*.

Some people will resort to anything to find a creative solution to retirement planning. We saw an extreme example in the 2007 *New York Times* article "A Financial Plan that Comes with Mug Shots."[1] The story involved "financial visionary" Timothy Bowers, who solved his retirement income shortfall by robbing a bank and immediately handing himself over to the police. Bowers figured that if he were sentenced to a minimum-security prison with "quality programming for an aging offender population" and remained in jail until Social Security and Medicare kicked in, he would be able to meet his retirement-income goal.

Few of us are desperate enough to go to that length. However, this story underscores the need for our retirement plans to succeed, again, not just for most people but for everyone individually. That is why we produced this book, covering key issues in today's retirement field. To gather a wide variety of experienced commentary on these issues, in 2006 we started the monthly *PIMCO DC Dialogue* series in which we interview various retirement experts, including consultants, academics, plan sponsors, financial advisors, attorneys, and others. This book discusses a number of points from conversations with them and covers key questions and proposed solutions discussed at the *Pensions & Investments* Custom Target-Date Summits held in both 2008 and 2009.

EVOLUTION OF DB AND DC PLANS

To see where you are going more clearly, it is helpful to understand where you are coming from. For that reason, we asked David Wray, president of the Profit Sharing/401(k) Council of America (PSCA), to share some historical background about the evolution of DC plans in America. Wray explained that while most people think that DC plans began with the invention of the 401(k) plan, the plans actually got their start in the late 1800s with the implementation of company profit sharing plans for employers "to build partnership in the workplace and manage labor relations."[2]

Procter & Gamble led the way with this type of plan in 1887, but then found that employees were spending the money instead of using it as a financial reserve or as money that could go toward their retirement. So in 1904, "to encourage saving, P&G introduced a stock-purchase and matching program in which they would match contributions made by the employee, with an additional amount based on the profitability of the company." This, Wray noted, was the genesis of company matching.

Then the Revenue Act of 1921 initiated tax advantages for employment-based retirement plans, allowing plan contributions to be tax free until the employee withdrew funds from the retirement account. "This law established the value of the DC plan from a tax perspective," Wray explained, "which remains the real advantage of these plans today."

These early DC plans flourished in the early part of the twentieth century, but when so many companies were forced out of business during the Great Depression, only about 300 plans remained at the beginning of the

1940s. However, World War II marked a rebirth of retirement plans and employee benefits. As Wray noted:

> *At the time, wages were frozen but there were no government limits on benefit plans. Competing for high-quality—and now scarce— workers, companies improved their benefit plans and started offering both health insurance and retirement programs. There was an increase in both traditional defined benefit plans, with which most people are familiar, as well as DC programs.*
>
> *By the 1950s, the DC system had grown and evolved into three kinds of tax-advantaged plans:* pure profit-sharing plans *where the employer contributed the entire amount;* cash and deferred profit-sharing plans *in which companies allocated a profit-sharing bonus to the employee, who could take all or part of it in cash or defer all or part of it into a profit-sharing trust; and* thrift savings profit-sharing plans, *into which the employee contributed a certain amount of his or her income on an after-tax basis and could receive a tax-deferred employer matching contribution.*

The year 1974 saw the creation of the Employee Retirement Income Security Act (ERISA), which focused on defined benefit (DB) funding issues, but also impacted DC programs. "Unfortunately," Wray pointed out, "ERISA failed to authorize the continuation of cash and deferred profit-sharing plans and, as a result, no new plans were formed and some companies withheld contributions waiting for a clarification."

Recognizing that there were at least 1,000 of these plans and that they "were excellent programs for workers to build retirement savings, as well as for companies to build a positive partnership in the workplace," legislation was passed in 1978 to change the tax code and correct this oversight. However, the language inadvertently went further, opening the door "to a new type of deferred compensation savings plan, the 401(k).... For the first time, workers were allowed to save not only bonus dollars, but also regular wages on a tax-deferred basis." Following further clarification by the IRS in 1981, the modern 401(k) plan was born.

In 1982, Wray explained, when companies began to allow "employees who were already making after-tax contributions to the plan to make their contributions on a tax-deferred basis...the 401(k) then took off like wildfire. Within years, literally millions of people were participating in these programs."

This full-speed-ahead rush to save a significant amount of tax-deferred wages in these plans was not to last. Concerned about lost tax revenues, Washington and the Internal Revenue Service (IRS) first tried to repeal the law but, with the Tax Reform Act in 1986, succeeded only in adding "onerous discrimination tests" and putting a cap on how much employees could contribute annually to a 401(k) plan. "This change in legislation," Wray explained, "led to the termination of most cash and deferred profit-sharing plans, as the new government restrictions made them impractical."

The great irony of this legislation is that Section 401(k) was intended to reinstate cash and deferred profit-sharing plans, but the government's revenue concerns regarding the potential success of 401(k) led to changes that killed cash and deferred profit-sharing plans.

When we asked Wray if he agreed with the general consensus that the Pension Protection Act of 2006 had caused many companies to close or freeze their defined benefit plans more rapidly, he agreed. He also concurred with us that, with so few companies now offering DB plans to workers, 401(k) and other DC plans are more important than ever and are currently undergoing a complete transition. "While they were created initially for profit sharing," Wray explained, "today the employee deferral using the 401(k) has become the predominant form of DC plan. More companies every year are adding the opportunity to save in a 401(k) plan, even those that already offer very rich profit-sharing plans. We're approaching 50 million actively employed workers who have a balance in a 401(k) plan and 60 million in DC overall." Wray is confident that the DC system will continue to grow in the coming decades.

MAKING THE MOVE FROM A DB PLAN TO A DC PLAN

We asked a variety of experts and plan sponsors to comment on how switching from DB plans to DC had changed the face of retirement. Deena Katz, associate professor at Texas Tech University, Personal Financial Planning Division, speaks about how having more than one choice in terms of retirement accounts has changed the way that they communicate with clients regarding their responsibilities. Almost 30 years ago, Katz related, when she first began in the retirement-planning field, there were DB plans "that could take care of a good percentage of a person's retirement-income needs."[3] Some of the plans even included cost-of-living adjustments to help clients keep up with inflation. "Many of us," Katz remarked, "grew up with a three-legged retirement-income stool composed of our DB plan, our own investments including defined contribution, and Social Security. Today, the truth is, we don't know where Social Security is headed. And our company-provided retirement benefits are typically limited to DC." Even in the many cases where DC plans offer a company match, plan participants are still responsible for deciding how much of their salary goes into those plans. "In essence, today we have a two-legged stool that tells us we're on our own in terms of investing for our future. As advisers, we need to help people understand that they must rely on themselves and how to plan, given the available programs and other resources."

However, Tom Idzorek, the chief investment officer at Ibbotson Associates, points out that the shift to DC as the primary retirement vehicle

> *doesn't necessarily reduce plan sponsors' responsibilities as they pertain to creating the best possible plan. Ultimately, as fiduciaries, plan sponsors still want to create a good lineup of options that enable employees to create their own diversified portfolios to meet their participant needs. In addition to designing a good lineup of single-asset-class fund options, these days we also see more plan sponsors adding a do-it-for-me option—either a target-date, target-risk, or perhaps a managed-account option.[4]*

Charlene Mims, vice president of benefits, HRIS and payroll at Dole Food Company, Inc. is creatively looking at the needs of the company's workforce, exploring a somewhat DB-like approach to the DC plan: "Basically we're exploring two directions. One is to give people an additional DC contribution based on years of service. A second is to offer a minimum or floor payout, again, based on years of service."[5] She feels that this somewhat "1970s approach" helps Dole to both attract and retain employees. Since over 50 percent of its workforce will be over the age of 55 within the next three to five years, this payout approach is a benefit that older employees who are nearing retirement find highly attractive.

David Wray of PSCA concurs that there is no such thing as a one-size-fits-all solution and that looking at the unique needs of the population is important in designing the DC plan. "I'd suggest the plan sponsor take a hard look at its workforce and what it's trying to accomplish. Often when companies transition from a DB to a DC-only system, they find very low DC participation. In this case, companies look for ways to make their DC arrangements more successful."[6]

Wray is looking for creative ways to achieve greater plan participation. One approach is auto-enrollment, not only of new hires but of current employees who are not participating. He explains: "While an educational process can work in some cases to raise participation, if you need to really jump-start the system and bring it up to a high level of participation right away, automatic enrollment makes a lot of sense. Auto-enrollment has gained ground rapidly, especially with the recent government support and incentives to add the feature to plans."

Wray also feels that adding "a hybrid, profit-sharing or other employer-funded program in which all employees are participants even if they don't make elective contributions like in a 401(k)" is a good strategy. "The idea ... is for everyone who works at your company to have an account that accumulates money for retirement. There are a lot of different ways to do that. The advantage of the DC system is that you can have a single plan with all these features integrated into it."

Mark Ruloff, the director of Asset Allocation at Towers Watson, points out that while DB plans continue to be "a key component of retirement security, we see them playing less of a role than in the past."[7] Now DC plans are the primary source of most workers' retirement income, and he notes that recent changes under the PPA have given employers the ability to improve asset allocation and increase participant's savings rates via automatic programs. These default strategies play an important role in an individual's ability to retire. However, like Wray, he does not believe in one-size-fits-all retirement solutions.

> *When we looked at the different types of target-date funds, we discovered that there's no silver bullet that solves all problems. In working with plan sponsors, we encourage participants to save more and to use an appropriate investment approach. Employers need to educate people to save more rather than simply rely on investment performance to deliver the retirement income that they need in the future. As we know, target-date strategies are garnering a lot of attention and assets. We hope that these asset-allocation strategies, combined with higher savings rates, will help participants better meet their retirement income needs.*

HOW DO WE MEASURE DC PLAN SUCCESS?

With all this in mind, it is important to look in more detail at how DC plan objectives have changed in recent years and how plan sponsors are defining "success." Because, as we discussed, plan sponsors now rarely offer a defined benefit plan, creating an effective employee DC plan has become the primary issue. During this transition, the DC plan objective has shifted from wealth accumulation to creating adequate and sustainable retirement income for all participants.

Today only 21 percent of U.S. private workers participate in a DB plan; given this reality, most plan sponsors—about 64 percent—view their DC plans as the primary company-sponsored retirement-savings vehicle.[8] Given this shift, it is important for plan objectives to change.

In one of our first *DC Dialogues*, we asked Josh Cohen, CFA, and Phil Enochs, CFA, of the Russell Investment Group, "How can a company measure its DC plan success?" Their answer: "A company should examine the retirement income-replacement ratio, a percentage of the pre-retirement income replaced by the accumulated DC savings."[9] They suggested that plan sponsors—especially those that use DC as primary retirement-savings vehicle—should evaluate the realistic likelihood that a plan will provide a sufficient level of income throughout retirement.

When we asked if there was a specific retirement-income replacement ratio that the DC plan should aim for, they said:

Financial advisors often suggest that a participant save enough to replace somewhere between 70 and 100 percent of pre-retirement income to enjoy the same standard of living after retirement. In the past, income replacement came from four primary sources: DC plans, DB plans, Social Security, and private savings. Today, a larger portion of that income needs to come from the DC plan.

Dallas Salisbury, leader of the Employee Benefit Research Institute, concured that "most individuals should plan to replace approximately 70 percent of their incomes, on top of Social Security."[10] He suggested that plan participants save 15 to 20 percent of their salaries throughout their careers to help them reach this figure. Clearly the amount needed will be impacted by the number of years the person saves, their retirement age and income needs, market performance, inflation, and other factors.

Cohen and Enochs also pointed out that what was considered an appropriate retirement-income-replacement ratio varied with each individual and his or her particular lifestyle preference. "Life expectancy, which continues to grow longer, and healthcare costs, determined by overall health, affects the percentage to a large degree as well."[11]

Consequently we asked, "Can a DC plan actually provide the same income level as a DB plan?" Cohen and Enochs replied, "Yes, so long as (1) people participate, (2) each person contributes a sufficient amount, (3) the company allocates each contributor's assets across diverse classes, and (4) the plan uses institutional investment vehicles to tap into lower fees."

Currently, we are in a strong position to create successful DC plans. Because of the Pension Protection Act, legislation now supports much of what Cohen and Enochs say about successful DC plan requirements.

In a *DC Dialogue,* we asked Marla Kreindler, a partner at the legal firm of Winston & Strawn, to discuss how the PPA impacted the design of retirement plans and paved the way to DC plans. Here are her main points, in summary:[12]

- The PPA cements the transition from DB plans to DC plans.
- It allows plan sponsors to add auto-enrollment to their plans easily by creating a "safe harbor" from fiduciary responsibility for auto-contribution arrangements.
- For plan sponsors that use Qualified Default Investment Alternatives (QDIA), it also provides a safe harbor from fiduciary responsibility.
- The auto-enrollment provision allows plan sponsors to transition from a wait-and-see position to more actively enrolling their participants in the QDIA.
- The PPA requires automatic escalation of contributions by plan sponsors. Auto-escalation must start from a 3 percent rate and go up by 1 percent a year to 6 percent. At that point, the plan sponsor can then choose to continue the automatic escalation all the way up to 10 percent.
- Firms that offer DC-bundled services, such as Fidelity, Vanguard, and the like, can now offer investment advice to their DC clients rather than use a third party.

In short, plan sponsors can now auto-enroll employees, auto-escalate contributions, and default to professionally managed asset allocations. What is more, many plans are moving in this direction already. In fact, 40 percent of companies already have auto-enrollment; this includes 56 percent of plans with 5,000+ participants that offer auto-enrollment, while only 16 percent of plans under 50 participants make it available.[13] The same is true for contribution escalation: 36 percent of firms have it, and others are likely to add it in the future. As for the default fund, 60 percent offer target date, 18 percent offer target risk, and 3 percent use professionally managed accounts. Target-date strategies should grow rapidly in prevalence as more plan sponsors seek to have participants' assets managed for them over a set time horizon. Since participants often ignore the investment mixes of their DC plans, offering investment solutions that reallocate for people as they age is becoming more popular.

WHAT IS A QUALIFIED DEFAULT INVESTMENT ALTERNATIVE?

As summarized in a Department of Labor (DOL) fact sheet, the PPA directed the department to issue a regulation to assist employers in selecting default investments that best serve the retirement needs of workers who do not direct their own investments. The final regulation provides these conditions that must be satisfied in order to obtain safe harbor relief from fiduciary liability for investment outcomes:

- Assets must be invested in a "qualified default investment alternative" (QDIA) as defined in the regulation.
- Participants and beneficiaries must have been given an opportunity to provide investment direction, but have not done so.
- A notice generally must be furnished to participants and beneficiaries in advance of the first investment in the QDIA and annually thereafter. The rule describes the information that must be included in the notice.
- Material, such as investment prospectuses, provided to the plan for the QDIA must be furnished to participants and beneficiaries.
- Participants and beneficiaries must have the opportunity to direct investments out of a QDIA as frequently as from other plan investments, but at least quarterly.
- The rule limits the fees that can be imposed on participants who opt out of participation in the plan or who decide to direct their investments.
- The plan must offer a "broad range of investment alternatives" as defined in the DOL's regulation under Section 404(c) of ERISA.

The final regulation does not absolve fiduciaries of the duty to prudently select and monitor QDIAs.

Qualified Default Investment Alternatives

The final regulation does not identify specific investment products; rather, it describes mechanisms for investing participant contributions. The intent is to ensure that an investment qualifying as a QDIA is appropriate as a single investment capable of meeting a worker's long-term retirement savings needs. The final regulation identifies two individually based mechanisms and one group-based mechanism; it also provides for a short-term investment for administrative convenience.

The final regulation provides for four types of QDIAs:

1. A product with a mix of investments that takes into account the individual's age or retirement date (e.g., a life-cycle or targeted-retirement-date fund)
2. An investment service that allocates contributions among existing plan options to provide an asset mix that takes into account the individual's age or retirement date (e.g., a professionally managed account)

3. A product with a mix of investments that takes into account the characteristics of the group of employees as a whole rather than each individual (e.g., a balanced fund)
4. A capital preservation product for only the first 120 days of participation (an option for plan sponsors wishing to simplify administration if workers opt out of participation before incurring an additional tax)

A QDIA must be managed by an investment manager, a plan trustee, a plan sponsor, or a committee comprised primarily of employees of the plan sponsor that is a named fiduciary, or be an investment company registered under the Investment Company Act of 1940.

A QDIA generally may not invest participant contributions in employer securities.

Other Significant QDIA Provisions

Recognizing that some plan sponsors adopted stable value products as their default investment prior to passage of the Pension Protection Act and this final Qualified Default Investment Alternative regulation, the regulation provides a transition rule. The regulation grandfathers these arrangements by providing relief for contributions invested in stable value products prior to the effective date of the final rule. The transition rule does not provide relief for future contributions to stable value products.

The final regulation clarifies that a QDIA may be offered through variable annuity contracts or other pooled investment funds.

The rule provides that ERISA supersedes any state law that would prohibit or restrict automatic contribution arrangements, regardless of whether such automatic contribution arrangements qualify for the safe harbor.

A summary of the legislation has been developed by the DOL. A copy of the QDIA regulation is available on the DOL's Web site at www.dol.gov/ebsa under "Laws and Regulations." We return to a broader discussion of safe harbors and legal issues in Chapter 4.

Understand Qualified Default Investment Alternatives

To help in our discussion of how to create a successful DC plan, it is important to clarify relevant terminology, as many different terms are used to describe various types of diversified investment strategies in DC plans. Over the last 25 years, we have seen the DC investment lineup evolve from plans offering a single balanced strategy, to those providing a set of target-risk strategies, to today's target retirement-date strategies. (Please note that the

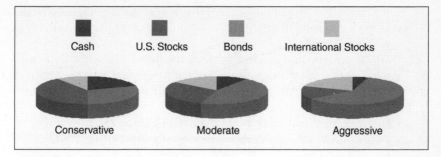

FIGURE 1.1 Sample Target Risk Strategies
Source: PIMCO. Hypothetical example for illustrative purposes only.

term "strategy" or "option" is used more frequently throughout this book than "fund," as a plan sponsor can create the asset-allocation options within its plan without the need to establish a fund as a separate legal entity and without registering the option as an investment company or "mutual fund" with the Securities and Exchange Commission.)

You can think of a balanced strategy as a single option, which is typically a blend of equity and fixed-income assets (e.g., 60 percent Standard & Poor's 500 and 40 percent Barclay's Capital Aggregate). By comparison, think of target strategies as a series of premixed investment options that focus either on risk or on maturity (in other words, "time until retirement"). Target-risk funds started in the 1990s and commonly are labeled "conservative," "moderate," or "aggressive." These funds rebalance to a target-risk level and have a static asset allocation. Many investment companies offer these strategies, as shown in Figure 1.1.

Gaining in prevalence, target retirement-date strategies are geared to the participant's time horizon rather than their risk tolerance and adjust their asset allocations automatically to become more conservative as the targeted retirement date approaches. The participant expects the year of his or her retirement to coincide with the strategy's maturity date. These strategies are offered in a series, such as a "today" or "income" fund, 2010, 2020, 2030, 2040, and 2050, and so on. However, investors should be warned that some investment companies manage their asset allocation to a target "retirement" date while others are focused on a "mortality date"; the latter funds typically take on far more risk, given an additional 20- to 30-year investment horizon. Many investment companies also offer target date funds. Target retirement-date funds, which have come later to the market than target-risk funds, have a shorter investment track record yet are already far more prevalent in plans than target risk.

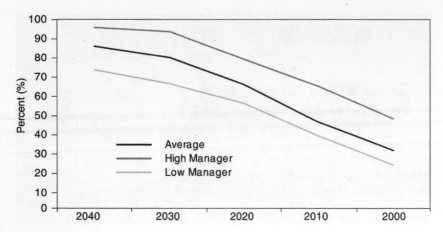

FIGURE 1.2   Equity Allocation Glide Paths Vary
Source: PIMCO.

Today, 83 percent of companies offer premixed strategies in their DC plans; among that group, 15 percent offer target-risk strategies, while 78 percent offer a target retirement-date approach, and 7 percent offer both. Target retirement-date strategies are gaining ground rapidly, as plan sponsors favor their simplicity from a communication and investor-behavior standpoint. Research by Benartzi and Thaler demonstrates plan participants' struggles in defining their own risk tolerances. Participants find it easier to state a likely retirement date. Target retirement-date strategies not only allow participants to focus on their retirement dates, they also provide automatic asset-allocation migration in the form of a changing "glide path" to the retirement-date target. (Note: As illustrated in Figure 1.2, glide paths vary significantly among retirement-date managers.)

Target retirement-date strategies rebalance on an ongoing basis and adjust allocations as a participant ages, so participants' inertia or lack of attention to their investments is likely to move them to a more favorable time horizon or age-appropriate asset allocation over time.

As mentioned, with the passage of the Pension Protection Act, we are likely to see even more interest in target retirement-date strategies as sponsors add auto-enrollment and default alternatives to their plans. No doubt the qualified default-investment alternatives regulations as drafted by the Department of Labor are designed to leverage inertia in participants' best interests.

Clearly, most of us would argue that it is best to engage a participant in determining his or her own asset allocation based on overall risk tolerance, time horizon, and financial profile rather than simply defaulting to a strategy. Yet in the absence of such engagement (and given participants'

	1999	2001	2003	2005	2007	2009
Money Market Stable Value	68	68	67	56	17	5
Balanced or Premixed Fund	28	31	30	39	13	12
Unspecified	3	1	3	5	1	1
Target Date Fund	0	0	0	0	50	69
Target Risk Fund	0	0	0	0	15	10
Managed Accounts	0	0	0	0	4	4

FIGURE 1.3   Default Fund Used by DC Plans
Source: Hewitt Associates, 2005.

typical lack of investment knowledge), a default to a target strategy is more likely to diversify DC portfolios (and take participants through retirement) better than other often-ignored approaches, such as investment-education and advice models, which have been relatively unsuccessful in the market to date. Given the typical time horizon for DC participants, defaulting to a target strategy is an improvement over the strategies that dominated in the past. As Zvi Bodie of Boston University told us in the March 2007 *PIMCO DC Dialogue*, "As you know, in the past the default alternative typically was a money market or stable-value fund. Or, in some cases, company stock was used as a default or match. Neither of them works. Money markets are highly liquid, but not appropriate for long-term saving and, on the other end of the spectrum, receiving company stock doubles participants' exposure to company-specific risk."[14] Thus, it is not surprising that DC experts believe target strategies will continue to grow at a rapid pace.

Figure 1.3 shows a continued increase over the past few years in the use of asset allocation strategies (including balanced, target-date and target-risk) as the default investment for automatic enrollment. Given the DOL's qualified default-investment alternative regulations, we anticipate a continued and more rapid shift away from money-market or stable-value default alternatives and toward alternatives such as target retirement-date strategies and managed accounts.

IS AUTOMATIC ENROLLMENT ENOUGH?

As we said, behavioral scientists have documented participant inertia within plans, showing that participants tend not to reallocate investments once they are in a particular plan.[15] However, while automatic enrollment is a good strategy to get people into a plan, according to Thaler, this is not enough. Auto-enrollment must be accompanied by auto-escalation of savings. Applying what he calls "simple principles of behavioral finance," Thaler and Benartzi have written an article entitled "Save More Tomorrow," in which they have outlined the three primary components in auto-escalation. In the June 2007 *PIMCO DC Dialogue*, they outlined the steps in this strategy: "First, we invite people to sign up for auto-escalation a few months before it takes effect. Second, we link contribution increases to pay raises and, third, we leave things alone until the person opts out or reaches an IRS or plan savings cap."[16]

According to Thaler and Benartzi's research, people can be persuaded to sign up for this type of auto-escalation because

> *they're more willing to entertain ideas of self-control if that control occurs in the future. As St. Augustine prayed, "Oh, Lord, make me chaste. But not yet!" People don't think they can afford to save more right now. Rather, they think they can later, perhaps. Linking savings increases to raises mitigates what we call "loss aversion"; people hate to see their pay go down, but they can imagine taking some of their raise and contributing it to the defined contribution plan.*

In this way, Thaler explained, the power of inertia can work *for* the plan participants rather than against him or her. Once people sign up for a plan, they usually stay where they are. Additionally, participants "almost never reduce their escalating contribution rates. A small percentage drops out of auto-escalation, but typically that's to stop future escalation. It's rare for anyone to set his or her saving rate back to a lower percentage. All these factors together lead us to think that auto-programs help the vast majority of people save more. We don't hear complaints."

Lori Lucas, defined contribution practice leader at Callan Associates, supports Thaler's finding that inertia can be made to serve the plan participant. She points out that when participants are auto-enrolled into a plan, they will be likely stay at the default contribution rate of 2 to 3 percent. But just getting them into the default plan then enables plan sponsors to use "auto-escalation to counter the contribution-rate inertia. In other words, plan sponsors not only auto-enroll employees, they also automatically increase the contribution rates over time. So, for instance, they may default in at the match percentage—say, 6 percent—and then increase it by 1 percent each year up to a maximum. This is another way to make inertia work in the participant's favor."[17]

AUTO-ESCALATION: HOW MUCH IS ENOUGH?

In terms of the Pension Protection Act of 2006, the safe harbor on auto-enrollment requires auto-contribution to start at 3 percent, then rise 1 percentage point each year until it reaches 6 percent, with the stipulation that it can go no higher than 10 percent. Most companies start at a 3 percent contribution level and stop at 6 percent. When we asked Thaler what he thought of those numbers, he stated that 6 percent should be considered a minimum escalation, in terms of qualifying for the safe harbor.

He also pointed out that the auto-escalation percentage rate also depended on the context of the plan. "If you also have a defined benefit plan, then 6 percent may be fine. If you have no DB plan, then that percentage is low and I suggest running it longer."[18] Thaler also suggested that plan sponsors could notify participants when their automatic contribution raises have leveled off at the 10 percent ceiling in order to give them the option of continuing to increase their savings contributions.

When we asked him what percentage of automatic escalation was considered tolerable, given his experience, Thaler reported that he had seen little resistance to 2 percent and that plan sponsors could even give participants the option of moving it down to a 1 percent if that figure was not within their comfort level. However, he did report that the first company to adopt Save More Tomorrow put their escalation increase at 3 percent, with a 14 percent ceiling, and that very few employees had dropped out.

According to Thaler, getting people to an adequate retirement income level—particularly if they do not have a DB plan—depends on where they start and whether they have a spouse who's saving, but a 10 percent savings rate was rarely too high.

HOW MUCH SHOULD WE SAVE TO BEAT INFLATION?

Olivia S. Mitchell, the executive director of the Pension Research Council and director of the Boettner Center on Pensions and Retirement Research at The Wharton School, also advocates savings, but at an even higher rate if participants want to have sufficient resources to cope with inflation during retirement years. The picture she paints is not an optimistic one:

> Our nation has no coherent retirement policy and we see it in many ways. Social Security is facing insolvency. Medicare is running short. Other institutions on which we've come to rely such as the Pension Benefit Guaranty Corporation also are falling short. Across the board, we haven't taken a hard look at the fact that we need to encourage people to save more and work longer in the face of ever-rising longevity.[19]

When we asked Mitchell what we needed to do to make that happen, she said that while DC plans were a powerful tool for diligent savers, the number-one challenge was getting people "to understand the need to save, to comprehend investment opportunities, and to keep money in a plan, so that assets don't leak out of the system early." She felt it was also vitally important "to help baby boomers realize they need to manage their assets sensibly during the de-accumulation or payout phase."

Like Thaler, Mitchell felt that auto-enrollment alone was not the answer to reducing future retirement shortfall. People who were automatically enrolled into a DC plan with a very low contribution rate and defaulted into a very low-return investment portfolio might "lull themselves into thinking they're doing the right thing. But then they may find at age 65 or 75 that they didn't make adequate contributions over the years." Contributing the minimum amount to one's plan is a formula for facing shortfall down the road.

When we asked Mitchell how much she felt people really needed to save, and at what rate plan sponsors should set auto-escalation, she spoke about the tension she was observing among plan sponsors between encouraging people to save more now so that they could live a better life during retirement or worrying that if they set the contribution rate too high, people would pull out altogether. She also pointed out that many other countries are having this same debate. "In Chile, a country where I work a great deal, the mandatory contribution rate is 10 percent of salary. In Australia they tried to get the mandatory rate up to 12 percent. They got as high as 9 percent, but then the tide turned and the politicians stopped there." While it is fair to say that Australia does not have a social security system, that does not negate the fact that higher mandatory contribution rates would significantly improve having enough money to meet retirement needs in the United States.

For Mitchell, the bottom line was that starting at 3 percent and escalating to 6 percent was a good start but much too low. As a solution she suggested "more education to help people understand that this isn't even a floor. It's a basement, and they should move up to a higher target saving rate." She also said that even contributions as high as 15 to 20 percent might still leave people falling short.

The challenge facing baby boomers today—which will become greater with each new generation coming into the labor force—is being aware of how much they actually need in retirement. According to Mitchell:

> My parent's generation was relatively secure when it came to retirement. They expected a strong Social Security system, they could lean on a fairly reliable Medicare program, and many had retiree health benefits from their companies. The baby boomers' story has changed dramatically. As a generation, we must be much less

complacent about all these institutions since many face insolvency in our lifetimes. Sadly, our children face even more serious risks.

This uncertainty suggests that we need substantially higher target saving rates. Each successive generation is likely to live longer and therefore need far more in retirement than one might extrapolate from looking at today's retirees.

PREPARING FOR RETIREMENT IN AN ECONOMIC DOWNTURN

In the June 2009 *DC Dialogue*, Anna Rappaport, president of Anna Rappaport Consulting and chairperson of the Society of Actuaries Committee on Post-Retirement Needs and Risks, agrees with Mitchell that 15 to 20 percent of salary should be considered as a basic savings rate for retirement. Referring to research in a TIAA-CREF paper recently presented at the Pension Research Council, Rappaport states that employees retiring at age 65 or later who have employer support for their health benefits in addition to their DC plan need "six or seven times [their] yearly income as an asset in addition to Social Security to provide a reasonable amount of retirement income.[20]

However, Rappaport also points out that there is a significant correlation between when people retire and what they actually need to supply them with inflation-adjusted income for the rest of their lives. If people can work longer, they can accumulate more savings as well as get significantly higher Social Security benefits. According to Rappaport:

People can claim retirement benefits as early as age 62 and as late as 70. If a person opts to start receiving Social Security at age 70 rather than age 62, she'll get much more money—often about 75 percent more income. In addition, if someone retires at 70 versus 62, she'll need the money for eight fewer years and she'll have eight more years to save and earn investment income before she starts using her savings. Also, at that age, she's covered by Medicare already.

In the recent past, individuals on average were retiring at the age of 62, but in our current economic downturn, people are expressing a desire to keep working longer. Rappaport points out, however, that plan participants cannot *count* on working until, say, age 68 or 70. In fact, there is often of gap between when people *hope* to retire and when they actually *do* retire.

More than four out of 10 people retire earlier than expected, often not by choice. So a person needs to ask, "What are the implications

*of different retirement ages and do I have contingency plans?" For
people who want to work longer, it's important to keep their skills
up to date. If they don't invest part of their time and some of their
resources in keeping those skills up to date, working longer may be
difficult or impossible.*

Rappaport also mentions other factors that can affect one's ability to
work past the median retirement age. Health issues are an issue since some
people become disabled or face major medical challenges that force them to
stop working. Also, in terms of retirement adequacy, in today's market crisis
many retirement models fail to take important factors into consideration,
such as the value of one's house. "The market crisis has affected people
whose houses are a huge part of their assets—many models don't handle
housing well. Some of them don't do it at all. At the other end of the extreme,
there's a model that assumes that home value is an asset that will be used
gradually." While some people plan to stay in their homes, others assume
that their house is one of their main retirement assets and count on being
able to sell it if they need to downsize. But as the recent economic downturn
has shown, using home equity to finance one's retirement is sometimes not
a reliable plan. Rappaport cites "a new 2009 study [that] reminds us what a
major part of the total retirement picture it is for many. People have diverse
views about how retirees should tap into housing equity. Some retirees think,
'I'll stay in my house and if I have a big emergency, like long-term care, I can
sell it.' Of course, that's not a reliable strategy because the housing market
might be bad right when you need to sell your house."

In the wake of the current economic crisis, Rappaport feels that even
fewer companies are offering DB plans—the number is now at about 20 percent, so DC plans are fast becoming the primary retirement vehicle for
many.

Hard economic times are also affecting employer contributions to DC
plans.

*Some employers have suspended or talked about suspending the
match to employee savings. Different surveys tend to look at different employment universes, and there's a lot of disparity in what they
indicate. For example, The American Benefits Council published a
survey at the end of 2008 reporting that 74 percent of employers
offering matching funds hadn't changed their matches, 15 percent
had increased or were considering an increase, 8 percent had decreased or were considering a decrease, and 3 percent had dropped
the match.*

Since plan participants and sponsors are now living in "a different [economic] environment," Rappaport suggests that it may take two to three years to get a "better idea as to what extent employers are helping people save for retirement effectively." In the meantime, she suggests that people should try to consider working "until the economy recovers somewhat," that they should keep their skills up to date, and that they should make sure they work diligently to pay off credit card debt.

WHAT THE FUTURE MAY HOLD FOR DC PLANS

The 2008–2009 economic downturn has also drawn the eyes of Washington to DC plans. In the September 2008 *DC Dialogue*, James Delaplane, Jr., a partner in the law firm of Davis & Harman, LLP, talked about the changes in regulations that might be up ahead for DC plans. He states that there have been many hearings on retirement plan issues and reports from the Government Accountability Office, which is an investigative branch of Congress. Many questions have arisen during this process, Delaplane points out:

> *For example, now that the 401(k) is the dominant plan for many American workers, is it functioning well for the average employee? What do the plans' investment menus look like? What are the investment choices' fee levels? How do we handle disclosure practices regarding investment options and fees, and should we change the legal standards governing these topics? Many Democrats in Congress are making the case that we do, indeed, need legal change regarding fee disclosure.[21]*

The DOL is also examining the regulations regarding fee transparency in DC plans.

Delaplane points out that Pension Protection Act of 2006 is under scrutiny and that Washington has been implementing "technical corrections to the PPA" that will have an impact on the DC plans. This scrutiny has resulted in many regulatory projects, which are keeping agencies such as the Treasury, the Internal Revenue Service, and the DOL very busy. "For example, the DOL worked through the PPA investment advice provisions and implemented regulatory guidance on qualified default investment alternatives. The Treasury and IRS also worked on all the defined benefit plans' funding regulations and auto-enrollment safe harbor regulations."

When we asked Delaplane what issues he felt would be rising to the top during the current presidential administration, he stated that there would be greater emphasis on encouraging Americans to save more in their retirement plans and to invest more in Individual Retirement Accounts (IRAs). There will also be greater emphasis on "how we can reach people who don't have a plan or IRA coverage and how we can reconfigure tax incentives for retirement savings." We look at legal and fiduciary issues in greater detail in later chapters, especially Chapter 4.

IN CLOSING

DC plans continue to evolve and have been helped by the passage of the Pension Protection Act of 2006, given its support of automatic enrollment, contribution increases, and asset allocation. Despite these advancements, DC plans are not out of the laboratory yet. No doubt the emergence of target date strategies provides a springboard for more successful plans in the future. In the next chapter, we take a close look at how the investment structures in DC plans have evolved as well as what is on the horizon in design change. It was not long ago that defined contribution plans were considered "something extra" with investment offerings that were simple. As we know, times are a-changing.

CHAPTER 2

Evolving DC Plan Design

In Chapter 1 we looked at the evolution of defined contribution (DC) plans and some of the issues associated with them, such as automatic enrollment and auto-escalation. In this chapter we are going to take a closer look at how DC plan investment structures have been evolving of late, including the use of brokerage and nontraditional or alternative investments. We also take a look at what we believe is on the horizon in DC plan design, such as retirement-income products. As with any design project, it is key to begin with a definition of success. How does one define success in a DC plan?

Over the past decade, the primary measure of DC plan success has been *quantity* rather than quality, as plan sponsors focused on plan participation rates. Measuring participation is a relatively straightforward process. Typically, using this measure, plan sponsors consider a plan successful if participation rates are in line with the industry or at least sufficiently high enough to enable all participants to contribute at their maximum allowable rates. Participation rates have remained relatively static over time, ranging from 74 percent in 1995 to 81 percent across employers in 2009, as seen in Figure 2.1. Let us hope the auto-enrollment has helped improve participation and that we may continue to see increases over time.

Today, plan sponsors consider more than just participation level. While that level is still important, the new measurement focuses on the *quality* of the plans in terms of their ability to facilitate adequate retirement income. As Pamela Hess, director of retirement research at Hewitt Associates, stated, "One of the biggest shifts is that employers now focus on plan outcomes as a top measure of success. Rather than gauge success merely according to the plan participation rate, companies now look at whether the plans are likely to facilitate adequate retirement income. They ask whether employees will have enough savings when they retire."[1] In other words, they typically look at final pay and project the percentage of pay that the plan is likely to replace in retirement.

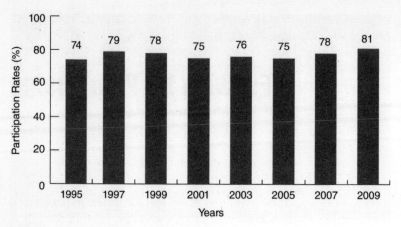

FIGURE 2.1 Participation Rates, 1995 to 2009
Source: Hewitt Associates, 2009.

For example, let us assume that as an individual goes into retirement, a defined benefit (DB) plan might replace up to 50 percent of her or his final nominal pay. If an employee earns $100,000 a year prior to retirement, $50,000 a year might be replaced, without inflation adjustment, throughout the individual's retirement years. Today, increasingly, we measure DC plans in the same way. Plan sponsors ask: "Can the DC plan replace an adequate level of an employee's final income?" Many plan sponsors seek guidance to determine how to design their DC plans to facilitate sufficient savings and investment returns to meet an acceptable income-replacement level, which often is combined with Social Security and other retirement-income sources. They tend to focus on the key risks participants face, including the market, inflation, and even longevity, as they consider the potential outcomes of their plans. Most important, plan sponsors look at both the overall success of the plans and whether each individual participant is likely to succeed in meeting retirement-income goals. Plan sponsors focus increasingly on the asset-allocation solutions that have the highest probability of facilitating an acceptable "real" income-replacement level for the majority of their participants.

Plan sponsors are not alone in identifying this new destination for their plans. Our nation's DC consulting community also focuses on this measure. In the 2008 PIMCO DC Consulting Survey, consulting firms reported that the probability of meeting the retirement-income adequacy goal is the most important factor plan sponsors should consider in selecting an asset-allocation default, such as target-date or risk strategies. Notably, they rank the volatility of returns as their second most important issue in terms of selecting asset-allocation strategies. It is much less important to them whether the plan offers the DC platform provider's proprietary product, and none of the firms considered brand name an important selection factor.

Why do plan sponsors focus first on income replacement and second on volatility? For better or worse, as discussed in Chapter 1, private workers in the United States increasingly rely on their DC plans as the primary source of retirement income from their employers. Consequently, plan sponsors know their DC plans need to work to facilitate adequate retirement income. In fact, a 2007 Hewitt Associates survey reported that 65 percent of plan sponsors consider their 401(k) to be the primary retirement plan for their employees.[2] Not surprisingly, as plan sponsors consider selection of a target-date or target-risk strategy, consultants report that they focus first on the probability of the strategy meeting a retirement income adequacy goal (see Figure 2.2).

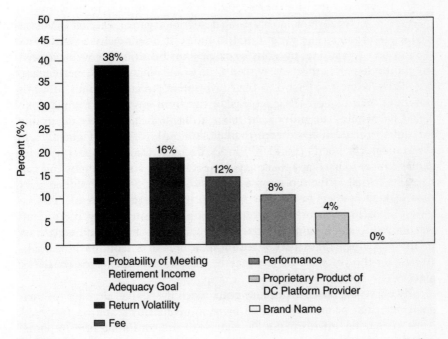

FIGURE 2.2 Most Important Factors in Considering Target-Date or Target-Risk Strategies
Source: PIMCO 2008 Defined Contribution Consulting Support and Trends Survey.

As Lori Lucas, CFA at Callan Associates, stated:

As many companies are eliminating or reducing their defined benefit and retiree medical coverage, they're now re-examining their 401(k) programs. Plan sponsors want to see how sufficient their plans are for the job that the plans now are being asked to do—serve as a primary retirement vehicle. In the past, when a company offered traditional pension and retiree medical plans, if employees weren't participating in the 401(k) plan or weren't participating in a very robust way, it was unfortunate, but it wasn't going to totally undermine their retirement-income adequacy. Now plan sponsors are saying, you know, people might receive nothing from the employer if they don't contribute to the 401(k) plan—at least to the match.[3]

Plan sponsors are not only concerned about retirement-income adequacy, they also want to manage volatility. One of the primary reasons that plan sponsors focus on volatility is the potential negative reaction to volatility by participants. The Hewitt 401(k) Index™ offers one way to analyze the impact of volatility, in terms of participant behavior. As we have seen, for the most part, especially with regard to auto-enrollment, participants are relatively inert in regard to their investment structure. That is, they do not move their money, chase returns, or run from given market conditions. Yet if participants do move their money, they will most likely do so during times of sudden downward market shifts. As we see in Figure 2.3, as the Standard & Poor's (S&P) 500 Index declines, the Hewitt 401(k) Index shows a jump in participant activity. Unfortunately, volatility may lead participants to sell at the worst time—when the value of their holdings dips, thus locking in their losses. For instance, in the first quarter of 2008, as the S&P declined, over 80 percent of money transferred by participants was moved to stable value and fixed income. While only a small percentage of the participant base may react to volatility on a daily basis, cumulatively over the years the impact may be far greater than it appears at first glance.

By observing how participants react when the market declines, we may determine that people seem to be more motivated by fear than by greed. Thus, managing volatility in a DC plan is of utmost importance to diminish participants' motivation to sell out of fear. Managing volatility is all the more important for participants who are approaching retirement, as reactively selling on a market decline may undermine their ability to retire comfortably.

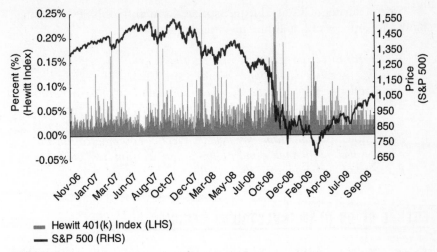

FIGURE 2.3   DC Participant Trading Rises as Market Falls
Source: Hewitt Associates, 2009.

With a focus on income-replacement and volatility management, let us look at how plan sponsors structure investment offerings in DC plans today.

INVESTMENT STRUCTURE OF DEFINED CONTRIBUTION PLANS

Let us start by taking a look at some studies examining broad trends in DC investment structures and then look at what some individual consultants consider to be an optimal plan design. We also consider questions regarding passive versus active investment offerings and discuss access to nontraditional or alternative investment strategies.

In a 2009 survey conducted by Hewitt Associates, the median total number of investment offerings in DC plans was 18, yet the number of core options was only 12.[4] Typically, the difference between total and core can be defined as the set of asset-allocation strategies that, for communication purposes, sponsors often offer as a separate tier. Increasingly, the asset-allocation strategies are offered as the default for plans that automatically enroll participants. Asset-allocation strategies include both target risk and target date, which this chapter examines in greater detail. Plan sponsors increasingly offer two or three tiers of investment choice: Tier I for asset-allocation strategies, Tier II for core funds, and possibly a Tier III for a mutual fund or full brokerage window. More recently, we have seen some plan sponsors also add a tier for index strategies.

Steve Charlton, CFA, and Ross Bremen, CFA, both of NEPC, comment on the advantages of a multitier investment structure:

> *While this three-tier structure offers ultimate choice, it's presented in such a way that participants are not overwhelmed. In the first tier, target retirement-date funds offer a turnkey solution for participants who are uncomfortable making investment selections or for more sophisticated individuals who prefer not to select or modify their asset allocations over time. We believe effective communication and education combined with smart plan-design decisions will guide the majority of participants to these options.[5]*

FUTURE OF DC PLAN INVESTMENT DESIGN

As we consider the future of DC plan investment design, let us take a look at each of the investment tiers. Regarding DC plan design, Charlton and Bremen suggest: "For participants to save adequately for retirement in today's environment, plan sponsors need to offer a range of choices that not only allow participants to construct portfolios with varying degrees of risk, but also appeal to the different types of investors." They also counsel plan sponsors to look not only at the financial aspects of a plan's investment lineup but also at elements of behavioral theory. They say, for instance, "While choice is good from a diversification perspective, participants can become overwhelmed by too many choices."

As we look toward the future, given the rapid adoption of target date strategies as the qualified investment default alternative within plans, we will likely see considerable assets driven toward this Tier I investment. Let us start with a close look at this tier.

TIER I: QUALIFIED DEFAULT INVESTMENT ALTERNATIVES—ASSET-ALLOCATION STRATEGIES

As introduced in Chapter 1, the 2007 Department of Labor (DOL) regulations, that support the Qualified Default Investment Alternatives (QDIA) safe harbor provided within the Pension Protection Act (PPA) of 2006, define this type of investment alternative.

As we have seen, automatic enrollment is key to keeping plan participants from becoming overwhelmed by their choices. The PPA provides government support for automatic investment programs within DC plans. This legislation encourages employers to enroll participants automatically, to increase their contribution levels or deferral rates automatically, and to allocate their DC retirement funds automatically through asset-allocation strategies or diversified strategies that the DOL defines within its QDIA regulations.

Through studies in behavioral finance, we know that once we auto-enroll people into a certain asset-allocation strategy, they tend to be relatively inert. Once invested in a plan option, they are unlikely to move assets from that investment, regardless of whether they selected it or—perhaps, even less so—were defaulted into it.

Given auto-enrollment and behavioral factors, when we look at the horizon to see what is ahead for DC plans, we believe that plans will shift from holding a majority of assets in a limited set of asset classes to holding perhaps the majority of assets within the QDIA option. This means that participants should have more diversified DC assets than in the past, as QDIAs require a blend of asset types. Further, the shift toward target date and other asset-allocation strategies will result in more professional oversight of the investment mix as well as a broader set of assets within the mix. This movement opens the door for significant advancement and improvement in DC investment management.

As Identified in Chapter 1, QDIA regulations list a set of premixed asset-allocation strategies that include three possibilities:

1. Target-date or life cycle (e.g., 2010, 2020, 2030 . . .)
2. Target-risk or balanced (e.g., conservative, moderate, aggressive, or a single-fund approach)
3. Managed accounts (typically overseen by an outside asset-allocation or advisory firm that creates an asset mix for the individual

Notably, stable-value strategies are left off this list. There are a few exceptions, however. As the regulation states, plan sponsors can select whichever default plan they prefer; they simply need to justify it. But it is important to note that if an investment is not one of the stated qualified defaults, it may be outside of the QDIA safe harbor protection.

Target-date strategies (Tier I), which typically modify their allocations over time based on a participant's age, have become the most prevalent type of DC plan default. When an employer offers automatic enrollment, over two-thirds of the plans default their assets into a target-date strategy, as seen earlier in Figure 1.3. We expect this trend to continue, as do many others.

As Pamela Hess stated in a 2008 *DC Dialogue*:

> *Target-date strategies are the clear winner, with half of all plans defaulting to these portfolios. Now that the Qualified Default Investment Alternative (QDIA) regulations are final, we anticipate many more companies to move in that direction. Target-date strategies*

Percent of Plans 2009

No change	57%
Changed default fund from money market/stable value fund to target-risk or target-date fund	25%
Changed default fund from balanced fund to target risk or target date fund	8%
Changed default fund from money market/stable fund to balanced fund	4%
Other (e.g., changed default to managed account)	6%

FIGURE 2.4   Change in Default
Source: Hewitt Associates, 2009.

are a simple solution because participants can be defaulted to the appropriate fund according to their age. People consider them as superior to balanced or target-risk funds since it's more challenging to default a participant into a risk level. Even if we could, participants' risk tolerances typically change over time, and employees often fail to reallocate their balances once defaulted. Target-date portfolios fix these problems and more easily allow for default behavior.[6]

Over the last couple of years, Hewitt reports, many companies have changed their default retirement plans to portfolio target-risk or target-date strategies. This includes a shift away from not only stable value and money market but also from balanced risk and more static-type investments. We expect to continue to see quite a bit of change in this area, as illustrated in Figure 2.4.

Given the significant movement toward auto-enrollment and defaulting to asset-allocation strategies, plan sponsors ask: Will my plan succeed in meeting its primary objective of facilitating adequate retirement income? To a large extent, this question becomes: Is my asset allocation optimal relative to my plan's retirement-income objective? We return to this question as we evaluate asset allocation or glide-path design in Chapter 8. For now, let us turn to Tier II and the evolution of core investment offerings within plans.

TIER II: CORE INVESTMENT OFFERINGS IN DC PLANS

In their infancy, DC plans offered a limited array of investment choices as a single list. The thought of structuring investment choices into tiers was a long way off. In the mid-1990s, plans had only 6 investment choices on average, as opposed to 14 choices a decade later.[7] Many plans did not even offer a balanced fund. At the time, some plan sponsors talked about the need for a balanced fund, but often they dismissed such an addition, reasoning that "since we offer an equity fund and a stable-value fund, participants can mix their own balanced fund."

Likely influenced by the development of their DB plan investment structure, DC plan sponsors may have thought that since they did not offer a balanced investment choice in their DB plan, there was no need to offer one in their DC plan. In these early years of DC plans, research on participant behavior was just beginning. Plan sponsors and their provider call centers were riddled with incessant questions from their participants: "Where should I invest my money?" "Tell me which funds to pick." "What do other people pick?" In other words, participants wanted asset allocation advice. With the best of intentions, some benefit representatives may have answered. "Others simply spread it around." And plan participants many did just that: They spread it around in what some refer to as a "1 over *n*" (1/*n*) approach: Given 10 investment offerings, they would invest 10 percent in each.

What are the investment offerings of today, and how are participants allocating among them? As shown in Figure 2.5, according to a 2009 Hewitt

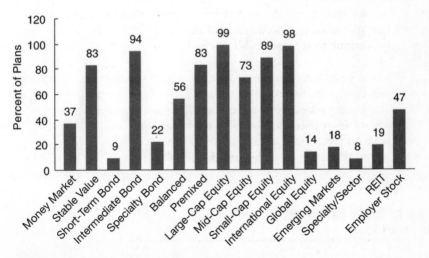

FIGURE 2.5 Types of Investment Options Available
Source: Hewitt Associates Trends and Experience in 401(k) Plans, 2009.

survey, the most common core investment offerings in DC plans are:

Large cap, 99 percent
International, 98 percent
Intermediate bond, 94 percent
Small cap, 89 percent
Stable value, 83 percent

The remaining options may include a specialty bond, such as high yield, emerging market debt, or Treasury Inflation Protected Securities (TIPS). More plans also offer real-estate investment trusts (REITs). Recently, we have seen plans add other nontraditional assets, such as commodities, and even alternatives, such as private real estate and absolute return strategies. As we discuss later, less liquid strategies may be blended into core offerings or added as diversifiers within asset-allocation strategies such as target-date structures.

Now that we know which investments are available, let us look at where people invest their money. Across the asset spectrum, Hewitt Associates reports in Figure 2.6 that asset allocation strategies (balanced and premixed)

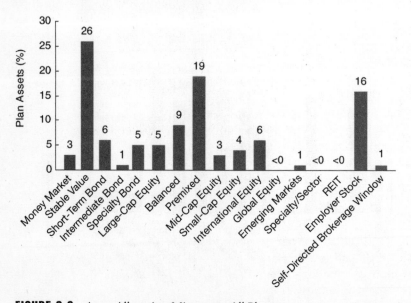

FIGURE 2.6   Asset-Allocation Mix across All Plans
Source: Hewitt Associates Trends and Experience in 401(k) Plans, 2009.

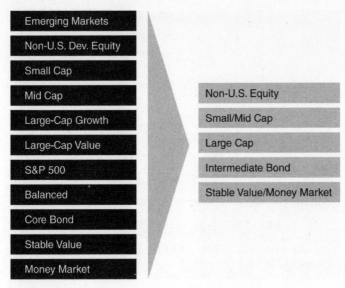

FIGURE 2.7 Common Core Investment Lineup
Source: PIMCO.

hold 28 percent of plan assets, followed by stable value with 26 percent of plan assets, and then by company stock at 16 percent.

While we typically have 12 to 18 investment choices within individual plans, we concentrate the vast majority of money in just a handful of these options. When we total the allocation across all offerings—stable value, large-cap equity, and company stock—over half, or 61 percent, of the assets fall into one of these three primary asset types.

Since the inception of 401(k) plans in 1981, plan sponsors have added about one investment choice to their plan every other year. As we study the investment choices that have been added over time, we recognize that most have been additions to the array of equity or stock investments. In fact, the typical lineup of investment offerings in DC plans tends to be over 70 percent equity. Figure 2.7 illustrates the common core investment lineup as well as the primary asset classes offered in DC plans today.

In Chapter 9 we take a closer look at the asset classes offered in plans as well as nontraditional investments. For now, let us suggest that the current investment lineup in DC plans may have been driven at least in part by the economic conditions which may have enticed sponsors into selecting what was hot yesterday, in other words, investing in the rearview mirror. In other words, plan sponsors may have responded to participant demand for investments that showed excellent performance of late. Falling prey

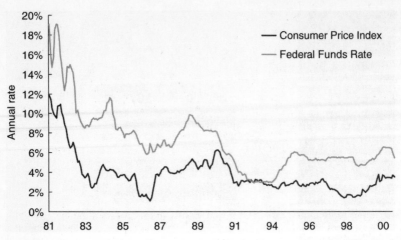

FIGURE 2.8   Economic Environment, 1981 to 2000
Source: Bloomberg Financial Markets.

to participant demand and yesterday's performance may explain, in part, the addition of a wide range of equity offerings, from small cap or even technology funds in the late 1990s, to real estate (primarily REITs) and more recently emerging markets strategies. While the addition of these investment strategies provides diversification benefits, it is important to note that as we design investment lineups, undoubtedly we are influenced by the current economic cycle and its impact on asset performance.

Briefly consider the economic times that we have lived in since 1981, the inception year of the 401(k) plan. Until recently, we have enjoyed a time of relatively strong economic growth and low inflation. When we consider the time period from 1981 to 2000, we see in Figure 2.8 a period of easy money reflected in low federal funds rates as well as low inflation as measured by the Consumer Price Index (CPI).

In times of such low rates and low inflation, equities tend to perform well relative to other assets, as indeed they did over this time frame. As shown in Figure 2.9, stocks mightily outperformed bonds, as well as commodities, TIPS (simulated prior to 1997), and inflation (measured by CPI). This is the picture we have been educated to expect: Stocks outperform assets in the long run. But is that always true? Can we question conventional wisdom?

Whether we agree that stocks are likely to outperform other assets in the long run or not, to structure a DC investment lineup for success, we must consider the range of economic environments that plan participants may face. In particular, we need to think about the sensitivity human beings

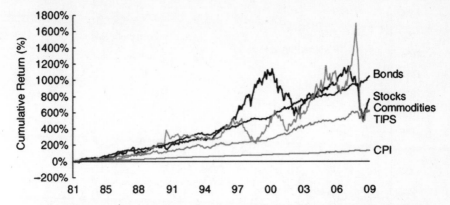

Stocks are represented by the S&P 500, bonds are represented by the 10-year U.S. Treasuries; commodities are represented by the Gorton and Rouwenhorst Commodity Index Plus DJ-AIG Commodity TR Index (starting January 1991); and TIPS Total Returns were calculated in the periods before TIPS were issued by combining actual U.S. CPI (NSA) inflation with estimated price returns and real yields. Estimated real yields were calculated by subtracting 12-month ahead forecasted CPI (NSA) from 10-year U.S. Treasury yields. The forecasts were from the Livingston Survey of Economists' Forecasts. The price returns were calculated by multiplying the monthly changes in these estimated real yields by an assumed duration of 7 years. From February 1997 through the most recent date, TIPS Total Returns were represented by the Barclays Capital U.S. TIPS Index.

FIGURE 2.9 Asset Class Performance, 1981 to 2000
Source: Morningstar.

have to the economic times they will live through as they both approach and enter retirement. It is critical that we look forward in our design to offer the asset classes that will provide appropriate diversification throughout changing market cycles.

Let us take a look at another timeframe from 1962 to 1980. During this time, conditions were nearly reversed as we observed high inflation as well as rising federal funds rates, as shown in Figure 2.10.

Not surprisingly, this economic environment prompted far different results among investments in the markets. In this environment, as shown in Figure 2.11, both bonds and stocks failed to outperform inflation. While TIPS were not offered as a security until 1997, we know that they would have outperformed inflation by the interest they pay since the principal invested in TIPS is adjusted by the CPI. During this period, commodities outperformed both stocks and bonds as well as simulated TIPS (i.e., CPI plus an assumed TIPS coupon) and inflation. Notably, the commodity data tracked excluded exposure to oil.

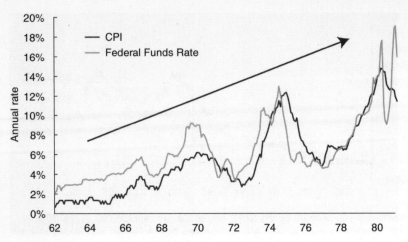

FIGURE 2.10 Asset Class Performance 1962 to 1980
Source: Bloomberg Financial Markets.

Returning for a moment to the consideration that many participants may follow a 1/*n* strategy of investment—evenly spreading their money across all of the investments in the plan—we may need to rethink the core investment lineup to make sure that we have not provided unintended advice by its very structure. We should be careful to offer a diverse and balanced array of investment offerings within the core that are appropriate throughout various market cycles. In Chapter 9 we return with our suggestions. For now, let us return to Tier III.

TIER III: BROKERAGE OR MUTUAL FUND WINDOW

Perhaps the most debated investment tier is the one that includes options for brokerage or mutual fund windows. These types of strategies are gaining in prevalence but currently are found within less than a quarter of DC plans. Plan sponsors and their Employee Retirement Income Security Act counsels often debate the merits of offering brokerage windows, arguing on one hand that participants "may unwisely invest all of their money in one-penny stock" and on the other that they "have a right to manage their money to meet their unique investment goals." Over the years, the number of plans that offer brokerage has continued to grow from 12 percent of plans offering brokerage in 2001 to 26 percent in 2009. While the percentage of plans that offer brokerage continues to climb, on average, just 3 percent of plan assets are invested in this option.[8]

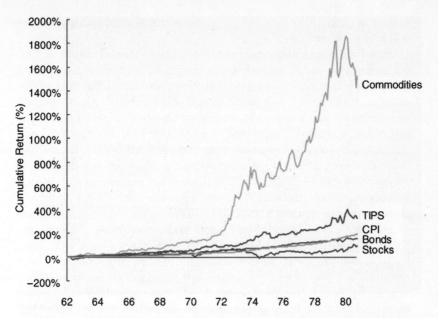

Stocks are represented by the S&P 500, bonds are represented by the 10-year U.S. Treasuries; commodities are represented by the Gorton and Rouwenhorst Commodity Index Plus DJ-AIG Commodity TR Index (starting January 1991); and TIPS Total Returns were calculated in the periods before TIPS were issued by combining actual U.S. CPI (NSA) inflation with estimated price returns and real yields. Estimated real yields were calculated by subtracting 12-month ahead forecasted CPI (NSA) from 10-year U.S. Treasury yields. The forecasts were from the Livingston Survey of Economists' Forecasts. The price returns were calculated by multiplying the monthly changes in these estimated real yields by an assumed duration of 7 years. From February 1997 through the most recent date, TIPS Total Returns were represented by the Barclays Capital U.S. TIPS Index.

FIGURE 2.11 Asset Class Performance, 1962 to 1980
Source: Morningstar.

We believe brokerage has gained in popularity for several important reasons:

- It allows plan sponsors to declutter their DC core lineup without taking away beloved mutual funds (i.e., mutual funds can be eliminated from the core yet participants are assured these investments are still available in the brokerage window.
- It allows the plan sponsor to focus the core lineup on institutional investment offerings, including blending managers (i.e., selecting two or more investment managers for one strategy) and at the same time

satisfying participant demand for name-brand mutual funds that they will find in the window.

- It keeps the higher-paid, longer-tenured, higher-balanced employees (often executives) happy since they can invest in the funds of their choice as well as in stocks, exchange-traded funds, and individual bonds, plus often with the ability to allow a personal investment advisor to manage the brokerage account. Note: Participants with higher salaries and higher DC account balances tend to participate in brokerage windows. According to Hewitt Associates, "the average participant who invested in a self-directed brokerage window had a total account balance of about $190,000 in 2008, which is three times as large as the average balance across the universe." Hewitt also notes that "10.3 percent of those earning more than $100,000 and 14.4 percent of those with a balance higher than $100,000 had assets in these accounts."[9] Similarly, "Younger participants and participants with lower tenure were most likely to use premixed portfolios. Eighty percent of participants with less than one year of tenure invested in a premixed portfolio in 2008." While all types of plan participants used premixed portfolios, the ones most likely to have them would be employees who were auto-enrolled.

- If we look at longer-tenured employees, we can see that 36.5 percent of those tenured between 20 and 30 years use premixed portfolios; only 33.5 percent of 30+-year employees do so. The plan balance on average for the brokerage window is $190,000, which is more than "three times as large as the general balance across the universe." In fact, "The average 401(k) participant's total plan balance was $57,150 at the end of 2008, declining from $75,570 in 2007."

Perhaps a more compelling reason to offer brokerage is that participants may be more satisfied with their plan overall by adding it, even when they choose not to invest in the window. This satisfaction may derive from knowing they have the choice to invest beyond the core options in the plan, just in case they desire this option.

David Fisser, consultant and former chairman of the Southwest Airlines Pilots' Association (SWAPA), confirmed that the brokerage window offering was quite successful for the plan. He revealed that SWAPA "started a brokerage window in the summer of 2000, but limited investment to 25 percent of the overall account. Since then, we've been trying to get them to raise that limit. The small group of people that chooses to use the brokerage window loves it, and wants to be able to put 100 percent in there."[10]

The number of people who do use the brokerage window is nowhere near the majority. In fact, Fisser says that "brokerage is not part of the overall plan and amounts to just 5 percent of total plan assets. So it's not a big draw but, again, the few who use it love it." Clearly an effective plan needs to cater to a variety of different types of investors to consider itself successful, and offering a brokerage window is a simple and effective way to do so.

While plan sponsors may, at times, fear that brokerage window participants might sue if they lose money, probably an equal number of sponsors believe they are less likely to face a suit if participants have access to the nearly unlimited choice within a window.

We anticipate that brokerage windows, like target-date strategies, are here to stay. While investment in these strategies can be as small as 1 percent of total plan assets, the fact that higher-income participants tend to invest via the window, combined with the benefit of greater plan design flexibility, increased participant satisfaction, and, for some, potentially positive legal considerations, may all work together to tilt the scales increasingly in favor of adding brokerage.

TIER IV: PASSIVE INVESTMENT STRATEGIES?

A popular question from plan sponsors over the past year has been "Should we add a tier of index funds such as the S&P 500 to the plan?" While some plans have added this additional passive investment tier primarily out of concern that they should include some low-priced investment offerings, the vast majority of plan sponsors have not gone this direction. Rather, they have evaluated whether to add active or passive strategies as they consider each asset class for the core lineup. Similar to DB plans, nearly all DC plans offer both actively and passively managed investment strategies in the core. Today, 97 percent of DC plans offer an S&P 500 fund, while only 42 percent offer a Barclay's Aggregate fixed income and fewer offer Europe Australia Far East (34 percent) or the Russell 2000 (35 percent).[11]

Investment consultant Roger Williams of Rogerscasey offers this insight relative to selecting active versus passive strategies. Since their clients usually have a combination of both active and passive managers in their core lineups, at their year-end review, some questions tend to come up about active management. What has surprised clients recently is that there are "some very prominent, highly regarded firms that have had surprisingly poor performance—in some cases...the worst performance in 20 years."[12]

In terms of equities, Rogerscasey advised clients that during the recent market turmoil, stocks were trading on emotions rather than on fundamentals. For that reason, "frequently active management doesn't work in this kind of environment. When people's fears and emotions stop driving the markets, and fundamentals come back into vogue, active managers should come back strong. So we advise our clients not to buy high and sell low on active management."

However, while some firms consistently outperform the benchmark, replicating these results in a passive bond portfolio is a challenge. "When clients ask about active and passive, we show them a variety of rolling time periods and where passive management ranks relative to the active manager."

Williams warns that statistics are not always reliable either. "While on average active fixed income doesn't always fare well, there are a number of fixed-income managers with the resources and the wherewithal to outperform consistently." But on the other side of this issue, there are also many firms that do not have sufficient resources and, therefore, consistently underperform. Unfortunately, Williams adds, "There are more of the latter than the former and, therefore, the passive returns tend to drift up relative to the active managers."

David Fisser basically sees this issue as an old debate where some people argue that active is better and others say that passive is best. "Over the long haul we focus on net return and we don't care if the strategies that maximize those returns are managed actively or passively."[13]

Fisser points out that SWAPA has had issues with certain asset classes, especially in the area of small-cap growth. "We picked three or four small-cap growth managers, but there's always an issue after we pick them. Their performance suffers, or there's turnover in the management, or there are operational issues. Finally, we got tired of changing out the people all the time." However, when they did their homework, they were disappointed, so a decision was made, in this instance, to go with index "so people don't have to worry about the manager leaving or things like that." Overall, SWAPA's approach is to go with whatever brings the best returns, regardless of management style. "Generally, we're looking for the best fund, the best return, and a reasonable level of volatility, to provide the best option for the participant, regardless of whether the strategy is managed actively or passively."

EVOLVING STRUCTURES AND ALTERNATIVE INVESTMENT STRATEGIES

As we have seen, when faced with designing their own retirement portfolios, plan participants often feel confused about how to proceed. However, one of the benefits of the Pension Protection Act of 2006, which allows for auto-enrollment, is that it enables plan sponsors to create a default plan. This means that employees, many of whom feel overwhelmed by choices or lack investment savvy, are no longer burdened with having to make their own asset allocation calls. All of this can now be done for them by investment professionals with a depth of knowledge about the complexities of the market. This has opened the door for sponsors, consultants, and/or investment managers to add much greater diversification to the plan by including nontraditional assets in the target date or other asset-allocation strategies. These assets may include for example high yield, international small cap, private equity, TIPS, emerging markets, commodities, and REITs. In our view, one of the best ways to incorporate these nontraditional or alternative strategies is in custom target-date strategies.

Ross Bremen of NEPC points out that one good reason to include alternatives in custom strategies is that they can perform relatively well "in a year like last year, 2008, when the equity markets were down significantly." He goes on to say that when "custom target-date funds...incorporate strategies that are not perfectly correlated with the equity markets, that less than perfect correlation has led to what have been very good results in what has been a very difficult market environment."[14]

Other consultants have pointed out that using alternatives such as commodity-based stocks, TIPS, international small cap, or REITS can provide a better return profile without introducing the question of liquidity. Another important benefit is that traditionally DB plans had access to a greater number of core strategies. Adding alternatives to the DC core gives them this DB-like flavor. Last, many alternatives, such as real estate, have longer cycles. A skilled manager can use his or her knowledge of the market to make some good long-term alternative investments.

Stuart Odell, director of retirement investments at Intel, talks about how the company has moved from 100 percent passive management to active management of investments in its DC plan, including incorporating alternatives into the target-date strategies. Ten years ago, Intel's profit-sharing plan was "100 percent passive to the S&P 500. Today it's a fully diversified portfolio with an initial allocation to what you would call alternatives...about 20 percent of the portfolio."[15] Odell shared that this allocation to alternatives was increased again in 2009 to 25 percent, including raising the percent invested in hedge funds from 5 percent up to 10 percent.

Although Intel is still very selective about which alternatives it puts into its plan, Odell feels that as the company becomes more confident in its ability to select capable managers for asset classes, it will incorporate a wider selection. In fact, Intel leaves many of the allocation decisions to their portfolio managers: For instance, Odell shares that his opportunistic fixed-income manager may "have the ability to make the bets on whether this is a good time to be in mortgage-backed securities or a good time to be over-weighted in investment grade credit."

In a 2008 *DC Dialogue*, Ross Bremen and Rob Fishman of NEPC spoke about their reasons for including alternatives in target-date strategies, referring to it as the "DB-ification of DC plans," a trend in which plan sponsors were "looking for ways to bring into their DC plans the broader investment opportunity set that is available to DB plans." Some nontraditional assets that they use include TIPS, commodities, global asset-allocation (GAA) strategies, absolute return strategies, and direct real estate. The goal of these sorts of investments is to "help reduce risk by incorporating additional uncorrelated asset classes and permitting diversification away from equity-centric portfolios." If the ultimate aim is to increase the probability of a participant reaching his or her income-replacement goals and reducing longevity risks, they believe that most of these 'less-traditional' asset classes are more suitable for inclusion in diversified target-date strategies."[16]

In this "new world" of DC plans, Bremen and Fishman see a strong advantage to including alternatives in their custom strategies:

> If sponsors have taken the time to build a well-diversified core lineup of best-in-class investment options with low fees, it makes perfect sense that they'd want to construct target-date strategies with the same philosophy. The core options serve as the initial building blocks that then can be complemented with these less-traditional asset classes. Many record keepers give sponsors the ability to blend asset classes into custom target-date strategies without offering these asset classes as standalone offerings.

Bremen and Fishman point out that while some of these nontraditional investments are not "hot knock-the-cover-off-the-ball funds," they do offer inflation protection and, with the right managers, alpha potential as well. They have the potential to "smooth the ride," especially for participants who are approaching retirement age and have a much lower tolerance for loss of principle.

When we asked them to tell us how sponsors are using alternatives within DC Plans, Bremen and Fishman talked about how to use each specific product type appropriately. They pointed out that when considering alternatives in a DB plan, many people tend to think of hedge funds and private equity, which are associated "with high fees, low liquidity, and low transparency." However, the nontraditional core offerings commonly used in DC plans are "emerging-market equity, emerging-market debt, commodities, TIPS, GAA, and real estate"—in other words, products that are valued daily and offer daily liquidity.

When DC alternatives are broken down into categories, there are two basic camps: equity alternatives and bond alternatives.

Equity alternatives include GAA strategies and unconstrained equity strategies. Bond alternatives include real-return assets such as TIPS and real estate (primarily REITs). Beneath the broad equity- or bond-alternative label, we have different products within each classification, and different benchmarks as well. And while GAA typically might fit in the equity-alternative category, GAA strategies might look to outperform inflation, or a global equity and global fixed benchmark.

Alternative strategies improve the risk-versus-return profile. Equity alternatives include many strategies that provide equity-like returns with more bond-like risk levels, which is attractive for a DC plan. Investing in these alternatives allows us to reduce the traditional equity exposure and improve diversification for participants without sacrificing return. We can achieve this particularly well in target-date strategies.

Matt Rice, chief research officer at Dimeo Schneider & Associates, discusses how the company works with plan sponsor clients to help them integrate nontraditional assets into the structure of their investment menus. "Our clients have long struggled with the limitations of off-the-shelf products, the lack of thorough and thoughtful diversification and over-reliance on a single fund family to manage every single asset class in participants' portfolios. Our clients want more flexibility to drive costs down, enhance diversification, and freedom to use best-in-breed underlying managers."[17]

In addition to the investment products in the core lineup of their target-date strategies, most clients

also include other asset classes they don't want to include in the core menu, such as emerging markets, real estate, high-yield bonds, foreign bonds, Treasury Inflation Protected Securities (TIPS) or commodity futures. The benefit of customization is that you get to use multiple managers from different investment management firms, and you can employ a more thoughtful allocation structure and broader diversification.

When we asked Rice why he would want to include assets in the target-date fund that is not in the core lineup, he pointed out the difficulty of educating participants on the more esoteric asset classes such as commodity futures.

While a 5- to 10-percent allocation to commodity futures within a portfolio may be appropriate for most participants, you don't necessarily want them to have the flexibility to allocate 100 percent of their portfolios to that asset class. Adding a commodity fund, with no constraint, to a core lineup almost dares participants to jump into it with both feet. The same is true of other, more esoteric investments such as emerging markets, foreign bonds, high-yield bonds or real estate investment trusts. Too much flexibility to invest in esoteric asset classes, combined with participants' naïve desire to chase performance, can be a dangerous combination.

BRINGING IT ALL TOGETHER: DC INVESTMENT STRUCTURE AND GUARANTEES

Now that we have discussed the multitier approach to plan design, we would like to suggest the structure shown in Figure 2.12.

This suggested structure offers the three tiers, including Tier I for target-date strategies, Tier II for core options, and Tier III for a brokerage window. We are not suggesting a tier for passive strategies, as we believe both passive and active should be selected for inclusion within the core lineup based on their merit. Further, we suggest that nontraditional assets be considered for inclusion within the custom target-date strategies.

In Chapter 9 we return to an in-depth discussion on the specific asset classes and value of including each within your DC plan. For now, let us suggest that designing a multitier plan is appropriate to help participants meet their unique investment objectives. Offering tiers enables plan sponsors to simplify communication without losing the value of diversification. Rather, the complexity of broadly diversified investment offerings within a wrapper of straightforward plan design is most beneficial to participants. Offering fewer core investment strategies that blend together asset classes helps in both communication and volatility management.

In Figure 2.12 we also introduce the idea of providing participants with guaranteed products, such as living benefit, annuities, and longevity insurance. In the PIMCO DC Consultant Survey 2009, 78 percent of consultants said that their plan sponsor clients are "somewhat to highly likely" to add a guarantee product to their plan.[18] Plan sponsors may be particularly interested in guarantee products, given the significant market blow endured in 2008. There are many flavors of guarantee product.

Consultants note that their greatest interest is in living-benefit programs that may be integrated within target-date or other asset-allocation approaches, including custom target-date strategies. These products provide market hedging by offering a guaranteed floor rate of return as well as longevity protection by providing income for the full life of the

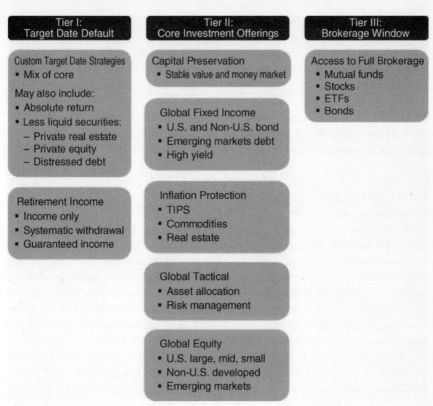

FIGURE 2.12 Suggested DC Plan Structure: Broader Asset Diversification and Customization
Source: PIMCO, 2009.

participant. Their second greatest product of interest is annuities, which may be fixed or variable in structure; both annuities and living-benefit programs provide longevity insurance; annuities also offer participation in market returns. Third most popular is longevity insurance, which begins paying out income to retirees who live beyond 85 years of age. While many of these products are attractive, consultants report that plan sponsors worry about insurance company default risk, cost, transparency, and fiduciary oversight. Given these concerns, adoption of these products continues to be slow. Some believe that to speed their adoption by plan sponsors, more support from Washington will be needed, such as a safe harbor for plan sponsor selection of an insurer and its product. Further, even with plan sponsor adoption, experience shows that few participants invest in these products when they are offered. We return to this discussion in depth in Chapter 13 when we look at guarantee products and other retirement income structures.

IN CLOSING

Over the past five years, DC plan design has experienced more of a revolution than an evolution. Plans today offer tiers for participants who prefer the do-it-for-me approach via target-date strategies and for those who prefer the do-it-myself approach, which allows participants either to select among core offerings or to invest in a brokerage window. Tiers of investments to satisfy the varying needs of plan participant will no doubt continue. What is exciting about this revolution is how the restructuring of plans has opened the door to institutional investment management. For the majority of participants who say "Tell me how to invest my money," sponsors can now offer a lineup of investments such as target-date strategies that answer that question for them. Today, participants receive more than an array of investment choices that are simple to understand. They are offered far more complex investment choices, presented in a reasonably understandable and accessible way. New hires can now simply default into target-date strategies that take care of their asset allocation from their first day of work, all the way to retirement. What could be better than that?

In the next chapter we look at the development of target-date approaches and, more specifically, at why plan sponsors are interested in custom target-date strategies. Now that you have a firm grounding in how and why plans have developed over the last three decades, you will be able to see why there is a growing trend toward custom target-date strategies and, furthermore, why they are an effective approach for creating a safe and secure retirement.

CHAPTER 3

Target-Date Strategies: Packaged versus Custom

Given the rise in importance of target strategies, many plan sponsors now are focused on how they can provide the best target-date lineup possible. While it is possible to turn to packaged products in the market, increasingly plan sponsors are creating their own blend of custom strategies. These plans typically create custom strategies by providing a mix of core options, as shown in Figure 3.1. Sponsors may also add investments to the custom strategies that are excluded from the core investment lineup, such as nontraditional asset classes.

We know that target-date strategies have grown rapidly in prevalence since they qualify as one type of qualified default investment alternative. The QDIA regulation has sped the trend toward these types of products. Plan sponsors have favored target-date strategies over balanced or target-risk approaches primarily because of their recognition of human behavior in terms of saving for retirement—that is, we know from decades of defined contribution (DC) record-keeping data that participants tend not to rebalance their investments. In fact, a 2009 Hewitt Associates survey shows that:

- 49.6 percent of employees preferred to invest in a premixed portfolio, if one was available to them.
- Over one-third of those participants had their retirement savings invested fully in a single portfolio.
- Even when market volatility was at record levels during the economic downturn of 2008, only 19.6 percent of plan participants made any type of transfer of funds in their retirement accounts.

Hewitt notes that, "despite the significant decline in the stock market during 2008, most participants did not change their saving and investment

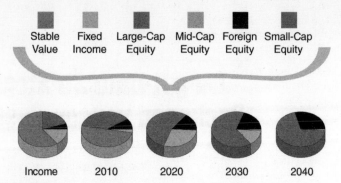

FIGURE 3.1   Sample Target Retirement-Date Strategies
Source: PIMCO. Hypothetical example for illustrative purposes only.

behavior throughout the year. Overall participant rates across the universe remained flat from last year."[1]

Since participants generally fail to rebalance their investments on their own, target-date strategies present an attractive solution as they automatically rebalance asset allocation for participants throughout their lifetimes. It is possible for new hires to join a plan at 25 years of age and never reallocate their balances over the course of their entire career with a company. Of course, it is rare for people to remain with a single organization for that long. However, if they move to another employer and decide to leave their current DC account with the first employer, investing in a target-date strategy offers them the hope that their account will be appropriately managed over their time horizon to retirement.

Taking on the responsibility of managing assets throughout participants' careers is a serious venture. Plan sponsors want to make sure the default strategy is appropriately managed so participants have the greatest likelihood of meeting their retirement-income goals. Even with the weight of this responsibility on their shoulders, plan sponsors continue to move toward custom target-date strategies. According to the 2009 Casey Quirk/ Profit Sharing/401(k) Council of America (PSCA) Target-Date Funds Survey, 61 percent of plans default to target-date funds. Among plans that offer target-date strategies, PSCA reports that 11 percent offer custom-designed target-date strategies as opposed to selecting packaged or "off-the-shelf" target-date funds. Whether a plan offers custom strategies or not appears to be largely dependent on plan size. While overall only 11 percent of plans have custom target-date strategies, this number increases for plans with over $1 billion in assets. The Casey Quirk/PSCA study reports that 33 percent

TABLE 3.1 Changes under Consideration by Plan Sponsors

Choice	Response %
Switch from off-the-shelf to custom-designed funds.	15
Change underlying managers or provider.	20
Change glide-path construction (target-date only).	16
Change model or approach to customized glide path (target-date only).	13
Add or change annuity/payout features (target-date only).	17
Add new asset classes.	18
We would not consider changes to our target-date/ target-risk funds.	

Source: Casey Quirk/PSCA Survey, 2009.

of these larger plans offer such strategies. What is more, according to an April 2009 PSCA survey, when plan sponsors were asked what changes they would make to their target-date/target-risk funds over the next three years, 15 percent answered that they were considering "switching from off-the-shelf to custom-designed" target-date strategies. (See Table 3.1.)

Yet that is not to say that small plans are not offering custom strategies. They are. Plans with asset sizes as small as $1 million provide custom. As we discuss in Chapter 5, custom strategies can be set up in different ways depending on the record keepers' capabilities. Smaller plans may set up their strategies in one way, while the largest plans may select another approach.

WHY PLAN SPONSORS CREATE CUSTOM TARGET RETIREMENT-DATE STRATEGIES

Plan sponsors create their own target retirement-date strategies for many reasons. This choice enables them to:

- Have greater control over their plans
- Reduce overall plan cost
- Leverage investment-manager selection and oversight
- Blend investment structures and styles
- Broaden their asset diversification beyond core
- Tailor the glide path to their plan demographics

Greater Control

The number-one reason for customizing the plan is control: Custom target enables plan sponsors to maintain control over asset allocation structures, investment managers within the strategies, and overall plan costs. In their 2009 Target-Date Funds Survey, PSCA asked plan sponsors why they had developed custom plans. They found that sponsors valued the "ability to create a more diverse asset allocation" as well as having "control over underlying managers."[2] They also placed value on the ability to create glide paths to address their unique demographics, have greater fee transparency, and address their fiduciary concerns over buying off-the-shelf products. Anecdotally, PIMCO found that plan sponsors also greatly value the ability to reduce overall plan cost by offering a custom approach. Next we discuss in greater detail many of the ways they gain control.

Reduce Overall Plan Cost

Creating custom target strategies not only allows plan sponsors to maintain control over the investment lineup but also allows them to reduce plan expenses. This savings is typically a result of tapping into an institutionally-priced core investment lineup, which often causes fees to decline as assets increase. Plan sponsors may even benefit from a relationship price offered by investment managers involved in both their DC and defined benefit (DB) plans. In that case, both plans benefit from the custom strategies since the assets that accumulate in the plans drive the basis-point cost for investment management down to a lower level. Charles Claudio, pension manager at Ahold USA, Inc., pointed out that his company's retirement plan has been able to save "a substantial amount of money" by using the same investment managers for both their DB and their custom target-date DC plan:

> Let's say a manager offers us a fee schedule that pools in its fund the assets of both our 401(k) and pension plans. Since they base the price on a graded-fee schedule, we'd see a substantial reduction in the overall cost to offer that fund in both our target-date and pension plan. We don't need to unitize to get this fee advantage; rather, we receive relationship pricing that accounts for both the DB and DC assets.[3]

The investment lineups of most large plans offer an array of high-quality institutional investment options, including institutionally priced mutual funds, separately managed accounts, and collective investment trusts. As assets grow in target strategies, plan costs fall further because the cost of institutional investment management typically is on a sliding scale. That is, the basis-point fees of institutional investment management strategies typically decline as assets rise. Thus, tapping into these institutionally priced investment vehicles helps plan sponsors bring down plan costs not only by using lower-fee-structure funds within target strategies but by adding more money to the base of existing assets (rather than draining assets to new platform investments i.e., packaged target-date funds). Consultants estimate that the overall fee savings of custom funds versus packaged target funds range from 20 to 68 percent for plans with over $200 million in assets. For plans that unitize their DB assets to include in their DC plans, savings are even greater and continue to grow over time as assets increase. For example, Hewitt Associates observed the cost savings across 10 plans (ranging in size from $200 million to $5 billion) that offer custom strategies as 16 to 61 basis points below the average target mutual-fund fee of 80 basis points. Hewitt noted that, on average, a custom strategy may cost 40 basis points compared to a packaged product at 80 basis points. From the participant's standpoint, the added wealth accumulation may be 11 percent, or $140,000 over a career, given typical savings and return assumptions. In retirement, this $140,000 difference may translate to nearly $1,000 per month for a 65-year-old male, given current single-life annuity quotes.[4]

Focusing on fee reduction will continue to grow in importance over the coming years. Recent class-action lawsuits underscore this necessity. We look at cost-saving issues in greater depth in Chapter 7.

Leverage Investment Manager Selection and Oversight

One major disadvantage of packaged strategies is that when a plan sponsor adds new funds to the lineup, that decision requires separate attention to selection and oversight, adding to a plan sponsor's due diligence tasks. By comparison, custom strategies allow a plan sponsor to leverage the investment-manager selection and oversight they already perform for their core funds—in essence, using a best-in-class lineup.

Plan sponsors value the ability to hire and fire core managers as well as being able to leverage core manager selection and monitoring, blend investment structures and styles, and broaden asset diversification beyond the core lineup. Plan sponsors carefully select the managers for each asset class (whether active or passive), and rarely place all plan investments with a single manager. These plan sponsors believe that selecting the strongest manager in each investment category is in plan participants' best interests. Importantly, plan sponsors retain control of when to replace a manager. Typically, the larger the plan, the greater the investment flexibility afforded to plan sponsors. That is, midsize to larger plans have more control and choice over investment structure and providers than smaller plans, which may have little or no choice beyond that provided by their plan record keepers.

John LaCara described how this control worked when he was director of the Commonwealth of Massachusetts Deferred Compensation Plan and it launched custom target-date strategies in July 2007. "We decided to create target dates to allow for broader asset diversification and to simplify the fund-selection process. By leveraging existing relationships with investment managers, we built the target-date funds using institutionally-priced investment funds. The approach also allows us to maintain control of the underlying investments and tailor the glide path to plan demographics."[5]

Dan Holupchinski, a retirement plans manager for Deluxe Corporation, expressed great satisfaction with the manager selection and control advantages available through creating custom strategies:

> *With custom strategies, we retain control of the asset allocation and investment managers, which we monitor on a quarterly basis. When our governance committee meets to review core managers and investment options, the target-date strategies fall right into that process. We can add or change managers as needed and feel we're doing our due diligence. We're much more nimble than if we used a proprietary fund, which would give us no influence at all. So I feel we have a stronger platform.*[6]

Blend Investment Structures and Styles

Custom target strategies can use the same core investment-strategy lineup regardless of whether the options are structured as separately managed accounts, collective investment trusts, or mutual funds. This is important, as some types of investments, such as stable value, are not available in a mutual fund format, while others may be more attractive in a collective investment trust or separate managed-account format. Further, nonmutual funds can be desirable from a cost- and investor-impact standpoint. This approach also allows the plan sponsor to combine active and passive management styles depending on its views and core investment selection. (Note: Off-the-shelf target funds are typically 100 percent passive or active rather than a blend.)

Broaden Asset Diversification beyond Core

Custom strategies also offer the ability to include asset classes believed to best optimize the strategies' potential even if the desired asset classes are not offered as core investment options. For example, plan sponsors may decide to add inflation protection or other securities to a custom strategy and to the core lineup, or possibly only to the custom funds. Georgette Gestely, director of the New York City Deferred Compensation Program, adds Treasury Inflation Protections Securities (TIPS) to their custom plan portfolios as workers approach and enter retirement in order to provide greater diversification and inflation protection.[7] The Commonwealth of Massachusetts includes real-estate investment trusts (REITs), high-yield debt, TIPS, and money market accounts in its custom plan. When we asked why they decided to add these asset classes, the answer was the same as Gestely's: diversification and inflation hedging.[8]

Given the flexibility a plan sponsor has in adding more sophisticated diversification and professional asset-allocation oversight to a custom strategy, experts believe this investment approach appeals not only to novice investors as a default but also to more knowledgeable investors.

Tailor the Glide Path to Plan Demographics

Finally, custom strategies may be attractive as they allow a plan sponsor to tailor the target date "glide path" to participant demographics. Sponsors appreciate having control over designing the target date, being able to decide how conservative or aggressive they wish to be with this asset allocation. For instance, for participants who have other pension funding available, the plan sponsor may weight the glide path more heavily toward higher-risk assets, such as equities.

Charles Claudio, of Ahold USA, Inc., includes more equities in the glide path. When we asked him how he tailored its $900 million plan to serve participant demographics, he explained that many considerations make them different from other companies. Ahold includes both union and nonunion plan participants as well as a decentralized workforce, since it is a "holding company for supermarket chains throughout the Northeast United States" with 110,000 associated, including 75,000 union members "spread out across supermarkets, distribution facilities, and regional offices."[9] Nonunion employees have access to a DB plan and a 401(k), but in January 2009, this plan was closed to new hires. Union members usually do not participate in the Ahold DB pension plan since they have their own multiemployer plan "to which we contribute on their behalf." However, a greater number of union members do participate in the Ahold 401(k) plan. As time goes on, Ahold plans to focus less on the DB plan and more on the benefits of the 401(k).

Recently, Claudio told us, Ahold has redesigned its 401(k), and it is in the midst of doing the same for its pension plan.

Individuals will be offered a choice to either stay in the pension plan or opt out. In return for opting out of the pension plan, they would get an enhanced 401(k) benefit. Effective in 2010, the company will introduce a results-based contribution, that is, a year-end contribution based on the company's profitability during 2010 and future years as well. That would be in addition to any match that they normally would receive.

Essentially, Claudio explained, the "results-based" contribution is similar to the idea of a profit-sharing contribution.

When we asked how Ahold structures its plan from an investment standpoint, he explained that, since the beginning of 2009, the focus has been on simplifying and streamlining the investment menu. Ahold has moved to the traditional three-tier plan design, offering custom target-date strategies as Tier I, core funds in Tier II, and a full brokerage window for Tier III. It also has reduced its core fund lineup from 15 funds to six: "money market, core bond, two large-cap stock, small-/mid-cap stock and international equity." By redesigning the focus to target date, Ahold hopes to "give people access to diversification and professional management." Those who wish to diversify their retirement portfolio beyond these six core funds can use the brokerage window, "which offers access to approximately 4,000 mutual funds, plus individual stocks and bonds."

Ahold is also in the process of gradually liquidating its stable value fund and transferring the proceeds into a money market fund. While Claudio agrees that the yield on stable value is typically higher than money market, he points out that it is a common misconception to associate stable value with no risk. He explains why Ahold feels this move benefits plan participants:

One redesign goal was to weed out the underlying risks in our different funds. Number two: Our stable-value fund was an encumbrance to overall plan redesign because of equity-wash rules around which we had to maneuver. We want our participants to be able to move in and out of any fund without any restrictions. If we'd simply liquidated the stable-value fund, we would've been subject to market pricing, and would've taken too much of a loss. So we'll phase it out over time.

When we asked Claudio why Ahold decided to create custom target-date strategies in the first place and how that benefits its demographic, he explained that this plan design change flowed naturally from Ahold's DB plan, for which it has a well-established investment and management process. "We asked ourselves, 'If it's good enough for the pension plan, isn't it good enough for the 401(k) plan and, in particular, the target-date strategies?' We wanted to use in our 401(k) plan some of the managers from our DB plan." Another question they asked was

> *"Why build target-date strategies using funds that aren't offered in our core fund menu?" We wanted to incorporate our Tier II funds into our Tier I target-date strategies. As a value-added proposition we also wanted to get some of the funds from our DB plan into our target dates. So we looked at our target-date strategies, which essentially are a mix of what's in the Tier II core-fund lineup and which use some of our same pension plan managers.*

When we asked Claudio how Ahold developed the asset allocation and glide path for its target-date strategies, he explained that it was fortunate to find a manager who could not only help to build the glide path itself "but also strike a daily price on the target strategies for our current record keeper, and give communication support—a turnkey package." The glide-path design takes many factors into consideration: company demographics, deferral rates, the benefit employees would receive from the DB plan, and current investment policy.

One of the main points Ahold noticed was that income-replacement ratios widely varied in its pension plan, depending on whether the plan participant was a higher-paid salaried employee or an hourly worker. When Ahold looked at this factor, he realized that deferral rates were lower than he had thought.

> *Given the lower deferral rates, the expected investment return rates going forward, as well as the anticipated drawdown in post-retirement years, we found that people would come up short—they would not have enough money to make it through their expected retirement years.... That's the most important consideration. Because of this study our glide path probably is more heavily oriented toward equities than other glide paths you might see... Now we have a glide path that is exclusive to Ahold.*

John LaCara also sees benefits in creating custom strategies since a prepackaged product would not take their demographics into consideration: "We couldn't control a retail, prepackaged target date's assumptions. But by providing our demographics to a glide-path or lifecycle manager, the manager can use that information to build a glide path tailored to our demographic base."[10]

Choosing to create a custom target-date plan allows Gestely to provide answers for a very complex demographic. The New York City Deferred Compensation Program has 300,000 New York City employees, including the uniformed forces—fire, police, corrections, and sanitation—all the mayoral agencies, and all of the city's schools and hospitals. The primary retirement vehicle is a DB, even though approximately 15 percent of its $9 billion in assets is invested in a custom DC plan. However, since many employees in the uniformed services take their retirement in their mid-forties but stay in the plan indefinitely, a traditional glide path ending at age 65 would not be appropriate for them. The solution is to custom-tailor 12 portfolios, which allow participants to "receive an automatic annuity from the DB plan in retirement, which can allow them to be a bit more aggressive on the DC side. Since those portfolios didn't make sense [for everyone], we added three more portfolios to the roll down. Within the nine existing strategies, we raised the equity pieces a little. Then we pushed the target portfolio down to the lowest, adding three more at the tail end."[11] (See Figure 3.2.)

INTEL: BUILDING IS BETTER THAN BUYING

In 2004, the Intel Corporation led the way for plan sponsors by creating its own custom strategies using its plan's core investment options. Today, Intel remains delighted with that direction as the company enjoys the investment flexibility and lower cost gained by having built rather than bought an off-the-shelf product. We asked Stuart Odell, assistant treasurer, retirement investments, to tell us about the company's innovative and leading-edge approach as well as recent enhancements and plans for the future.

As one of the pioneers in creating custom "lifecycle" or target-date strategies, Intel has much to teach about creating an effective DC plan structure. It currently offers two retirement plans: a 401(k) and a profit-sharing plan.

> *The profit-sharing plan represents the Intel contribution to its employees' retirement and is equivalent to an employer 401(k) match, except that Intel manages the asset allocation on its employees' behalf, with a guaranteed-minimum-floor defined benefit. Part of the reason for offering a profit-sharing plan instead of a 401(k) match is that the company wants to provide an equal benefit to all employees, regardless of participation.[12]*

This plan enables Intel to provide a discretionary annual contribution—higher historically than the typical 6 percent—to all employees.

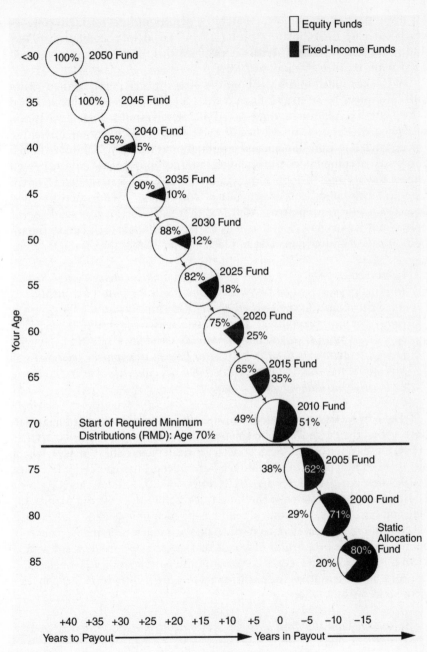

FIGURE 3.2 Fourth Attempt: Target-Date/Risk Portfolios
Source: New York City Deferred Compensation Program.

Even without an employer match, 75 percent of Intel's 50,000 employees participate in the plan, creating $9 billion in total combined 401(k) and profit-sharing assets. Across both plans there is an average combined participant balance of about $170,000.

We asked Odell to tell us about the 401(k) plan's investment structure and how lifecycle strategies fit into the plan. He explained that in April 2004, Intel created a new three-tiered 401(k) investment lineup consisting of five core asset-class funds, five lifecycle funds (which at time of writing has expanded to eight funds), and a mutual fund window. "The core funds, comprised of commingled trusts and separate accounts generically are named 'Stable Value Fund,' 'Global Bond Fund,' 'Large Cap US Stock Fund,' 'Small Cap US Stock Fund,' and 'International Stock Fund.'" While there are only five core investment choices, Odell said that each one may be made up of one or more managers. Some, such as the International Stock Fund, contain both passive *and* active managers. Odell explained that the

> *combined approach of active and passive management allows the fund to generate some potential alpha while keeping our overall investment management expenses low. Generically naming the core funds and using commingled trusts with underlying multiple managers also permits us to control individual manager selection. The flexibility allows us to offer a "best of breed" in manager selection and is an important consideration when deciding whether to build or to buy your own lifecycle funds.*

These five core strategies allow financially knowledgeable participants to put together their own well-diversified portfolio. Participants also can choose premixed selections of the eight core target retirement-date strategies, which Intel calls "Lifestage" funds: Lifestage Retirement, Lifestage 2005, Lifestage 2010, Lifestage 2015, Lifestage 2020, Lifestage 2025, Lifestage 2035, and Lifestage 2045. The dates in the fund titles signify the year the participant plans on retiring. Each Lifestage fund has its own unique glide path, which becomes more conservative as participants approach retirement, primarily by increasing the proportion of bonds to stocks. These funds are designed as an investment vehicle for all or most of the participant's 401(k) assets.

As a final alternative, for participants seeking a more specialized investment strategy, Intel offers

> *a mutual-fund window with 65 investment options, primarily institutional mutual funds and commingled trusts. We offer both active and passive alternatives in most major asset classes....So, with emerging markets, for example, we offer both debt and equity*

individual options within the window. Similarly, we have funds that take advantage of small-cap stocks, developed international, commodities and real estate. For most people, the core or lifecycle strategies provide all that participants need to develop a well-diversified portfolio, regardless of their investment horizon.

When we asked Odell why Intel had decided to create custom retirement-date retirement strategies, he explained that the decision was largely a response to behavioral finance findings. These findings showed that no matter how much education or advice participants were given about their retirement-fund choices, inertia seemed to be the most powerful force driving their behaviors and choices. Therefore, they needed the automatic mechanisms inherent in lifecycle or target retirement-date strategies to move them away from that inertia and adjust their portfolio as they neared retirement.

We asked why Intel decided to create their own custom strategies rather than select a packaged retirement-date approach like those offered by mutual fund companies. He replied that during 2003, when Intel was looking at providers of these types of funds, the products it was reviewing seemed too simple for the company's needs. "What concerned us was how little thought they'd put into the products' actual underlying asset allocations, or glide paths. We also were concerned with the underlying assets or particular funds used."

Intel's concern was that if it bought into one of these packaged solutions, it would be stuck with it. "If we weren't satisfied with the provider's asset allocation—glide path—or an underlying manager's performance, we wouldn't have a lot of recourse beyond pulling and replacing every single fund. With our built strategies Intel can replace a single underlying manager if it needs to—without disrupting the rest of the fund." Ultimately, having control was an important deciding important factor for Intel.

We asked Odell if Intel had considered plan costs as well; he stated that fees had been a major factor in the company's decision. Not only did the off-the-shelf providers' fees vary widely, but some

charged a fee on top of the underlying active manager's fee, while others focused primarily on passive index products and, thus, featured lower management fees. There weren't a lot of institutionally-priced products that you could buy off the shelf. By building the strategies ourselves, we took advantage of competitive institutional pricing right from the start, and kept our overall fees lower than most off-the-shelf products. Our strategies' all-in investment management fee is just 10 to 12 basis points.

The lowest-cost passive funds were in the 20- to 25-basis-point range. However, our funds feature both active- and passive-management components, so it's not quite an apples-to-apples comparison. Off-the-shelf active target-date funds had much higher costs—as high as 100 basis points or more. So we brought the cost down 50 to 90 percent compared to the mutual funds.

Concerning the added costs associated with custom strategies—trustee fees, communications, and additional administrative expenses—Odell pointed out that they were very reasonable, given the overall cost savings: "only around one basis point."

Another question we had was whether Intel considered the ability to blend active and passive investment approaches an attractive benefit. Odell agreed, pointing out: "By building one's own, the plan sponsor both has the flexibility to determine the active-passive mix, and maintains control over the offered asset classes and allocations by age group," determining the plan's glide path.

Odell also appreciates how custom strategies gives Intel the flexibility to add asset classes, such as real estate or commodities, that an off-the-shelf product may not be able to provide because it lacks professionals qualified to manage a particular asset class. By contrast, building your own custom plan gives you greater flexibility. "In the future, as part of a well-diversified lifecycle asset allocation, you even can consider alternative investments—hedge funds, private equity, or direct real estate, for example, which traditionally have been unavailable to DC participants." According to Odell, these alternative or nontraditional asset classes offer valued diversification and higher risk-adjusted returns. While currently these asset classes make up only a small portion of a participant's portfolio, Odell believes that, over time, "more plan sponsors will embrace alternatives in DC structures—particularly within lifecycle strategies."

Intel is very pleased with its decision to build rather than buy because it gives the company a lot of flexibility and "the ability to add managers or change an asset allocation without disrupting our participants. For a large plan sponsor that has a dedicated investment staff monitoring its DC core funds all the time anyway, this kind of flexibility is very beneficial."

When we asked Odell if he believed that, in the coming years, most DC plans would offer a default approach using custom strategies, he stated that retirement-date or lifecycle funds were definitely the future because the Pension Protection Act of 2006 and the Department of Labor supported this approach. He also felt that the flexibility of custom strategies was extremely appealing to plan sponsors.

VERIZON: WELL WORTH THE EFFORT

Michael Riak, director of savings and affiliate plans at Verizon, spoke with us about how Verizon has restructured its DC plan and launched its custom target-date strategies, tapping into its core investment offerings to do so. He specifically described the structure of Verizon's Management and Business DC plans, which include 70,000 active participants, 35,000 inactive participants (retirees), and just under $10 billion in assets. Verizon also has a DB plan for longtime employees, but in 2006 this plan was frozen to new hires and the DC plan became the primary vehicle for retirement savings.

When we asked Riak how Verizon made the decision to create their own custom strategies, he listed several reasons for this approach. First of all, it allowed Verizon to address the needs of both types of plan participants, those who were inexperienced investors (and could therefore be automatically enrolled in an age-appropriate glide path) and those who were financially sophisticated enough to make some of their own investment decisions. "Target-date funds allow our participants to choose funds based on specific goals and based upon the length of time the assets will be invested. And, of course, the key decision we made was that we were going to use our core investment lineup to create the target-date funds. We weren't going to use a packaged target-date product or retail mutual fund lineup."[13]

Riak also stressed the enormous amount of effort put into evaluating, selecting, and monitoring the investment managers for the DB and DC plans, so that Verizon provided participants not only with the "best building blocks for our target-date funds" but also the "best-in-class" managers. The company uses the same managers in its custom DC plan as it uses in its $28 billion DB plan (as of 10/1/09) because Verizon is comfortable with these tried-and-true individuals.

> *Our investment philosophy for our fund options is to use a multi-manager structure to control the overall risk and return characteristics of each investment option's asset class. Our multi-manager structure helps us reduce risk in the plan, and also keeps costs down. We also have control over the investment mandates for each investment strategy used in our plan, which is something we couldn't achieve with a packaged target date product.*

Another advantage to creating custom strategies is that the plan sponsor can create cost savings by selecting some of the already existing DB assets and unitizing them over into DC. Riak remarked that one of the issues Verizon was struggling with when creating the emerging-markets option was how many of the assets would flow over into the DC fund. Choosing a custom strategy design enabled Verizon to avoid the quandary of having just one emerging-markets manager running the fund, as is often the case for an off-the-shelf product. Instead, Verizon was able to utilize three DB managers with whom it was already comfortable. The unitization also helped the company acquire advantageous investments in emerging markets. "Since we lacked the initial asset base in the DC plan for the multimanager emerging market strategy, we decided to unitize this asset class over from our DB plan. In essence unitizing allowed the savings plan to buy emerging markets units along with the DB plan. Structurally, the emerging markets fund master trust holds assets for both the DB and DC plans in a unitized structure."

When we asked Riak about the custom core investment lineup, he explained that the plan offered 13 core investment options, plus company stock. The 10 target-date strategies were created from assets within the core, with the goal of broadly covering the asset classes available in the market.

As we have already seen, a great advantage to designing custom strategies is that they allow plan sponsors to leverage the investment manager selections and oversight they already perform for their core. Many of Verizon's core offerings are comprised of several investment managers, representing different styles or approaches. The company offers U.S. large- and U.S. small-company funds as well as an international actively managed fund. Each of these funds has five managers. "Some of the managers are growth-oriented, some are value-oriented, and some are core-oriented. Our Emerging Markets and Global Opportunity Funds each have three managers. We select managers that we know well and that are complementary to one another." This clearly shows the advantages of the custom strategy approach.

Although most of the investment management in Verizon's DB and DC plans is active, participants also are offered two passive strategies, each run by a single investment manager, the U.S. Large Cap Index and an International Index. While Verizon believes that active management "does offer the ability to get above average returns...we also wanted to offer passive investing, especially for participants who are seeking index pricing."

Custom strategies also allow plan sponsors to add desired asset classes and inflation securities to their lineup. Verizon offers cash, REITs, and private real estate (hard real estate assets such as malls, office buildings, and apartment complexes) in its lineup to provide the liquidity component for its strategy. "It's another excellent diversifier for an investment lineup. Real estate is a key component of our DB plan as well." Verizon chose private real estate as well as REITs because the latter

> tend to act like the general stock market and tend to correlate closest to the small cap value assets. By comparison, private real estate is less correlated to the general stock market. So, again, it's

a great diversifier relative to the stock market. And we wanted to give employees the ability to have alternative asset classes, not just the usual large cap/small cap US equity and international equity.

Riak also considers real estate a good inflationary hedge, along with TIPS.

When we asked him the extent to which his glide path structure was impacted by plan demographics, Riak remarked that the majority of participants who had been placed in the default option of their plans almost always stayed there. Therefore, Verizon

felt that the target-date funds will be the best vehicle to use as the default option for investors to accumulate assets by having more appropriate risk levels over a long period of time. In other words, since target-date strategies change the asset allocation over time as the participant ages, we believed this would be a more prudent approach than a static investment default option such as a money market or stable value fund.

While the glide path is "more heavily weighted toward equity for the younger populations who have longer time horizons for investment," for those closer to retirement, there is available "a relatively high weight in equity" because people are living longer and retirement income has to last much longer.

When we asked him what sort of work went into setting up his custom target strategies, Riak admitted that there were a lot of challenges, with timing being one of the biggest. "We set a deadline to have the new plan up and running on the first of the year to go along with our plan changes, including auto-enrollment, contribution escalation, and the diversification of company stock. So, it was a lot to get done all at once." Meeting this deadline was a team effort, requiring

weekly meetings with their project team, management and outside professionals. They also put their human resources, finance and legal professionals to work on various project requirements, including plan design, fund descriptions, documentation and so on. We needed everyone's insights to help us make important decisions necessary to moving the project to completion.

Riak stressed, however, that he did not believe that the difficulty of the project should stop companies from setting up custom strategies. "We're offering broad investment choice and low fees, plus we maintain the control we need to monitor the managers and make changes as needed over time." In the end, everyone considered it well worth it because now Verizon has "a well designed plan that offers participants an excellent opportunity to reach their retirement goals."

IN CLOSING

Custom target-date strategies are likely to continue to gain ground for one simple reason: They make sense. Plan sponsors for both DB and DC plans have historically selected a best-in-class lineup of investment managers to include in their plans. They have enjoyed the freedom to determine which asset classes to offer, how to structure asset mixes, and when to hire or fire investment managers. As assets continue to build in target-date strategies, plan sponsors increasingly will seek the control they have enjoyed for decades in designing retirement programs. Custom target-date strategies provide the control that plan sponsors need to design plans for their unique populations as well as to implement and evolve the investment structures to meet the needs of both participants and retirees. What is more, custom strategies allow plan sponsors to modify the design over time without upheaval in the plan. They can change an underlying manager or the asset allocation without removing an entire series of funds. In essence, they can redesign the kitchen without rebuilding the entire house.

Development of Custom Target-Date Retirement Strategies

Legal and Fiduciary Considerations

As plan sponsors consider establishing custom strategies in their defined contribution plans, the first concerns they voice are "Will custom strategies raise my level of fiduciary responsibility or risk?". At the 2009 Pensions & Investments Custom Target Strategies Summit, Employee Retirement Income Security Act (ERISA) attorney Marla Kreindler of Winston & Strawn LLP suggested that the plan sponsor's fiduciary risk need not be greater when it decides to set up custom strategies rather than using prepackaged target-date funds. In either case, as discussed in Chapter 1, the plan sponsor may be supported by the new provision added to ERISA by the Pension Protection Act (PPA) (and applicable regulations adopted by the Department of Labor [DOL]) for qualified default investment alternatives (QDIAs) under participant-directed defined contribution (DC) plans. These rule changes extend ERISA Section 404(c)–type fiduciary relief for decisions to invest plan assets in default investment funds, when those funds meet the QDIA requirements. Under ERISA Section 404(c), fiduciaries of individual account plans are not responsible for participant investment decisions when, among other requirements, participants have the right to exercise control over their investment decisions. Default investment options have not been eligible for Section 404(c) relief because participants do not make the affirmative investment decision but instead are "defaulted" into the default investment option. The QDIA rules solve that problem by in effect extending Section 404(c)'s protections to QDIAs.

Kreindler explained that the QDIA rules effectively transfer the potential liability associated with investment decision-making responsibilities from the plan sponsor to employees, so long as the plan sponsor prudently selects and monitors the plan investment options and provides choice and disclosure on the investments. She went on to suggest that "custom strategies may actually position a plan sponsor better from a fiduciary perspective," as they may allow plan sponsors to manage conflicts of interest and to gain control as well as transparency of the glide path, selection of investment managers, and the fee structures employed.[1]

Custom strategies may also protect participants from the activity of other plans or investors, given the use of separate accounts rather than mutual funds or collective investment trusts that commingle investments of plans that may not have the same investment horizon or objectives. Plus, plan sponsors have the ability to outsource fiduciary risk by selecting and hiring a consultant, investment manager, or investment advisor to oversee the glide path and perform other duties, such as selecting and monitoring the underlying investment managers.

Advisors can be experts who come in and help with the glide path on a nondiscretionary basis to support fiduciary decisions. Or they can come in and make discretionary decisions on the plan sponsor's behalf, even helping select fund managers. Some sponsors have considered hiring an outside advisor; others have considered two advisors, one for the glide path and one for fund selection. There are very different ways of approaching using advisors. Of course, using advisors comes with a cost. Yet, outsourcing this oversight can help reduce concern with fiduciary risk.[2]

In this chapter we answer some of the most common questions plan sponsors have asked us. We share views on these issues and other topics from lawyers Marla Kreindler and Julie Stapel of Winston & Strawn. In addition, we share observations on the special hearing at the Department of Labor and the Securities and Exchange Commission on June 18, 2009, regarding the 2008–2009 bear market and target funds as investment options. We also consider what consultants and plan sponsors feel are some of the greatest legal concerns regarding designing, managing, and monitoring custom strategies in defined contribution plans.

COMMON LEGAL QUESTIONS REGARDING DC PLANS

Here are the six top questions that people often ask us about the PPA and other new laws governing custom DC plans.[3]

1. Do we need an outside fiduciary, or even an investment manager, to design and monitor the strategies of our glide path?

Lawyers with whom we have spoken have advised us that this is not required. Rather, plan sponsors can create and monitor their own glide paths. Nonetheless, a plan sponsor may still desire outside consulting and oversight. The sponsor even may want an ERISA Section 3(38) investment manager (i.e., a registered investment advisor, a bank, an insurance company) to oversee the fund, although this may be unnecessary or at least redundant in instances where the investments that make up the strategies are all mutual funds or already are managed by Section 3(38) investment managers.

In the April 2008 *DC Dialogue*, we asked Georgette Gestely, director of the New York City Deferred Compensation Program, to tell us her view on the matter. She said that her program had solved this problem by having specific "contracts with each of the investment managers we hire. We look at exactly the way the separate-account investment policy is written so that there are no diversions that create a greater liability."[4]

Another area where companies are concerned about fiduciary responsibility and potential liability is in creating their own mix of core funds in their DC plans. We asked Pam Hess, director of retirement research at Hewitt Associates, to share her views on this matter. She pointed out that most companies Hewitt works with do not see a difference in the liability or fiduciary responsibility between choosing an off-the-shelf fund and designing a custom plan. Even if the sponsor chooses the packaged product, she said, it still has to make decisions regarding asset allocations. She also points out: "Many employers that create their own mix choose to partner with a consulting firm or fund manager to manage the allocation and possibly serve as fiduciary for them."[5] This is one way to ensure greater protection against liability.

Phil Suess, DC practice leader at Mercer Investment Consulting, said that in some cases, he has seen companies retain outside consulting firms to direct and decide the plan's entire investment lineup. Figure 4.1 shows the prevalence of plan sponsors seeking the support of an independent investment advisor with fiduciary responsibility (which may include hiring a consulting firm to direct and decide the investment lineup).

Suess adds: "Consultants often are willing to accept the risks and responsibilities required to oversee the plan's investments. We're likely to see more delegation in the future, as fewer companies are comfortable making these decisions and prefer to hire an expert third party." In cases where a consulting firm is willing to accept responsibility for overseeing DC investments, it often excludes company stock because it is "concerned about making decisions regarding an individual security." Suess states that there are "trust-company banks [that] are willing to assume this role and focus solely on company stock."[6]

2. Are custom target strategies considered to be mutual funds, that is, are they investment companies that require Securities and Exchange Commission (SEC) registration?

Many target mutual funds are made up of sleeves of mutual funds, and the target fund itself also is registered. Yet custom target strategies within a DC plan, when designed properly, are not themselves considered an

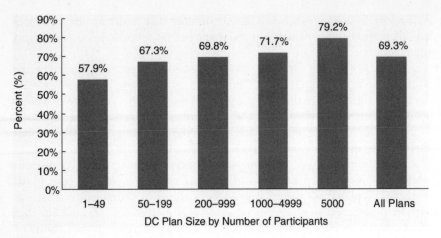

FIGURE 4.1 Percentage of Plans that Retain an Independent Investment Advisor to Assist with Fiduciary Responsibility (Separate of Record Keeper)
Source: Profit Sharing Council of America, 2008.

investment company that requires SEC registration. Rather, these custom strategies typically shift assets into and out of underlying plan investments—whether they are mutual funds, collective trusts, or separately managed accounts—based on model allocations or strategies that are custom designed by the plan sponsor. To the extent that a fund includes plan assets other than those from a single plan or a group of closely affiliated companies, the question should be addressed based on the specific facts and circumstances. Where plan interests are registered pursuant to a Form S-8 (i.e., a form used to register securities that will be offered to employees via employee benefit plans), as with any new investment option, plan sponsors should incorporate these new investment options into the plan's Form S-8 disclosures, as appropriate.

3. Do custom strategies qualify under the Pension Protection Act as a safe-harbor qualified default investment alternative (QDIA)?

The answer is yes. The final regulations applicable to QDIAs under participant-directed individual account plans permit a QDIA to be managed by an investment manager, a plan trustee, an investment company registered under the Investment Company Act of 1940, *or a plan sponsor*.

4. If the underlying funds are required to charge redemption fees to frequent traders within a plan, will custom target strategies be hit with fees from reallocations?

This plan sponsor concern is regarding the redemption fee described in SEC Rule 22c-2 of the Investment Company Act of 1940, as amended by the Pension Protection Act of 2006. As summarized in a press release by the U.S. Securities and Exchange Commission:

> *The rule would require all mutual funds to impose a 2 percent fee on the redemption proceeds of shares redeemed within 5 days of their purchase. The fund itself would retain the proceeds from the redemption fees. The rule is designed to require short-term shareholders to reimburse the fund for the direct and indirect costs that the fund pays to redeem these investors' shares. In the past, these costs generally have been borne by the fund and its long-term shareholders. Thus the redemption fee would be a "user fee" to reimburse the fund for the cost of accommodating frequent traders.[7]*

To clarify, let us explain this rule in a bit more detail. This rule requires the boards of funds issuing redeemable securities to either (1) adopt a redemption-fee policy, or (2) determine that a redemption fee is not necessary or appropriate. Practically speaking, we do not anticipate that this policy will apply to target strategies, since we believe the record keeper can establish cash-flow rebalancing in a way that will not trigger redemption fees for underlying funds. Plan sponsors should check with their record keepers and underlying fund providers to confirm whether their strategies are affected or whether, in fact, the underlying funds even impose redemption fees. Practically speaking, by defaulting or reenrolling participants into a single target retirement-date strategy, plan sponsors likely will find little movement between funds and thus minimize this concern.

5. Can custom strategies invest in funds that are not offered as core investments to plan participants? For instance, can a target strategy include an allocation to inflation-protected securities (such as Treasury Inflation Protected Securities [TIPS], real estate, or commodities) or even less liquid alternatives that are not available to participants otherwise?

The answer is yes, you can include investments in the custom strategies that are not core asset classes while precluding plan participants from directly investing in these asset classes. You may even blend into the strategies less liquid securities such as private placements, yet you need to consider carefully any potential pricing issues for investments that are not daily valued or that have liquidity constraints. While many less liquid alternatives or hedge funds generally are unavailable as core investments in participant-directed defined contribution plans, these investments may be appropriate as diversifiers within custom strategies. Again, given pricing and liquidity issues, you should manage carefully the allocation to such alternatives.

6. Is implementing a custom strategy the same as taking discretionary control of a managed account? That is, do these strategies constitute the provision of advice to participants?

Custom strategies and managed accounts are different. In the past, custom strategies generally were structured to fall within the safe-harbor fiduciary protections of ERISA, potentially as a combination of Section 404(c) compliance along with the additional benefit of hiring a Section 3(38) investment manager. By comparison, managed accounts sought to use the Section 3(38) investment manager structure but did not rely on Section 404(c) protections because participants give up control over their account balances to the managed-account providers. Both alternatives qualify as safe harbor-qualified investment alternatives under the QDIA regulations.

It is the fiduciary responsibility of plan sponsors to always review plan documents. They should make sure that target strategies are appropriately authorized or addressed in the plan's governing documents, including the summary of the plan documents and investment-policy statement. Also, they should make certain the expenses are permitted and charged in a manner consistent with DOL guidelines, plan documents, and participant disclosures as well as plan expense policies and procedures.

Finally, regarding Section 404(c) compliance structure, plan sponsors can, in essence, regard these strategies in the same way as any other core funds and structure the target strategies in compliance with the plan's Section 404(c). However, they should make certain that any selected advisor or manager accepts appropriate responsibility for developing and maintaining the strategies, including the performance monitoring and communication support necessary to satisfy Section 404(c) compliance.

INVESTMENT POLICY STATEMENTS AND GOVERNANCE

Other issues that have been under discussion recently are investment policies and governance. Phil Suess talked to us about the changes he was seeing in how plan sponsors were rewriting their investment policies as they were making the shift from defined benefit (DB) plans to DC plans as their primary retirement income vehicles.

In the past, there wasn't a lot of discussion necessarily as to plan objectives, other than providing access to key asset classes, making sure they're different materially in the context of, say, Section 404(c), and perhaps having an alternative for participants who weren't comfortable making asset-allocation decisions. Now, we're starting to see plan sponsors take a step back and look at their objectives from a higher level.[8]

In the past, Suess pointed out, "companies that offered DB and DC plans designed the DC plan for wealth accumulation." Now, as DC plans are rapidly becoming the only retirement plan offered, the focus is shifting toward seeing that plan as a vehicle for retirement savings. For this reason, it has become important to indicate the new purpose of the DC plans in the language of the company's investment policy. In fact, Suess stated, most companies are now writing these policies to clarify their "governance issues in the context of the selection, evaluation and replacement of investment funds." The Profit Sharing Council of America's 2008 survey reports that 85 percent of plans have an investment policy statement, up from just over half of plans (54 percent) having such a statement in 1999.[9]

In regard to structuring the retirement plans, Suess described how changes on the DB side impacted the DC side. A company might increase matching contributions in the DC plan or even add profit sharing or money purchase as a supplement to the plan.

Many times, the investment options in these company-funded plans are different from those offered via the participant-directed 401(k)s. For example, in the company-funded plan a sponsor may provide only target-date funds or a single plan-sponsor-managed balanced fund. Companies also review the array of funds in their existing plans with concern that participants rely more on these funds or this plan for retirement. Sponsors ask whether the investment array is doing its job or whether it may be too complex. They evaluate target-date options and often work to simplify their lineups.

Suess also explained how all the changes in investment structure and plan design, were causing sponsors to revise their investment-policy statements, stressing that plan sponsors were evaluating risks such as longevity and expanding retirement income adequacy to help determine what "contribution rate and investment array [is] necessary to provide a reasonable probability of meeting adequate income goals."

In addition, he pointed out that defining guidelines for the evaluation of the plan's investment options was also a high priority. Some of the strategies contained in these guidelines are causing investment policies to become more structured, focus more on process, provide a greater amount of documentation, and plan the "action steps that they'll need to take if an option fails to meet ongoing evaluation criteria." In essence, DC policies are being written with a lot more attention to detail than they were in the past, when DB plans received the plan sponsor's more rigorous attention. This is becoming essential now as DC plans gain a larger asset base, which requires a "heightened marketplace awareness of governance and compliance issues."

Suess also believes that fee litigation may drive plan sponsors to add fee issues into their policy statements.

> *Up to this point, it's been pretty limited and targeted. But having said that, from our perspective, it begs the question if somebody comes at you with respect to fees, "What are you going to say?" Plan sponsors will want to point to a policy with respect to fees. They'll want to show that they review fees on an ongoing basis and how the fees have changed over time. You want to have a defense to the extent questions are raised, and I think the best defense is being able to point to a policy and a process you followed.*

When we asked Suess what final words he had for plan sponsors in terms of writing their investment policy statements, he suggested "defining the responsibilities, the delegation of those responsibilities, and the processes that are in place to oversee the plan" so that if someone asks how decisions were made, the plan sponsor will have something clear and concrete at which to point.

TARGET-DATE STRATEGIES ON THE HOT SEAT

In the August 2009 *PIMCO DC Dialogue*, we talked again with Marla Kreindler as well as with her colleague Julie Stapel about recent activity in Washington related to defined contribution plans, with a particular focus on target-date strategies. Among other things, they discussed the five main themes they see emerging as Washington considers target-date offerings. These themes are:

1. **Conflicts of interest.** How best to address these in target-date strategies
2. **Transparency.** A look into how the company's target-date strategies work and the relative risks
3. **Disclosures.** At both the level of the plan sponsor and the plan participant
4. **Fees and expenses.** Especially in regard to funds that employ layers of managers and advisors
5. **Relative risk.** If investment funds are within target retirement-date strategies, including whether there should be adjustments to account for longevity

Kreindler and Stapel feel that these themes "provide a useful framework to consider the current proposals and best practices in designing target date funds" and that they even "extend beyond target-date funds and probably represent a starting point for analyzing any type of retirement plan strategy or investment product."[10] Let us take a look at each of these themes in greater detail.

Conflicts of Interest

In the wake of the financial upheavals of 2008 and the general market decline throughout 2008 and the first half of 2009, Washington has turned its attention to target-date strategies and Congress has been raising issues about them, particularly in regard to retirement strategies for plan participants who are closest to retirement and, therefore, the hardest hit by the financial downturn. The DOL and the SEC are also asking questions in this area.

There have also been questions in Washington in regard to a number of other contexts related to target strategies. For example, the DOL's regulations in the area of investment advice, which were once considered near final (but which have been withdrawn), have become the center of many discussions, and it is expected that they will be rewritten or legislative proposals may be adopted to again change these rules. Concern has been raised over how conflicts of interest could come into play in the context of providing investment advice, impacting plan participants.

Kreindler and Stapel discussed how conflicts of interest might appear in target-date strategies specifically, in certain prepackaged target date products where the investment advisor may have conflicts in selecting the funds that comprise the target date product. For instance, some have asked whether an investment advisor may include new investment strategies that do not have a track record in their target-date funds in a way that could be viewed as furthering the advisor's interests and not necessarily in the best interests of plan participants. In addition, the DOL received a request for an advisory opinion that suggested that ERISA could be interpreted to prohibit certain conflicts of interest inherent in mutual funds, which are operated as "funds of funds" by investing in other proprietary mutual funds of the mutual fund provider.

While the DOL since provided it's view that its prior interpretations of ERISA do not support that conclusion, raising the question does it provide "another way to consider the core theme of conflicts of interest, including in the context of target date funds."

We asked Kreindler and Stapel if this focus on potential conflicts of interest in target-date mutual funds might suggest that plan sponsors consider open architecture or custom target strategies or perhaps even managed accounts. They agreed, saying that these kinds of conflicts could be eliminated by using either an off-the-shelf solution, "where an independent advisor selects the various investment options," or in situations where "the plan sponsor can control the fund's architecture."

Transparency

Kreindler and Stapel feel that the theme of transparency is directly related to conflicts of interest because "one of the objectives of being transparent is to enable the plan sponsor and plan participants to evaluate what conflicts may exist." They mentioned several pieces of legislation that have been introduced in Congress recently, including a bill introduced by Congressman George Miller (D-CA) that would "require different kinds of fee and expense disclosures for plan participants, with an emphasis on making the plan investment options more transparent to the end user of the plan."

Two other significant players in the push to create greater transparency in target-date strategies as a response to recent market downturns are Senator Herb Kohl (D-WI), chairman of the Senate Special Committee on Aging, and SEC chairperson Mary Schapiro. Early in 2009, Kohl wrote to the secretary of labor and the chairman of the SEC, "urging them to examine target-date strategies" and to ascertain whether there was sufficient transparency "in terms of the asset allocation, particularly the degree of risk as participants approach retirement." In the early summer of 2009, Schapiro addressed the Senate about "the question of whether there is adequate transparency in and disclosure of target-date strategies."

Disclosures

In terms of what has been proposed by the DOL regarding disclosure requirements, Kreindler and Stapel described regulations that would require fee disclosures by service providers to plan sponsors under Section 408(b)(2) of ERISA and to participants under Section 404(c) of ERISA. For instance, the DOL regulations would require service providers to disclose to plan sponsors detailed explanations of any conflicts of interest presented by the service provider's fees or provision of services. These regulatory proposals would also require that information about fees and expenses associated with various different types of products be more transparent at point of sale, regardless of the legal form of the product. Currently, there are different reporting obligations depending on the structure of the investment product. Is it a mutual fund? Is it a separately managed account? Or is it a collective trust or some other vehicle? Depending on the structure, the fee disclosures can be different. These regulatory proposals seek to provide for a minimum level of consistency in disclosures regardless of legal structure.

However, Kreindler and Stapel pointed out that no one knows when such regulations would be finalized or whether legislation such as the Miller bill, which has disclosure as its cornerstone, would override the new DOL regulations. In other words, there is a great deal of uncertainty involved with predicting exactly how disclosure rules are going to change. However, with the change in administration, it is expected that increased disclosure requirements will remain a top priority. Other players include Senator Kohl's committee, which has been focusing on disclosure as well. Kreindler and Stapel feel that "the SEC will also take a leading role on this issue as its inquiries on target funds have been disclosure-focused as well."

One issue that has been jointly raised by Kohl and the SEC is "whether the very name 'target-date fund' is not an adequate disclosure of the fund's strategy, particularly if there is confusion about the meaning of 'target.' For example, do plan participants believe that by the time they reach their retirement date, they should be risk free and ready to retire?" Since there is such a "wide variety of asset allocations among the target-date strategies offered in the market," Schapiro has questioned whether regulations or guidance may be needed on the name given to these types of funds. "Should funds that 'target' the expected retirement date use the name 'target fund,' the same as funds that 'target' the expected mortality date?" Phyllis Borzi, assistant secretary of labor of the Employee Benefits Security Administration, has raised similar concerns. We explore these issues as we discuss glide-path design in Chapter 8.

Fees and Expenses

Kreindler and Stapel pointed out that "making sure that plan sponsors are able to access information about fees and expenses, as well as making sure that participants can evaluate and compare fees and expenses across available plan investment options," was an issue included in all of the potential new regulations and pending legislation. For example, the Andrews bill addresses concerns related to investment advice. A concern is whether investment advisors receive a higher profit by directing client revenues toward higher-revenue investment products. The Miller bill, if passed, "would go as far as to require DC plans to offer at least one passive investment choice, such as an S&P [Standard & Poor's] 500 index fund. The theory here seems to be that offering at least one index fund would ensure at least one low-cost plan investment option." Representative Richard Neal (D-MA) has also introduced a bill on fees and expenses; however, this legislation would not require that plan sponsors "offer a passive investment option."

Relative Risk

The questions raised in Washington about relative risk have largely been fueled by the economic downturn that began in 2008 and the significant losses in equity allocations, especially in 2010 target-date strategies. Kohl has raised concerns regarding "the wide variations among glide paths and specifically the wide variation in the percentage of equities in 2010 strategies." Kreindler and Stapel relate this issue to the question of whether target-date strategies are accurately named. They point out that if "the investment objective is to give you enough money to last until you're likely to die, that would mean one thing for your asset allocation. If it means having a hard stop at retirement, that would mean another thing for your asset allocation." In other words, are these funds being managed for retirement or for mortality? This question has become very emotionally charged of late because of testimony offered in Washington by retirees who have lost as much as 30 to 40 percent of the assets in their target-date funds. The general consensus is "How on earth could such a thing happen?". Even the popular television show *60 Minutes* aired a segment in April 2009 entitled "Retirement Dreams Disappear with 401(k)s." This show focused on the double tragedy of unemployed plan participants who were also watching their 401(k) plans shrink dramatically.

When we asked Kreindler and Stapel whether they thought that the qualified default investment alternatives safe harbor would be impacted by these concerns and discussions in Washington, they suggested that there were two issues related to this question: Would plan sponsors change the way they included QDIAs in their plans, and how were Congress and the regulatory commissions going to respond?

While they pointed out that congressional "hearings before the ERISA Advisory Committee have again broached the topic of including stable value as another QDIA," they added that "it is not clear that any formal proposals to reopen the QDIA regulations, or to override them through legislation, will prevail." The only real trends that seem to be emerging are calls for greater transparency and more disclosure by Congress and other regulatory agencies.

Kreindler and Stapel felt that the primary effect of these developments was causing plan sponsors "to re-examine their QDIAs in a renewed attempt to understand the investment strategy structure, the risk profile of the glide path and investment strategy, the fees and expenses, and any potential conflicts of interest presented by the structure." In conclusion, they stated:

> *Whatever legislative proposals come out of Washington likely will impact 401(k) investment options across the board. But there may be certain actions that are going to have more of a specific focus on*

target-date funds; for instance, requirements on naming of the funds and disclosures in terms of how the funds are managed to a target retirement or mortality date. We also expect the whole concept of QDIAs will continue to evolve, such as by clarifying when fiduciary protection is available.

WHAT MAY LIE AHEAD IN LEGISLATION OF TARGET STRATEGIES

On June 18, 2009, the Department of Labor and the Securities Exchange Commission held a joint hearing about whether, in light of the severe bear market in 2008, target-date retirement strategies were still a viable structure for retirement plans. Senior officials of both organizations heard testimony from more than 30 plan consultants, fund managers, and pension plan sponsors. Their goals were "to better understand target funds as a product and determine whether current regulations promulgated by the respective agencies adequately sponsor investor understanding of target funds."[11] One of the main issues they were investigating was why the performance of retirement funds with the target date of 2010 had varied so widely in performance. The 31 target funds they chose to review had lost an average of 25 percent of their value, with general losses ranging between 3.6 to 41 percent, depending on the plan. Two questions regulators were investigating were why target-date funds were so heavily invested in the equities market, which made them vulnerable to any market downturn, and whether plan participants understood what they were investing in. In other words, were education and communication adequate?[12]

Here is a summary of some of the main points of this hearing and the decisions made.

One question that has been under wide scrutiny of late is whether the name "target-date" is misleading and whether it is necessary to regulate what these retirement funds are called in order to help participants understand them better. Jodi DiCenzo of Behavioral Research Associates gave testimony at the June 18 SEC/DOL hearing about workers' misperceptions about target-date funds. Her firm conducted an online survey of 250 American workers to understand better their perceptions of target-date funds. The firm provided the workers with typical descriptions of target-date funds compiled from actual marketing materials of the top three target-date fund providers. The survey showed that the majority of plan participants do not really understand what target-date retirement funds actually provide for them.

DiCenzo highlighted these points: "61 percent of people say that target-date funds make some type of promise," and "when asked to describe the promise that target-date funds make, nearly 70 percent of respondents perceive a promise that does not in fact exist." Here are some sample quotations showing what some American workers think the funds promise:

- "Funds at the time of retirement."
- "Secure investment with minimal risk."
- "It's like a guaranteed return on investment even when the market bottoms out."
- "A comfortable retirement."

DiCenzo continued: "Alarmingly, over 60 percent of employees say that investing in target-date funds means they will be able to retire on the target date." As evidence, she presented these statistics: "38 percent think target-date funds offer a guaranteed return" and "30 percent of workers think they can save less money and still meet their retirement goals if they invest in a target-date fund."

She continued: "Worse yet, when workers ranked five tasks based on their importance to their overall retirement planning, selecting a savings rate, arguably the most critical determinant of retirement success, was ranked first by the fewest number of people. Only 8 percent of people say it is the most important aspect of their overall retirement planning."

In terms of "how workers perceive the risk of target-date funds," DiCenzo offered these statistics:

- "Over 23 percent of workers believe that there is little to no chance that they will lose money either before or after the target date.
- "41 percent think there is little to no chance of losing money in any one-year period."
- "70 percent think they are equally as likely or less likely to lose money in any one-year period, as compared to investing in money market funds."[13]

DiCenzo's testimony and that of others was helpful to the Investment Company Institute (ICI), which had formed a committee to study this issue. ICI's conclusion was that simply changing the name of the retirement funds would not create greater understanding of their investment structure and function—and would be more likely to create greater confusion in plan participants. Instead, the ICI working group recommended greater transparency. It "concluded that if the disclosure in the prospectus clarified that the target date in the target fund's name is the date the investor is assumed to stop making contributions to the fund (i.e., the key event in the design of all target funds), then any investor confusion about the relevance of the target date in the target fund's name would be resolved."

The next major issue on which the senior officers of the DOL and SEC heard testimony was why target-date plans ending in 2010 produced such widely differing return values. The reason given was that fund managers have different investment strategies and different ways of structuring the DC plan, depending on the plan objectives. Some plans aim to create as much income as possible during the participant's working years so that he or she will have a large lump sum to take at retirement. Other plans aim to create sufficient income to last throughout the participant's retirement years, so that he or she does not outlive plan returns. Again, the recommended action was greater communication and transparency. Given the difference in philosophies and objectives in the timing horizons of different plans, "many panelists agreed that the disclosure in the target fund's prospectus should clearly delineate the target fund's Investment Objective and time horizon to help plan fiduciaries evaluate a target fund."

In addition, panelists further testified that individual plan structures were driven by plan sponsors' evaluation of risk factors such as "longevity risk (the risk of outliving one's savings, which has increased recently because of longer life expectancies), inflation risk, market risk, and withdrawal risk." These risk factors were taken into consideration when decisions were made concerning what percent of a plan's assets should be allocated to equities at a particular time period on the glide-path arch. Decisions about this asset allocation varied among plan sponsors, however. One plan sponsor testified that his plan was allocated 32 percent to equities upon retirement. Another said that his plan put this number at only 25 percent because he believed that "market risk should be more limited at retirement." Other fund managers believe that equities should be set at 50 percent—or even 60 percent—at retirement and only gradually decline to 20 percent in order to provide adequate income throughout retirement.

> *The testimony of the various fund managers illustrated that there is no consensus as to what constitutes an optimal target-date strategy, asset allocation, or glide path. Each of the fund managers, along with other panelists, agreed that any potential regulation should not mandate a particular glide path because glide path diversity is necessary to accommodate investors' different risk appetites, retirement goals, and financial situations. These panelists argued that a one-size target fund could not fit all investors' financial situations and, therefore, plan fiduciaries should be allowed to make decisions on behalf of their participants' particular goals.*

There was consensus that greater disclosure in the prospectuses of target funds was necessary to help investors understand the funds in which they were investing. Since target funds typically are designed as investment vehicles for less sophisticated investors, plan sponsors should be sure to take this fact under consideration when deciding on levels of disclosure and communications strategies. "There was broad agreement among panelists that investor education is the first step in attempting to help investors understand the methodology used to construct the underlying portfolios."

The last issue discussed at the hearing was "target funds that use proprietary funds of their parent fund complex as underlying funds." Because of the lack of transparency in evaluating the fee structure of proprietary funds, many panelists remarked that "no fund complex can possibly have the 'best in class' fund for every asset class." In other words, retirement funds that invest only in proprietary funds are not necessarily operating in their participants' best interests, because some managers invest in proprietary fund complexes that include "underperforming or expensive funds." In such cases, these investments can generate higher fees for the managers.

Returning to the argument that plan managers must choose plan investment options according to overall plan goals, the general panel consensus was that managers should still be allowed to use these types of funds in their plans. However, there was also some discussion of whether "the group controlling such decisions should be subject to ERISA fiduciary standards."

In conclusion, in the future, "the SEC and the DOL are expected to promulgate some regulations governing some aspects of target funds, in order to protect investors by providing greater disclosure, especially regarding the glide path." While both agencies are "interested in potentially substantive regulation...whether either agency would go as far as governing the construction of a glide path or mandating particular asset allocations at various dates remains to be seen."

At the time of writing this book, hearings on target-date strategies continue in Washington. For instance, on October 28, 2009, the Senate Special Committee on Aging held a hearing to examine the report "Target Date Retirement Funds: Lack of Clarity among Structures and Fees Raises Concerns" in which three concerns were identified:

1. Lack of disclosure and consistency in the design of target-date funds
2. Excessive fees
3. Conflicts of interest

Among the conflicts of interest, it was noted in the hearing that packaged target-date products fail to offer the plan sponsor a choice of selecting the underlying funds and "as a result, some investment firms may include low-performing funds in their portfolio in an effort to garner more assets."[14] By the time you read this book, we may have more clarity on this issue. Right now, however, we believe that the concerns with conflicts of interest will drive more organizations toward creating custom target strategies or seeking packaged target strategies that offer multiple investment managers as well as independent oversight of the underlying fund selection.

IN CLOSING

From a legal perspective, plan sponsors should feel as much regulatory support in offering custom target strategies as they would in selecting packaged target date funds. Custom strategies fall within the QDIA regulations, which guarantee safe-harbor protection for plan sponsors. To gain greater comfort in moving to custom strategies, plan sponsors may outsource the management of the glide path to a consultant, investment advisor, or investment manager. It may be argued that custom strategies may actually reduce risk for plan sponsors, as such strategies can address potential conflicts of interest, increase transparency to managers, improve disclosure to participants, control fees and expenses, and prudently manage risk. Custom strategies may free plan sponsors to manage investments in the best interest of participants, which is the core of their fiduciary duty.

CHAPTER 5

Record Keeping and Trust

T he operational setup of custom target-date strategies may appear daunt-ing or insurmountable on the surface. Given the concern with complexity, smaller organizations may believe that their plan asset size precludes them from offering custom strategies. We want you to know that the setup does not have to be a hurdle to open architecture, even for the smallest companies. Organizations of all sizes are offering custom strategies to their participants. What is important to realize is that company size may drive the use of different operational approaches. In this chapter, we take a look at how record keepers and trust companies support custom target strategies. We share information on the two primary operational approaches to target strategies and discuss the trust company's role. Finally, we suggest questions for you to pose to your record keeper.

To gain insight into how the largest record keepers support custom strategies, in 2009 PIMCO surveyed 30 firms representing plans with $1.6 trillion in defined contribution (DC) assets under administration. Our survey highlights these facts:

- The vast majority of record-keeping firms (93 percent) support custom asset allocation strategies including target date.
- The majority of firms (71 percent) support the model portfolio approach on their record-keeping system.
- One-third support trust unitization of custom strategies via an internal or external trust company.
- Additional fees vary on a firm-by-firm basis, depending on the level of support, with many not adding charges, especially for the model portfolio approach.

From an administrative perspective, custom target strategies are relatively easy to set up. To the market, these strategies appear as newcomers, but the operations that support them are well established. Record keepers and trustees have supported blended-manager institutional options for decades, and blending investment-manager options is common for stable-value investment options, which may hold multiple contracts or managers. Custom target strategies leverage the same operational approach and systems as blended strategies. Next we turn to the approaches record keepers and trust companies may present to you.

TWO BASIC APPROACHES TO SETTING UP RECORD KEEPING

There are two basic ways in which target-date strategies can be set up:

1. **Model portfolio approach** (some may call this the "paper portfolio" approach). A record-keeping system solution where the plan administrator creates a set of model target-date portfolios using all or a portion of the core funds.
2. **Trust unitization approach** (some may refer to this as the "custodial model" approach). A trust and record-keeping system solution where each target-date portfolio is set up as a separate account within the trust and as an individual investment option on the record-keeping system, using all or a portion of the core funds. This approach also offers the option to include investment strategies outside of the core fund lineup.

Some record-keeping providers offer a combination of these two approaches where, for example, the investment and rebalancing tasks normally provided by the trust are performed by the record keeper. An important step in designing the custom target-date strategies that you envision is exploring with your record keeper the approaches it supports.

CUSTOM TARGET STRATEGIES LEAD TO NEW RECORD-KEEPING APPROACHES

Matthew Rice, the principal and chief research officer at DiMeo Schneider & Associates, talked with us about how the company works with plan sponsors on structuring DC plans to meet retirement-income needs, including the different kinds of operational approaches to offering custom retirement-date strategies. Since many plan sponsors believe that creating custom strategies is feasible only in large or mega-plans (e.g., plans over $100 million), we asked Rice about his experience in this matter. He assured us that, in terms of custom target-retirement strategies, DiMeo has clients of all sizes, with plans ranging from $2.5 billion down to $20 million. For him, the most important issues had to do with whether the sponsor remapped the plan assets to the target-date funds as well as record-keeping constraints. Rice felt that there were distinct advantages to this remapping. First, it allows the sponsor to create a larger asset base, making the cost of the custom strategy more feasible. Remapping also allows plan sponsors "to cross the asset hump and make the jump to customization. If you add custom target strategies as new investment options and don't map, it can take a long time for assets to find their way to these strategies—even with the best education and communication efforts. Inertia is the most powerful force in the universe, especially for 401(k) participants!"[1]

Rice discussed the pros and cons of the two basic operational approaches when offering custom strategies: the trust unitization approach and the model portfolio approach. The disadvantage Rice saw to the unitization approach is that it "requires the record keeper or trust to create separate accounts of the underlying funds, and strike daily net asset values for each target-date strategy." He felt that the larger plans, or those that decided to remap assets to create a sufficient asset base to get established, would be the ones most likely to be attracted to the trust unitization approach.

For smaller plans—those below $100 or $50 million—Rice felt that the model portfolio approach might be the only viable option for many sponsors, due primarily to the potentially higher cost of the trust unitization approach.

> *The model portfolio approach resides on the record-keeping system at the participant level. Model portfolios are simply predetermined allocations to underlying funds. For example, if a participant selects the 2020 model, the system automatically allocates 20 percent of their account to Fund A, 12 percent to Fund B, and so on, based on the model's target allocation. As the 2020 model's target allocation changes over time, the record keeper simply rebalances each participant's account to the new targets.*

One advantage of the model portfolio structure, Rice pointed out, is that it requires fewer resources. Record keepers for this type of structure would be less likely to charge additional fees because they might not need to manage cash flows in and out of a trust account or to strike a daily net asset value (NAV). Another advantage is that in the model portfolio structure, "a participant's contributions are allocated simply based on a predetermined, percentage mix, and rebalanced at the participant account level," enabling smaller plans to create cost-effective custom strategies. This is contrary to the general conception that custom target strategies are feasible only for mega-plans, as sponsors often assume.

Another frequent question plan sponsors ask is whether all record keepers support the model portfolio approach to target strategies. While the 2009 PIMCO Record Keeping Survey assures us that most do, Rice encourages sponsors to talk directly with their record keeper to ascertain this. "More record keepers are developing the capabilities to support custom strategies, though some are more reluctant than others to do so. Many times the record keeper is also a mutual-fund company. In that case, it may have incentives to discourage custom strategies because it instead wants to distribute its own proprietary [off-the-shelf] target retirement-date funds." However, Rice also feels that in the future, more record keepers will be getting on board with the model portfolio approach because those who do not offer those services are actually losing clients.

PROS AND CONS OF ALTERNATIVE OPERATIONAL APPROACHES

Since all plan sponsors are at different places in terms of plan design and current needs, each of the two types of approaches has certain unique qualities that might be more advantageous for their plan. The size of a plan, whether its assets are above $20 million or below $20 million, is also a consideration regarding which approach is best. It is important to discuss the cost associated with the unitization approach with your trustee and not assume based on your plan assets that this approach is cost prohibitive. Tables 5.1 and 5.2 summarize some of the pros and cons of each approach.

QUESTIONS TO POSE TO YOUR RECORD KEEPER

There are many different issues plan sponsors need to discuss with their current or prospective record keeper regarding finding the approach that best fits their plan. With this in mind, PIMCO has created some key questions that a plan sponsor can use to identify a record keeper's capabilities in supporting custom target date funds.

1. Do you support custom target-date strategies?
Yes or No. If "Yes," continue.
2. How many custom target date clients do you support today?
3. Which operational approaches do you support?
Trust unitization/Model portfolio/Both

4. If you support trust unitization, are you using an internal or external trust (or either) for these services?

5. Describe your best practices support for custom target strategies.

6. Do you allow the plan sponsor or a consultant/advisor to provide the custom glide path (versus only supporting a proprietary glide path)? Yes or No.

7. What type of investment vehicles do you allow within the strategies? Mutual Funds _____ Collective Investment Trusts _____ Separate Accounts _____ Company Stock _____ Stable Value _____ other_____

8. Describe your support for custom strategy fund fact sheets and other participant communication.

9. Do you require a minimum plan asset size or investment amount to support target-date strategies? Yes or No. If "Yes," what is the requirement?

10. Do you limit the number of target-date strategies that you will support on your system? Yes or No. If "Yes," what is the limit?

11. How often can the glide path be modified and updated via your systems (e.g., monthly, quarterly)?

12. Will participants' statements show a single value for the target strategies, or will they only see the underlying fund values?

13. Can participants invest in both the target-date strategies as well as core funds, or is the choice all or nothing?

14. How are cash flows to the target-date strategies managed?

15. If you are using the model portfolio approach, are accounting reports provided at the fund and subfund level? Yes or No.

16. Can your administrator also provide the glide path management? Yes or No. If "Yes," confirm the associated fees.

17. How will you and your record keeper coordinate subsequent changes to the underlying funds, as well as manage communication of these changes?

18. Can the record keeper support an expense allocation through the NAV, individual participant allocations, or a mixture of both? Yes or No.

19. When/if historical transaction adjustments are necessary, does the record keeper retain each glide path for the established relative time period? Yes or No.

TABLE 5.1 Trust Unitization Approach

Pros	Cons
This approach gives plan sponsors the ability to include funds not offered within the plan's current core lineup, which provides more diversification of strategies and asset classes within the custom strategy without directly exposing participants to alternative asset classes. This not only produces additional alpha potential but shields the fiduciary from extra liability. This approach also allows for seamless switching of underlying managers with potentially limited or no change to participant communication materials. This approach would allow for the most flexibility in future changes.	There are likely additional trustee costs associated with utilizing a large trust. According to PIMCO's 2009 Record Keeping Survey, all administrators unitizing funds via an internal trust company, and nearly three-fourths (71 percent) of those unitizing funds via an internal or external trust company, charge an additional fee. Therefore, due to the cost, small plans may not be able to take advantage of this approach, whereas large plans actually may be able to decrease overall plan fees, given their asset base. (In discussing with one trust company, adding a customized fund as an additional account costs approximately $5,000 to $8,000 annually.)
The trust strikes a daily NAV to update nightly record keeping as well as to provide a clear and easy metric for participants and plan sponsor to track overall strategy performance.	The plan sponsor and record keeper need additional administrative support for trustee interactions, cash flow management, and striking a daily NAV. Most of these tasks should be easily leveraged.
The approach provides potentially lower fees, due to the ability it gives plan sponsors to utilize institutionally priced investment strategies.	A minimum asset level will be necessary to justify adding various asset classes to the strategies given the use of trust separate accounts.
All fees for investment management and operations can be folded into a single expense ratio to share with participants, as done with mutual funds.	
This approach provides for a clear audit trail when conducting investment fund reconciliations because the trustee holds a separate account for the specific fund and tracks the cash flows accordingly.	The additional fees for creating custom target-date strategies must be disclosed and allocated to participant accounts or covered by the plan sponsor.

TABLE 5.2 Model Portfolio Approach

Pros	Cons
This approach charges minimal to zero fees. The majority of record keepers (55 percent) who participated in the PIMCO Record Keeping Survey did not charge an additional fee.	This approach often is limited to the asset classes offered within the core lineup. Plan sponsors may be reluctant to offer directly to participants certain alternative asset classes that they would like to include in the custom funds, such as commodities, emerging markets, or alternatives. Full communication is necessary regarding any changes in the underlying asset classes.
System and operational enhancements are necessary. Allocation percentages (the model portfolios) are simply programmed into the existing record-keeping platform.	Since a daily NAV for model portfolios is generally not created, the performance of the target-date strategies may be difficult to track and report to participants.
No minimum asset size or initial funding is necessary to initiate each strategy. All future contributions will simply be invested according to predetermined allocations.	In the account statements as well as via the Web, plan participants will not see their assets in a single target-date strategy. Rather, they will see their assets in each subfund, which may lead participants to move out of the strategies if they are unhappy with the performance of an underlying fund.
Rebalancing of the model portfolios can be automated to occur at specific time intervals or based on a percent deviation from the policy glide path.	Participants may be required to invest in the target-date strategies as "all or nothing." They could not have 50 percent in the target model portfolios and the remainder in the core investments they select.
	For plan audit reports, the specific transactions cannot be isolated in accounting documents by the specific fund. The cash flows are included in the core fund analysis. It can be more difficult to monitor trends or report out.
	Redemption fees for frequent trades between funds may result.
	It is more difficult to monitor the performance, fund detail, and fees associated with this approach. There is more risk knowing the DOL will be addressing requirements for participant reporting of fees in the coming months.

KEY CONSIDERATIONS TO DETERMINE WHICH APPROACH TO CHOOSE

As you consider which operational approach makes the most sense for your plan, consider these issues:

- **Plan asset size and investment in the target-date strategies.** Most record-keeping providers will have a plan or investment-level minimum for custom target-date strategies. If plan assets are below a certain threshold, model portfolios may be the best direction for you to pursue until assets reach the provider minimum.
- **Additional plan costs.** As noted, record keepers often do not impose additional fees for the model portfolio approach. The trust unitization approach, however, likely will add both trust and record-keeping costs as the separate accounts are set up, priced daily, and supported on the system. Plan sponsors will need to determine how to cover and disclose these additional costs. Typically, these costs are passed directly through to participants in the target-date strategies. Both approaches may incur a fee for custom glide-path development and ongoing management. More on cost allocation is presented later in this chapter and in Chapter 7.
- **Alternative asset class use.** Some plan sponsors may want to use asset classes within their custom target-date strategies, but not as an investment option in the core lineup. The asset classes most commonly considered for addition to the custom strategies include non-U.S fixed-income, high-yield, emerging markets, commodities, real estate investment trusts (REITs), and hedge funds. In general, the trust unitization approach is required if alternative asset classes are desired within the target-date glide path.
- **Record-keeper limitations.** Plan sponsors should have discussions with the plan administration provider very early in the custom target-date analysis stage to understand its capabilities, requirements, and limitations.
- **Plan sponsor limitations.** Adding and maintaining custom target-date strategies may require additional support by the plan sponsor. These activities can be outsourced to investment managers or consultants. For instance, you may want to hire a glide-path manager as well as a communication provider, or perhaps a consultant or other provider to manage the entire implementation and ongoing oversight of the strategies. Some firms provide all of the needed oversight and act as investment managers and fiduciaries overseeing the glide path. You may also decide to divide these responsibilities across different organizations.

ESTABLISHING AND MAINTAINING OPERATIONS

To establish custom strategies, you first need to determine the operational process that you prefer or that your record keeper supports. Depending on the direction you select, you will then follow the steps outlined in Table 5.3.

CONVERSION OF TARGET RISK TO TARGET DATE

Many plan sponsors are interested in converting from custom target-risk strategies (e.g., conservative, moderate, and aggressive portfolios) to target-date structures. In essence, target-date strategies may be viewed as a series of target-risk strategies that dynamically reallocate as the participant ages. Making a change to target-date strategies may be accomplished by relabeling the target-risk strategies to target date and modifying the asset allocation within the strategies as needed. Additional target strategies are then created to offer a sufficient set of alternatives for the plan's population. Prior to actually mapping participants to the new strategies by age, a sponsor must communicate the upcoming change and allow participants to take another course of action, if they prefer. Part of the communication should mention any short-term trading restrictions that apply.

FEE ALLOCATIONS AND DISCLOSURES

At the 2009 Target Retirement-Date Strategies Conference, Tom Eichenberger, vice president and Senior Executive for State Street's institutional investor business, shared his insights on the type of decisions plan sponsors must make when implementing the trust unitization or what he refers to as the "custodial model" of record keeping. State Street manages approximately 2,000 funds used by 140 customers, and roughly 475 of these are custom target-date strategies.

An important decision a plan sponsor must address is how to allocate expenses throughout the plan. This issue is complex because it is one that is currently being scrutinized by Congress and legal practitioners. (See Chapter 4.) Eichenberger suggests a number of ways to achieve these expense allocations. The first would be to build them into be NAV of the portfolio, resulting in them getting allocated equally across the board. This approach requires transparency into the NAV. But he warns: "Even though it's easier from an administrative standpoint to just bundle it into the NAV and send it

TABLE 5.3 Steps to Establish Custom Strategies

Step	Model Portfolio Approach	Trust Unitization Approach
1. **Add strategies to your record-keeping system.** Your record keeper will need to know how many target strategies you would like to add to the plan. For instance, if you decide to offer targets by decade—for example, income for those retiring in 2010, 2020, 2030, 2040, and 2050—the record keeper will set up five model portfolios or new funds on the system. (Note: The setup process and ongoing operations vary by record keeper.)	No	Yes
2. **Establish trust accounts.** You will need to set up each strategy on a trust system to enable the calculation of a NAV. Since these strategies are not mutual funds, your plan trustee may refer to the NAV as a "super" or "synthetic" NAV. The trustee may start each strategy with a $10 NAV, which then is revised daily, based on the performance of the underlying holdings (e.g., based on the allocation to the plan's core and possibly the plan's added funds). To minimize cost, plans that also offer a defined benefit (DB) plan may wish to consider unitizing DB assets through a master trust, using them as core investment options in the DC plan. If the savings justify the effort, the unitized core assets then may be folded into the target strategies' synthetic NAV calculations.	Not needed. There are no new funds at the trust. All investments are made to the existing core lineup.	Yes
3. **Determine the rebalancing frequency.** Your record keeper and/or trustee will need to know how often to rebalance the funds back to the target allocation. Many plan sponsors request a quarterly rebalance, yet some may request it as infrequently as annually or as frequently as daily, depending on the rationale developed during the structuring process. Your record keeper and/or trustee also may offer the ability to rebalance based on a percentage deviation from the initial allocation (e.g., when the strategy achieves a deviation percentage without regard to the date or frequency of	Yes	Yes

TABLE 5.3   (*Continued*)

Step	Model Portfolio Approach	Trust Unitization Approach
occurrence). Some may utilize a combination of these approaches. Whatever frequency or approach you select, it is important to have a documented rationale for it. Be sure to evaluate frequently any impact of trading on the underlying funds' cash positions and overall costs.		
4. **Communications.** Work with your record keeper on how you are going to communicate the required fund information. Some record keepers can create customized fund fact sheets that mirror the information provided for your core funds. This becomes easier in the trust unitization approach since it is set up as a separate fund. However, under the model portfolio approach, you can create this information by linking the participant via the Web to information on the subfunds, but that can be more confusing to participants.	Yes	Yes
5. **Modify asset allocation.** Your record keeper and/or trustee also will need to know when you wish to revise the strategy allocations. Most companies look at the mix once a year and then notify the record keeper and/or trustee of any allocation revisions. Major record keepers and trustees say that typically there is no cost to change allocations. Typically, the record keeper and/or trustee make the adjustments in the system, and the balances are adjusted with that day's normal cash flows. As appropriate, your plan trustee will work with the record keeper to rebalance any existing assets to the new allocation percentage.	Yes	Yes
6. **Monitor performance.** Periodically evaluate strategy tracking relative to the underlying sleeve allocations (i.e., core fund performance). Look at how the record keeper and/or trustee directs daily cash flows and transfers. Make sure your record keeper	Yes	Yes

(*Continued*)

TABLE 5.3 (*Continued*)

Step	Model Portfolio Approach	Trust Unitization Approach
and/or trustee is able to set up strategies without requiring a cash buffer or reserve. Beware of the fact that some record keepers cannot split the cash flows to the underlying funds and thus may require one fund in the plan to serve as the default. This inability increases the strategies' tracking error relative to the underlying core funds. Given a direct flow to the underlying funds, based on the custom allocation, your strategies should tightly track the performance of the underlying funds. (Note: You may wish to retain a consultant to perform this evaluation as well as the asset-allocation adjustments.)		
7. **Maturation of strategies.** As each retirement date approaches, the glide path of the earliest target-date strategy (e.g., 2010) may become identical to the current "income" or "today" strategy within the family. Once this happens, the target strategy (the 2010 in this example) is preset to map to the "income" or "today" strategy, and the target strategy fund can be replaced with a more aggressive strategy (e.g., a 2060 date), to accept assets from younger investors. It is important to note that when a fund reaches its target retirement date, this does not require elimination of the fund or an allocation that excludes equities. However, a more aggressive asset allocation may be appropriate for years past the strategy's marked retirement date.	Not needed	Yes

out, you'll probably spend a fair amount of time educating the participants to exactly what that fee is and what constitutes the fee."[2]

A second approach is to "break the fees down independently and pass those through on a participant level.... When they start seeing these fees broken out—could be a record keeping fee, investment management fee, custodial fee—that's going to raise a fair number of questions that you should be prepared to answer."

A third option would be to combine the two approaches, perhaps taking the investment management fee directly from the NAV and passing the other fees through directly to plan participants, using the target-date strategies.

REBALANCING THE TARGET-DATE STRATEGIES

Another important consideration is rebalancing the portfolios, along with deciding how frequently that should be done. PIMCO's 2009 DC Consulting Survey reports that the most common frequency for rebalancing the glide path is quarterly. Eichenberger feels that as providers become more comfortable with target date, and as more technology gets introduced into the business, rebalancing "may become somewhat more frequent." While there are several ways to rebalance, most often the trust custodian does the actual monitoring and rebalancing within the glide path, as directed by the glide path manager.

DELUXE CORPORATION: SEAMLESS OPERATIONAL SETUP AND ROLLOUT COMMUNICATION

When we asked Dan Holupchinski, retirement plans manager at Deluxe Corporation, to tell us how difficult it was for Deluxe to set up custom strategies from an operational perspective, he said it was easier than he anticipated. Working closely with service providers helped a great deal. "Since we're unbundled, we've been working with our plan trustee and record keeper for years. They helped us establish the appropriate structure, as well as the communication rollout. We gave our participants roughly a six-week window to choose auto-enrollment, auto-escalation, the target-date strategies, and opt-out opportunities."[3]

When the six weeks were up, Deluxe simply eliminated the balanced fund from the lineup and defaulted everyone who had not made an active choice into an age-appropriate target-date strategy. The most difficult and time-consuming task for Deluxe was the process of eliminating the balanced fund and communicating the default choices to plan participants. Also, working with their record keeper on the operations side to make all of the options clear to participants via the Web site took more time than anticipated. "During open enrollment, we wanted employees to be able to go to the Web site look at their investment choices, and reset their asset allocations as they saw fit. So we tried to make the Web site robust enough to convey their options and to link them to the appropriate pages to make their selections."

But, according to Holupchinski, once Deluxe had set up everything for the rollout, communications went very well. The company adopted a multi-stage approach, giving participants high-level information six months prior to the choice period and slowly building from there. Everyone even received an educational booklet, including those who were not actively employed.

Last, Deluxe invited its service provider to give presentations of the plan changes at each of its facilities. Having an expert in the room to explain the changes in the plan, rather than just depending on paper communication or sending people to the Web page to try to figure things out for themselves, helped immensely. "The combination of all the different communication and educational channels helped make it successful."

HOW RECORD KEEPERS AND TRUSTEES SUPPORT OPERATIONS

Deluxe's record keeper also supports the company's operations and online communications. Once Deluxe has provided the record keeper with its glide path, Holupchinski works with the investment-data company on an ongoing basis. "Our service providers work together closely to ensure that they update information appropriately, on an ongoing basis." Deluxe does periodically review the data to make sure it reflects the company's expectations. It relies on the service provider to modify the data appropriately if need be. This takes a lot of the burden off the company's shoulders. "We rely on our trustee to establish everything appropriately regarding configuration and structure, and we rely on our record keeper to do the same."

When we asked Holupchinski what duties the Deluxe trustee performs, he explained that the trustee has the same spreadsheets the record keeper has, detailing the asset allocation targets for each target-date fund. The trustee and record keeper use this information to rebalance the glide path each quarter and strike the daily NAV for the target-date funds. This means that while Deluxe touches base with the record keeper periodically, it does not direct active rebalancing itself, although it may tweak the glide path from time to time and convey updated information to plan participants.

We were curious about how this rebalancing work was done and whether Deluxe had any minimum-asset size issues. Holupchinski explained that the company's rebalancing is done using core funds.

On a daily basis, the record keeper and trustee monitor cash flow. We still have the same number of fund managers we had prior to implementing the target-date strategies. So, ultimately, we just need to convey the cash-flow activity, in total, to those investment managers. This includes fund transfers, withdrawals and the quarterly rebalancing activity. We had to watch minimum funding or asset size. We had to ensure that the balances were large enough in each target-date strategy to strike a NAV appropriately.

As mentioned, the biggest challenge Deluxe faced when it created its target retirement-date strategies was phasing out the balanced fund and remapping the money into age-appropriate target-date strategies. However, working closely with each investment manager and keeping them informed of the changes enabled Deluxe to make this transition easily. Also, there are some trustees that will automatically manage the rebalancing process for you and communicate those trades to the appropriate fund managers.

During this conversion, Deluxe relied on its record keeper to provide periodic information about anticipated cash flow and status. "Four weeks before eliminating the balanced fund and mapping over all money to the target-date funds, we asked them to report on the remaining pool of money in the balanced fund and the anticipated effect on each investment manager." The record keeper also provided Deluxe with information about where the assets would flow, based on age, if a person took no action and defaulted into the target-date fund. The benefit of this was that it enabled the company to see "the potential cash inflow or outflow on a per-manager-level basis" and to apprise their investment managers of this information. A collaborative effort ensured that the changeover to target date flowed smoothly.

Deluxe is happy about switching over to target retirement-date strategies for a number of reasons. This approach provides assistance to participants who wish for additional assistance in selecting age-appropriate types of asset mixes. In fact, their glide path continues to change until the age of 85, when it remains static, which enables participants to remain in the plan all through their retirement years.

Deluxe also is happy that custom strategies allow it to retain control of asset allocations and investment managers, adding or changing managers as needed based on due diligence. Using custom strategies has also allowed Deluxe to keep its fee structure down. "By offering custom strategies, we tap into the lower fees and continue to feed assets to the core, thus further reducing total plan costs over time."

IN CLOSING

Custom strategies may be simple to set up or complex, depending largely on the record keeper and trustee that you use for your plan. Given the move toward custom strategies in the market, record keepers and trust companies are becoming far more skilled at supporting this approach. Many have established protocols for the setup process for plan sponsors, including record keeping, trust, and communication such as fund fact sheets, Web information, call center training, and even investment advice that integrates the custom glide path. PIMCO, working with several other investment managers and consultants, has gathered information on the best practices of 30 of the largest record keepers.

We encourage plan sponsors to design the optimal plan for participants and then determine whether the current record keeper can support this design cost efficiently. This is similar to building a house. You start with a vision, perhaps even drawings on paper. Then you hire an architect as your consultant to create professional plans and blueprints. Then you query builders—in this case, record keepers and trustees—to determine whether they can make your dream house a reality at a price you can afford. Many providers will guide you through every step along the way to make sure you have a well-functioning plan and delighted participants. The right partners can make the setup and ongoing operations painless and worry free.

CHAPTER 6

Communication Challenges
and How to Meet Them

In many ways, target-date strategies owe their very existence to communication challenges. I recall in the mid-1990s when plan sponsors and consultants questioned the need for even a single balanced fund within a defined contribution (DC) plan. At the time, only 35 percent of plans offered a balanced fund.[1] Instead, the typical plan had six investment choices, including a capital preservation fund, a bond fund, and an equity fund or two. Experts reasoned at the time that participants could create their own balanced strategy out of the core lineup of investment choices.

Since then, studies in participant behavior have instructed us otherwise. Over the last two decades, plans have evolved in their asset-allocation offerings as plan sponsors are recognizing that participants need help to set an appropriate balanced strategy *and* to modify that asset allocation as they age.

First to emerge was a simple balanced fund that generally offered a 60 percent equity and a 40 percent fixed-income static balance. That grew into a series of target-risk strategies designed for conservative, moderate, or aggressive investors. Today target-date strategies are structured to meet the needs of people retiring at different ages. With every step in their evolution, the communication has become a bit easier.

The first move—from the standard balanced fund to a target-risk series—seemed like a brilliant idea because it allowed participants to better match their needs. However, that brilliance dimmed when the realization hit that most participants did not really understand their level of risk tolerance and tended uniformly to pick "moderate" when confronted with a choice. And when they did take time to pick the appropriate risk level, once invested, they tended not to move their money, even though their risk tolerance was likely to change as they aged.

That leads us to the more recent move toward target-date strategies that both mix and modify the asset allocation over time as plan participants age.

Without a doubt, today it is easier to educate participants about target-date strategies. The communication can be as simple as a we-can-do-it-for-you message, especially when that message is part of your automatic enrollment briefing.

Despite the ease of communicating target-date investments, we need to be cautious of oversimplifying. Be careful that participants understand the risks they face and that these strategies are not designed to provide a guaranteed amount of income. The challenges are similar, whether you are communicating a packaged target-date fund or a custom strategy. Participants need information on the investment approach and how it will or should change over time. They need to understand the underlying investments, risk characteristics, and fees involved.

Some may argue that communicating the details of target-date plans is far more difficult with custom strategies than with packaged funds. We disagree. Although setting up communications for a custom strategy initially may require more effort, we believe that ongoing communication can be much easier, particularly when plan sponsors make changes to the lineup of underlying investment managers. As discussed in Chapter 5 on operations, this communication setup can be streamlined and managed by your record keeper. If that is not an option, plan sponsors may need to get involved personally or talk with a consultant about putting the optimal communication support in place.

COMMON MYTHS SURROUNDING CUSTOM TARGET-STRATEGY COMMUNICATION

When it comes to communications, each plan and participant is different. To feel comfortable about setting up custom target-date retirement strategies and communicating their benefits to plan participants, it is important to understand and move beyond the myths held by some plan sponsors.

Myth 1. **Custom target strategies preclude some of the communication support mutual funds receive.** In reality, custom target strategies can have communication support that looks nearly identical to mutual funds, including fund fact sheets from recognized mutual fund communication experts such as Morningstar. In addition, the custom strategy data can be fed into the advice models and other participant tools, the same as we do with mutual funds.

Myth 2. **Plan participants respond better to brand-name funds than to non–brand-name choices.** A study concerning participation rates, however, showed that there is actually little difference between the participation rates in plans that offer name-brand mutual funds versus those that offer generically labeled institutional strategies. In fact, there seemed to be a slightly higher advantage to the non–brand names, which may have been the result of more extensive communication campaigns.

Myth 3. Plan participants need to be able to look up their funds in a newspaper to feel comfortable about their investment options. A study conducted by Alliance Bernstein showed that only 3 percent of respondents actually look up investments in the paper. Rather, 97 percent of respondents said that they look only at their quarterly statements or at the data on either their company Web site or an Internet site.

The truth is that communicating custom strategies does not need to be challenging. Once the communication strategies are set in place, making changes to the asset-allocation structure or to the lineup of investment managers is not that difficult. If an underlying fund changes, you simply communicate the change to participants and the impact it will have, if any, on your glide path. In contrast, if you are not happy with the underlying investments or the asset mix of a packaged product, you may need to remove the series of funds entirely. That is a much greater communication challenge. What is more, plan sponsors often struggle with a decision to remove an investment fund from their core that is included in the packaged target-date strategy. How can they justify offering an investment in the packaged fund that their investment committee deemed unsuitable for the core lineup?

Communication of the packaged funds may appear simple on the surface yet may become more complex over time. Custom strategies are just the opposite: seeming complex on the surface yet far more straightforward over time.

COMMUNICATING THE BENEFITS OF TARGET-DATE STRATEGIES

At a recent Custom Target-Date Strategies Conference held in New York City, Barbara J. Hogg of Hewitt Associates, a senior retirement consultant who has had over 20 years of experience working with defined contribution plans, talked extensively about what she saw as the central communication challenges and solutions surrounding custom target-date strategies. She stressed the importance of demonstrating the benefits of target-date strategies to participants: "If we look at the evolution of custom target strategies in

DC plans, this move is really a good thing. Custom target strategies offer a lot of benefits to your employees, whether they completely realize that or not."[2]

The primary communication challenge, according to Hogg, was more basic, such as how to invest: "If you think about where employees are, investing is an overwhelming thing. They're intimidated by it. They don't want to do it. For the average employee, it's not their expertise. That's why target-date strategies are a great solution. By putting in target-date investments, we're really helping them learn how to invest in a way that's very easy for them to understand."

In the old "pre–target-strategy days," according to Hogg, investment education involved helping people understand asset allocations and how to choose the proper mix that was right for them. Of course, participants could not stop there; they had to look at their portfolio over time, rebalancing their investments. "And, oh, by the way, every so often, step back and think about your life circumstances, and how they've changed. Is it time to update that allocation?" So plan sponsors were actually asking participants to do many different things. However, enrolling employees in target retirement date strategies "automatically answers many of those questions for them. They get into an age-appropriate allocation that automatically rebalances, changing over time. A great many of the issues that required so much education are taken care of within these strategies."

There are other advances Hogg outlined that could be communicated to participants. For example:

- Going the custom route improves the plan sponsor's buying power and may reduce not only the cost of the target-date strategies but the cost of the core investment strategies as assets build.
- Plan fiduciaries provide valuable oversight in selecting and monitoring the core funds—the same funds that are used inside the custom target-date strategies. And, if changes are needed, the underlying funds can be replaced.
- The custom target-date strategies may include investment sleeves that are not available in the core funds, such as nontraditional investments. These additions bring value to the participant through diversification and opportunity for higher return.

COMMUNICATION: STRATEGIES TO KEEP IT SIMPLE

What is the best approach to keep employees from being overwhelmed with investing and get on a good track with their retirement plan investments? The answer, according to Hogg, is "Keep it simple. Simple really can be your best strategy when you're looking at communication and deciding how to move forward." In this spirit, she offers these five basic strategy points to help plan sponsors educate employees about the benefits of target-date options.

> **Point 1. Send a clear message that custom target funds are different from other plans employees may have.** According to Hogg, the question here is "How do we convey, within our custom target, that this is something more than just another fund in the lineup? We need to make sure people understand these strategies are different from whatever else they've done in the past."

> **Point 2. Guide employees onto the right path.** In the spirit of keeping it simple for the employees, Hogg suggests using the concept of a package. "Plan participants see packages everywhere in life, vacation packages, carwash packages, catering service packages—all put together to make things easier for the purchaser. So what we're doing within the custom target strategy is packaging investments for people who are looking for an easier solution. In other words, 'Here's a path you may want to choose because it's packaged in a way that serves your needs.'"

> **Point 3. Educate on the basics.** Do not try to cover everything. Instead, pick and choose the issues, focusing on what is most important to participants, such as the mix of the core fund, making it clear "that target date is a particular type of approach rather than a whole new investment they need to deal with."

> Because target-date funds are a 100 percent solution, you may need to (1) transfer current money into the new investment option and (2) redirect future contributions to the investment. "A lot of employees don't discriminate between those two things," Hogg explains. "There are two choices, and they've got to think about both."

> You also need to help participants understand when the custom target investment option comes with an additional asset-allocation fee. Generally, it is not much, and it is a fair fee for the services provided. "We pay for this like we do for any other service we purchase. For example, if we pay to have someone clean our house, we choose to make that expenditure because we don't have the time or the inclination to do it ourselves."

> **Point 4. If you are adding investment sleeves to the custom target-date options, explain them simply and briefly.** Hogg says: "Employees need to understand that by going the custom-target package route,

they are getting some enhanced investment vehicles that may improve diversification and/or long-term growth. It's a bonus for taking the whole package—an added value."

Point 5. Provide access to the details. It is also important to recognize that custom target strategies have features (such as new investment sleeves) that could bring in some more sophisticated investors who find them attractive. So it is important to also provide access to all the details. Hogg states, "I absolutely love simplicity, but I greatly respect information and details as well. You shouldn't ignore that. You're just structuring your communication so that you get the main points up front first." However, you still need to have the details and more complex information available for the interested plan participant.

COMMUNICATION TOOLS

When presenting target-date investment options to participants, plan sponsors often separate them into distinct tiers or investment paths. For instance, participants may be shown Tier I: A Mix Created for You and Tier II: Create Your Own Mix. The first tier is the target-date options, and the second tier allows participants to select among the core investment options. In some cases, plan sponsors offer a third tier, Full Brokerage. In fact, 22 percent of plans offer brokerage, including 14 percent that offer full brokerage and 8 percent that offer only a mutual fund window.[3] More recently, some plan sponsors have added a tier of passive investment strategies, which sometimes may appear as a third tier, either in place of or in addition to a brokerage window.

As Hogg stated, choices should be prioritized and kept simple. At a higher level, plan sponsors should provide opportunities for participants to dig deeper into the specifics of each strategy, including the underlying investment details. The goal is to guide employees to the tier that best meets their needs and then allow them to gather more information as desired. This depth of communication is important for the plan sponsor to satisfy Employee Retirement Income Security Act Section 404(c) or Form S-8 disclosure requirements.

Four types of basic communication tools are commonly used to educate employers about custom target-date strategies:

1. Promotional/introductory materials
2. Web information

3. Printed and online statements
4. Phone support or in-person communication.

How or if all four of these tools are used depends on a company's experiences regarding the types of materials that work best with its employees.

Promotional/Introductory Materials

Most plans push out communications materials when they launch new investment options. Their purpose is to help employees understand these options so that they can make new investment decisions. Ideally, these materials should address all investment alternatives within the plan rather than just introduce the new funds. Plan sponsors may provide participants with the tiered or path choices: "mix it for me" or "do it myself."

In addition, each custom target-date strategy may offer a fact sheet that provides a description of the option, including asset allocation, retirement-date target, and cost. You can create fund fact sheets to show the same information in the same format, regardless of whether it is a custom target strategy, collective investment trust, or mutual fund.

Charlene Mims, vice president of benefits, HRIS, and payroll at Dole Food Company, talks about how the company utilizes a playful approach in print mailings. As Dole introduced its custom target-date investments, it sent out a "Your Retirement Review" mailer to encourage plan participants to reexamine their retirement portfolio. Dole knows that people tend to stay passive in their investment strategies, sometimes over a decade, so it uses the campaign slogan "You've changed. But has your investment strategy kept up with you?" "We show different pictures of how someone may have looked when they first started. For example, we have a picture of a hippie and another one of how that person might look today—as a 55-year-old Baby Boomer."[4]

Web Information

Similar to written material, the Web should lay out the choices a participant can make. Again, you can present a path approach from which the participant may choose: custom target-date strategies or a mix of their own creation. Some plan sponsors make it an all-or-nothing decision, yet we believe this direction may be too rigid. How strategies are presented, relative to other plan investment alternatives, will undoubtedly impact selection. Participants are likely to research only at a broad level when selecting investments rather than digging deeply through the fact sheets or other information. The Web site can explain the details of the custom target-date strategy in the same way that it is explained in the printed materials, yet it has the additional advantage of being able to link to information on the underlying fund sleeves (i.e., the core investment offerings) to provide more detail.

Once participants have invested, the Web site can show a consolidated return for the strategy rather than each underlying fund's breakout (which can be available through a link to the underlying fund sleeves). This consolidated view should help participants make investment choices for the long term rather than chase returns.

Interestingly, many plan sponsors are seeing the Web as the leading-edge tool in providing online participant information. Mary Beth Glotzbach of Morningstar believes that electronic publications are the future of company communications, even though printed material still has its place with some clients and in some situations:

> *While there is still a need for printed, hard-copy materials, more and more we are seeing the drive towards as much electronic distribution of information as possible. For example, you might provide very abbreviated fund investment data in an enrollment kit and drive plan participants to the Web for greater detail. Many record keepers such as Hewitt Associates use our HTML format as part of their Web-based fund communication materials. We also offer print-friendly materials in PDF format to use on the Web or as hard copy, but again this material is really designed to drive employees to the Web as much as possible. For those providers that focus on the small or even micro-markets, where electronic communication isn't often viable, we produce much more print-ready content for them. But as print and postage costs continue to rise, any way to mitigate those fees is welcome.[5]*

Figure 6.1 presents an example of a Morningstar Investment Profile for a custom target-date fund.

In the May 2009 *DC Dialogue*, Barbara Kontje, director of retirement plan investments at American Express, talked about how the company offers participants online information/education about retirement plan choices.

> *About two years ago, when we made investment lineup changes and introduced the target-date strategies, we provided an extensive series of onsite and webinar information sessions for the entire population. Our 2008 goal was to walk them through general plan information, explain the 401(k), show them our investment lineup and how it works, and discuss asset allocation and the target-date retirement strategies. We also covered the basics—for example, making sure they name a beneficiary.[6]*

Release Date: 09-30-2008

2035 Target Date Retirement Fund

Benchmark	**Overall Morningstar Rating™**	**Morningstar Return**	**Morningstar Risk**
Blended Benchmark	★★★★	Above Average	Above Average

Rated against 237 Target-Date 2030+funds. **An investment's overall Morningstar Rating, based on its risk-adjusted return, is a weighted average of its applicable 3-,5-, and 10-year Ratings. See disclosure for details.**

Investment Strategy from investment's prospectus

The investment seeks total return for investors retiring in approximately the year 2035. The fund uses an asset allocation approach. The allocation changes, becoming more conservative, as the fund nears its maturation. The fund allocates assets among securities contained in various domestic and foreign indexes.

Category Description: Target-Date 2030+

Target-date portfolios provide diversified exposure to stocks, bonds, and cash for those investors who have a specific date in mind (in this case, the years 2030+) for retirement or another goal. These portfolios aim to provide investors with an optimal level of return and risk, based solely on the target date. These portfolios get more conservative as the goal date approaches by investing more in bonds and cash. Investment managers structure these portfolios differently; two funds with the same goal year may have different allocations to equities and therefore different levels of return and risk.

Volatility Analysis

```
                    Investment
                        ▼
  ┌────────┬─────────────┬────────┐
  │  Low   │  Moderate   │  High  │
  └────────┴─────────────┴────────┘
                        ▲
                     Category
```

In the past, this investment has shown a relatively moderate range of price fluctuations relative to other investments. This investment may experience larger or smaller price declines or price increases depending on market conditions. Some of this risk may be offset by owning other investments with different portfolio makeups or investment strategies.

Best 3 Month Return	**Worst 3 Month Return**
21.22%	−17.95%
(Oct '98 - Dec '98)	(Jul '02 - Sep '02)

Operations

12b-1 Fee	—
Redemption Fee	—
Expense Ratio	0.11% of fund assets
Fund Inception Date	08-01-97
Portfolio Manager(s)	Management Team
Management Company	ABC Global Investors
Telephone	—
Web Site	www.abcglobalinvestors.com

Notes

The fund performance illustrated above is not actual performance for this fund but reflects the investment manager's simulated returns for certain periods before the fund began operations. The simulated returns are hypothetical based on returns for similar funds and are solely for illustrative purposes. PAST PERFORMANCE, WHETHER HYPOTHETICAL OR ACTUAL, IS NO INDICATION OF FUTURE RESULTS.

Allocation of Stocks and Bonds

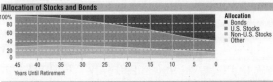

Allocation
- Bonds
- U.S. Stocks
- Non-U.S. Stocks
- Other

Years Until Retirement

Performance

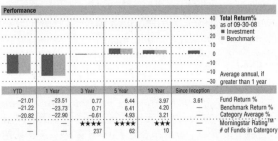

Total Return%
as of 09-30-08
- Investment
- Benchmark

Average annual, if greater than 1 year

	YTD	1 Year	3 Year	5 Year	10 Year	Since Inception	
	−21.01	−23.51	0.77	6.44	3.97	3.61	Fund Return %
	−21.22	−23.73	0.71	6.41	4.20	—	Benchmark Return %
	−20.82	−22.90	−0.61	4.93	3.21	—	Category Average %
	—	—	★★★★	★★★★	★★★	—	Morningstar Rating™
	—	—	237	62	10	—	# of Funds in Catergory

Performance Disclosure: The performance data quoted represents past performance. Past performance does not guarantee future results. The investment return and principal value of an investment will fluctuate so that an investor's shares, when redeemed, may be worth more or less than their original cost. Current performance may be lower than the performance data quoted. For performance information current to the most recent month end, please call the ABC Company Information Line, 1-888-XXX-XXXX or visit the plan website at www.abccompany.com.

At times, certain funds' performance may be extraordinarily high due to investing in sectors that achieved unprecedented returns. There can be no assurance that this performance can be repeated in the future.

Portfolio Analysis as of 09-30-08

Composition as of 09-30-08

	%Assets
● U.S. Stocks	63.7
● Non-U.S. Stocks	27.9
● Bond	5.6
● Cash	0.2
● Other	2.6

Morningstar Style Box™ as of 09-30-08(EQ); 09-30-08 (F-I)

Large Med Small / Value Blend Growth
High Med Low / Short Interm Long

Top 10 Holdings as of 09-30-08	%Assets
ABC Equity Index Fund	49.14
ABC International Index Fund	27.29
ABC Extended Equity Market Fund	12.18
ABC Global Real Estate Index Fund	6.64
ABC Bond Market Index Fund	4.75

Total Number of Holdings	6
Annual Turnover Ratio %	—
Total Fund Assets ($mil)	204.13

Morningstar Sectors as of 09-30-08	Funds%	Category%
🏛 U.S. Credit	24.43	3.33
🌐 Non-U.S. Credit	2.46	0.35
🏠 Mortgage	40.87	3.08
🏛 U.S. Government	29.51	1.71
💲 Cash	2.74	2.46

Morningstar Sectors as of 09-30-08	Fund%	S&P 500%
☁ Information	15.64	19.27
📊 Software	2.90	4.02
🔧 Hardware	6.84	9.48
📺 Media	2.20	2.72
📞 Telecommunication	3.70	3.05
☞ Service	46.86	40.95
❤ Healthcare Service	10.35	13.10
🛒 Consumer Service	6.41	7.45
🏢 Business Service	5.26	4.74
💲 Financial Service	24.84	15.66
⚙ Manufacturing Service	37.50	39.79
🏭 Consumer Goods	9.66	10.65
⚙ Industrial Materials	13.00	12.22
🔥 Energy	11.04	13.43
💡 Utilities	3.80	3.49

©2008 Morningstar, Inc. Morningstar Investment Profiles™ 312-696-600. All rights reserved. The information contained herein: (1) is proprietary to Morningstar and/or its content providers; (2) may not be copied or distributed and (3) is not warranted to be accurate, complete or timely. Neither Morningstar nor its content providers are responsible for any damages or losses arising from any use of information. Past performance is no guarantee of future performance. Visit our investment website at www.morningstar.com

 M⭘RNINGSTAR®

Sample report for illustrative purposes only.

FIGURE 6.1 2035 Target Retirement Fund
Source: Morningstar.

During the initial year, American Express provided plan participants with more than 120 on-site sessions and approximately 10 webinars. The company's on-site presentations "were well received. People came up to me after some of the sessions and said, 'I've been in the plan a long time but I learned something new today.' Many more people said that they had never expected investing in the plan to be so easy. So it was refreshing and encouraging that our education efforts hit the targets we wanted to hit."

Printed and Online Statements

Just as on the Web, participant statements should reflect each strategy's fold-up value, that is, the strategy's overall return versus the return of each underlying fund within the strategy. From an investor-behavior standpoint, experts believe this fold-up value is important as it reflects lower volatility and, therefore, is more likely to keep participants in the strategy. By contrast, showing the return breakdown for each strategy's underlying fund may scare participants away from a strategy if they see that an underlying asset class has performed poorly. Of course, if they want more detailed information, participants can obtain actual return data and more via an online benefit site. Again, plan sponsors should help participants focus on the long term rather than on short-term return variations. Participants should understand that even a target retirement-date strategy may have short-term losses yet in the long run it is designed to help meet their retirement-income needs.

Phone Support or In-Person Communication

Benefit specialists and investment education experts who support plan participants should have direct access to the same information made available to participants. Further, specialists and experts should be trained to help employees understand plan alternatives yet stop short of providing ad hoc investment advice. To the extent that plan sponsors are interested in offering advice to participants, they should train specialists and experts on the availability and operation of these tools, as appropriate.

In the July 2009 *DC Dialogue*, David Fisser, former chairman of the Southwest Airlines Pilots' Association 401(k) Committee, talks about how Southwest uses in-person communication tools via a two- to three-hour orientation to help familiarize new hires with its retirement plan options—even though they know the newly hired pilots usually have already done a lot of research on Southwest before they start working for them.

We give them a 15-minute quick and dirty on the 401(k), why it's important, and why they need to do this. We also hit tax savings and investment options pretty hard, and make it clear that the match is

7.3 percent. Most people realize that's free money lying on the table that they just can't afford not to take. They can also sign up for online retirement education forums, and our record keeper allows them to enroll for them online right then and there.[7]

HELPING PLAN PARTICIPANTS TO VISUALIZE THEIR POSTRETIREMENT FUTURE

These days plan providers and behavioral scientists are looking for even more effective ways to help employees make better decisions using defaults or other path-of-least-resistance programs. Professor Richard Thaler of the University of Chicago and points out that "In every dimension, people need all the help they can get."[8] Susan Bradley, financial planner and author of the book *Sudden Money*, states that "We need to help pre-retirees see the future."[9] In other words, plan sponsors must ensure that people have an *accurate* idea about the total value of their accounts and its *actual worth* in retirement. Clients need to understand how money translates into an annual income and the impact of inflation and various market environments. This is the only way they can plan to meet their needs as they prepare to retire.

Bradley speaks of the importance of educating individuals to see the future, and academics and behaviorists are saying the same thing. Sheena Iyengar of Columbia University, along with Shlomo Bernartzi and Alessandro Previtero of University of California at Los Angeles, have some very innovative ideas about ways to educate DC participants. According to this team, we have not been as successful as we could be in conveying ideas to participants because we are using cognitive/deliberative means rather than intuitive/affective communication. In other words, we have been appealing to the mind, not the gut and the heart.

Think of it this way: Instead of throwing numbers at participants, which engages the brain's cognitive/deliberative part, we also should give people visual and emotional examples that engage them on an intuitive/affective level. The difference between these two learning styles is radical. Cognitive learning is slower, controlled, analytic, and rule based, while intuitive learning is faster, automatic, holistic, and associative.

As an example, take a look at two antismoking advertisements presented in Figure 6.2. The top message, "Think. Don't smoke," is a cognitive message. This campaign actually produced a 36 percent *increase* in teen smoking! The bottom message presents words embedded in strong, sinister, visual images suggesting death and resulted in a 66 percent *decrease* in smoking—a huge difference in effectiveness.

Cognitive 36% Increase in Teen Smoking

Effective 66% Decrease in Teen Smoking

FIGURE 6.2 Advertisements Drive Different Behavior
Source: Iyengar, Benartzi, and Previtero.

If you save this percentage of your salary...	You could expect to accumulate this amount by age 65
0%	£0
4	125,000
6	200,000
10	295,000
11	350,000
12	365,000
15	475,000
16	499,000
18	545,000
19	595,000
26	795,000
28	875,000
31	950,000
41	1,250,000

FIGURE 6.3   Cognitive Version
Source: Iyengar, Benartzi, and Previtero.

Another example shows a hypothetical retirement plan that was presented to fully employed MBA students at London Business School, who then were asked to indicate their intended savings rate. Savings rates were displayed either as an *amount* of money they would accumulate by retirement (Figure 6.3) or as images of London apartments along with a blurb concerning what they could afford at retirement based on their rate of savings (Figure 6.4).

The intuitive/affective version, showing the savings rate and a picture plus description of the living space, noted that if you saved zero, you might end up living on the street. This version produced a 14.5 percent contribution rate, while the cognitive/deliberative version produced only a 10.9 percent contribution rate. Giving participants a visual that helped them *see* their futures raised savings rates by 33 percent.

Helping participants visualize the future is important as plan sponsors try to help people understand what they need to do to save for retirement successfully. Even with auto-enrollment and contribution escalation,

Cromwell Road

Penywern Road

Homeless Man

FIGURE 6.4 Retirement Lifestyle Based on Savings Rate
Source: Iyengar, Benartzi, and Previtero.

FIGURE 6.5   Buying Power
Source: Iyengar, Benartzi, and Previtero.

people still may not be contributing at the necessary rate. Sponsors need to encourage them in a visceral way to save what they will need.

A final visual example illustrates the effects of inflation planning. Figure 6.5 shows the different groceries that a person may afford given his or her retirement-income level.

Figure 6.6 shows the impact of inflation and decrease in the dollar value of retirement savings. When inflation occurs, you may have to give up

FIGURE 6.6   Inflation Impact Reduces Buying Power
Source: Iyengar, Benartzi, and Previtero.

certain things. Some higher-priced items you may value, such as wine and beer, vanish, as does your favorite cereal and other food.

The visual impact of giving things up hits the target. Rather than just providing an accumulated dollar amount—a value people have no idea how to translate into retirement—it makes financial communication real so that people truly see and *feel* it,

To educate more effectively, plan sponsors need to find comprehensive, creative ways of presenting clear choices to pre-retirees.

COMMUNICATIONS AND THE SWITCH TO DC CUSTOM STRATEGIES

Dan Holupchinski, the retirement plans manager for Deluxe Corporation, spoke about how Deluxe handled its change-over to custom strategies. It gave participants roughly a six-week window to choose auto-enrollment, auto-escalation, target-date strategies, and opt-out opportunities. At the end of that period, Deluxe eliminated the balanced fund and defaulted everyone who did not actively elect into an age-appropriate target-date fund. According to Holupchinski, "Eliminating the balanced fund and communicating the default choices took the most time and effort, especially working with our record keeper on the operations side to make the options clear to participants via the Web site."[10]

Deluxe delivered a good deal of this communication about the open enrollment choice via its benefits Web site. Holupchinski said that Deluxe "wanted employees to be able to go to the Web, look at their investment choices, and reset their asset allocations as they saw fit. So we tried to make the Web site robust enough to convey their options and to link them to the appropriate pages to make their selections." Setting up the Web site ended up being the most challenging part of the process, taking more time than anticipated, but it was extremely valuable.

However, the Internet was only one part of the campaign used by Deluxe for the rollout. According to Holupchinski:

> We had multiple communications—we provided high-level information to participants almost six months prior to the choice period—and we slowly built upon that. We even sent out an education booklet to every participant, actively employed or not. Our service provider delivered presentations at each of our facilities, which helped immensely. It helps very much to have a live person in front of you explain the changes, rather than just offer it on paper

*or ask people to go online to try and decipher it. The combination
of all the different communication and educational channels helped
make it successful.*

One communication advantage Holupchinski saw in taking a custom
target-date strategy approach was that Deluxe had already educated employees about the plan's core funds, which streamlined the process.

> *Our primary task was to explain what our target strategies were
> and how they worked. We didn't need to go into detail on the
> core strategies since people were familiar with them already. For
> instance, we had already provided fact sheets on each core fund. We
> built upon this to deliver information on the target-date strategies.
> An outside provider helped us with the fact sheets and updates.*
>
> *On the Web site, the participant could click on a particular
> target-date strategy. Then the screen brought up information about
> the target-date asset allocation and makeup, including links to the
> fact sheets of each underlying core fund.*
>
> *We provided the investment-data company with the glide-path
> and rebalancing details. The online information then reflects this
> data, by strategy, so that participants can see the current asset mix.
> What we didn't do at this juncture was to convert it into a hard
> document. Our mailing piece was more general. It explained the
> concept of a target-date strategy, how we created them, and the
> philosophy behind them. However, the mailing didn't show the
> glide path for everyone involved in that investment option. We
> referred them to the online pages for detailed information.*

Deluxe relies on its record keeper to update the online fund information automatically and keep the Web site current. After the plan sponsor or
glide path manager provides the record keeper with the current glide path,
the record keeper works closely with the investment-data company to ensure that information is updated appropriately on an ongoing basis. In this
way, the plan sponsor does not have to perform that task itself. However,
Holupchinski stresses that Deluxe has to examine the data periodically to
make sure that it reflects the company's expectations. "If not, we ask our
service provider to modify it appropriately. We rely on our trustee to establish everything appropriately regarding configuration and structure, and we
rely on the record keeper to do the same."

John LaCara, former director of the Commonwealth of Massachusetts
Deferred Compensation Plan, described the approach to communication
after the Commonwealth had launched its custom target-date strategies.

Prior to this, the plan offered three risk-based lifestyle funds—conservative, moderate, and aggressive—with static asset allocations among four asset classes. Risk-based funds represented just 6 percent of total plan assets.

> *We decided to create target dates to allow for broader asset diversification and to simplify the fund-selection process. By leveraging existing relationships with investment managers, we built the target-date funds using institutionally-priced investment funds. This approach also allows us to maintain control of the underlying investments and tailor the glide path to plan demographics.[11]*

When we asked him how he handled the broader communication issues regarding the new custom target-date strategies, he discussed the marketing campaign developed to accompany the plan's launch. LaCara explained:

> *The basic premise is that participants now have two paths in which to invest for retirement. Path 1 is to select a target-date portfolio based on age. Path 2 tells them how, with assistance, to build and monitor a personal portfolio. We wanted to contrast the differences between the ease of selecting a target-date portfolio and the effort required to do it yourself.*

(See Figure 6.7.)

Next we asked LaCara how he helped plan participants compare information about the 11 target strategies the Commonwealth plan offered. He explained that the record keeper/third-party administrator, in conjunction with the life cycle manager, developed fact sheets for each plan investment and strategy to enable participants to compare them more easily. These fact sheets are distributed by the field representatives and also can be found online.

For LaCara, a combination of written and electronic media and in-person educational tools seems most effective for communicating with diverse plan participants.

> *Multiple solutions can help when you're trying to meet the demands of various investor behaviors. We offer free asset-allocation services, both one-on-one and in seminars. People can do the same thing online. Complete a risk-profile questionnaire, and the system generates a recommended portfolio. If a participant wants a more comprehensive financial plan, we also offer a "for-a-fee" service. The participant meets with a financial planner who looks at all retirement assets and develops a financial plan.*

One-step funds, for a diversified portfolio in one simple step.

♦ The asset allocation strategy is managed by a
team of experienced investment professionals.

♦ Designed for people that don't have the time,
desire, or experience to build and monitor their
own investment portfolio.

If you prefer to select your investment options and fine-tune the amount you
invest in each asset class and fund, you'll enjoy building your own
investment portfolio with the investment options available through the
SMART Plan.

♦ Determine your own investment strategy.
♦ Select your own investment options.
♦ Monitor your own investment portfolio.

FIGURE 6.7   Two Paths for Retirement Investment
Source: Adapted from the Commonwealth of Massachusetts.

COMMUNICATION CHALLENGES DURING AN ECONOMIC DOWNTURN

The current economic downturn has provided communication challenges
for sponsors who are looking for effective ways to guide and educate plan
participants through this crisis. We asked Roger Williams, managing director
and head of defined contribution consulting at Rogerscasey, to tell us about
some of the communication issues they were facing. He explained that the
"one true challenge" is figuring out what to tell employees about the markets
and investing in general during these economically uncertain times.

> *We've had more than one conversation in which a committee has
> considered whether they should tell employees to "stay the course."
> To me that sounds like good advice: stay in the market; but to others*

that is investment advice. What happens if a sponsor makes that statement and the participant stays in the market while it continues downward? Could the sponsor be found at fault?[12]

Williams points out that if participants had been educated on this type of volatile market, they would all be better prepared about what to do. Unfortunately, most of us have no prior experience of this kind of dramatic downturn, and telling them what to do now is difficult. "What we hope is that the individual has looked at an appropriate level of risk already and done something about it so that if they're 63 and plan to retire at age 65, they have an appropriate asset allocation."

According to Williams, the real concern is the person who still has too much invested in equities. "They enjoyed the ride up in earlier years, but now they're unpleasantly surprised. How do we handle this individual?"

We asked Barbara Kontje of American Express to tell us how the education and support her company provided to plan participants was helping people through the crisis. Kontje explained that the goal was to calm people, to let them know that they should not panic, especially if they could look at markets historically, and realize that they have a good asset allocation. While the knee-jerk reaction would be to fly to safety, Kontje reports that about 90 percent of plan participants have not moved—thanks to Amex's educational efforts—and the 10 percent who did moved to stable value.

The company's current message to people is to not panic but to take the time instead to review their asset allocation.

Is it appropriate? Are you comfortable with the risk? Everyone thought international equity was great when it returned 40 percent. But you need to also consider the risk. We tried to educate people to look at the risks. If they're not comfortable with the risk, it's a good time to evaluate and perhaps redirect new money. We also tell people to consider that if they rebalance now or make changes to their asset allocations, they may be locking in losses.[13]

Kontje felt that the current crisis has helped people determine whether they are on the right path or not. She feels it can be beneficial to communicate to plan participants the need to determine whether they are on the correct path; if they are, they should continue to follow that course. But if someone is on the wrong path, he or she should make an adjustment and invest to get on the right path, the one that will lead to the person's retirement goal.

Kontje explained: "Some people tell me they're not changing their balances, but they are targeting future allocations to something more conservative because people are no longer comfortable with their risk levels. It's a time of evaluation."

IN CLOSING

The communication challenges that come with custom strategies should not scare plan sponsors away from this approach. Many of the supposed communication "problems" are actually myths that can be dispelled quickly. In reality, custom strategies can lessen the complexity of communication over time. Sponsors will find it easier to make changes in asset allocation as well as investment lineup. Further, they will be able to show participants logically how the underlying best-in-class investments are brought to the target-date strategies. Our challenge as professionals is to find ways to help participants save more effectively for retirement. Studies cited in this chapter show that helping participants visualize their living standard in retirement based on how they save today can make a difference. Helping them to reframe their view of retirement savings from accumulating a pool of money for retirement to saving to create a monthly income stream also is important. We come back to the value of reframing DC savings as retirement income in Chapter 12 when we discuss advice and retirement planning. Next we discuss evaluating costs.

CHAPTER 7

Evaluating Costs in Custom Strategies

Over the last several years, defined contribution (DC) plan costs have been under the microscope, both in Washington, D.C., and across the nation, as plan sponsors, consultants, and providers seek ways to render the plans more effective. Motivated in part by losses in market value during 2008 and diminished trust in investment professionals, legislators and litigators are asking whether there are conflicts of interest in plan payment structures and whether the total amount of fees imposed on participants are justifiable. As discussed in Chapter 4, making sure fees are reasonable and transparent at both plan sponsor and participant level are important responsibilities of the plan sponsor as fiduciary.

One of the primary benefits of custom target strategies, as we saw in Chapter 3, is their ability to bring down total plan costs. Both plan sponsors and investment consultants believe that large and even medium-size plans can reduce their expenses by creating custom target strategies, which leverage the low costs of the institutional core funds of the plans. In fact, experts estimate the net savings for larger plans to range from 20 to 65 percent relative to using packaged target funds. However, the savings will vary, depending on plan size and specifics. Clearly, you should run the numbers on your own or work with a consultant to determine your potential savings.

It is important to consider not only immediate costs but how expenses are likely to change over time as assets grow. For plans that use target-date strategies as a default, and especially those plans that reenroll participants into the target strategies, plan sponsors may find that asset growth is rapid. It is critical also to consider the impact on the core investments as assets grow in the target strategies. For instance, if money goes into the target funds but not to the core investment strategies, will the asset base in those core strategies begin to wither, resulting in rising fees in the core funds? In this chapter we look at why costs matter and how to evaluate total plan costs.

Finally, we return to the specific costs of implementing custom target-date strategies.

WHY COSTS MATTER

Reducing DC plan fees by a single basis point can mean big savings for a plan participant. Hewitt Associates showed us that custom strategies reduce cost by 40 basis points (.40 percent) on average. This savings may result in significant added monthly income in retirement.

Reduced costs are important not only to current participants; they also are meaningful to retirees. Institutional pricing within DC plans often compels participants to remain in the plan throughout their retirement years. This is a topic that we return to in detail in Chapter 13.

HAVE YOU CALCULATED AND REDUCED TOTAL PLAN COST?

So, clearly, by managing and reducing total plan cost, sponsors can make their clients' retirement incomes last longer. MacKenzie Hurd, formerly of Callan Associates, and Lori Lucas of Callan Associates talked about ways to achieve this goal effectively: "The key is ensuring that fees are reasonable given the services provided. And, really, that's the standard to which plan sponsors are held."[1] Figure 7.1 shows that the majority of cost—50 to

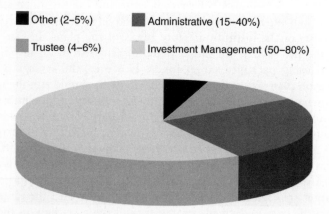

FIGURE 7.1   Costs Associated with Plan Delivery
Source: Hewitt 2006 Survey, Trends and Experiences in 401(k) Plans. Used with permission.

80 percent—is actually in investment management. Administrative comes in second at 15 to 40 percent, while trustee costs are 4 to 6 percent. The best way to calculate a total plan-cost percentage (e.g., 15 to 100 basis points [bps]) is to divide the total of all these fees by the total plan assets, then evaluate fee competitiveness across providers.

A primary advantage DC plans have relative to retail accounts is the ability to invest in structures such as collective investment trusts (CITs) and separately managed accounts, which often provide fees on a sliding scale. In other words, as assets increase, the price of investment management decreases. Employee Retirement Income Security Act (ERISA) plans can invest in these trust company structures and take advantage of pricing that is generally lower than retail-priced mutual funds. For example, in Table 7.1, notice that moving from retail-priced mutual funds, which have higher regulatory fees, to a CIT may lower fees by average of 27 bps (i.e., 0.27 percent)— that is a 28 percent fee reduction from an average fee of 95 bps to 69 bps. In the future, more companies will try to reduce costs in this manner. Asking your investment managers whether they have a lower-cost share class or investment structure should be at the top of your list as you evaluate total plan cost.

Plan sponsors should consider administrative costs next. This is primarily the cost for record keeping, for instance, supporting participant transactions, generating statements, and providing government reporting. While some once believed that administration services are provided for "free," in reality such services are either explicitly charged or bundled into the overall cost of plan services. For example, some DC providers may offer free administration when the plan sponsor selects investments from that provider's fund family or from a list of funds that carry sufficient revenue sharing to support the cost of administration. Of course, nothing is free. As a plan

TABLE 7.1 Comparison of Fees by Structure Type

Asset Classes	Mutual Fund (%)	Collective Fund (%)	Separate Accounts (%)
Intermediate Term	0.55	0.30	0.30
Large Value	0.85	0.55	0.51
Large Growth	0.93	0.56	0.52
Small Value	1.12	0.96	0.92
Small Growth	1.20	0.94	0.90
International	1.05	0.80	0.75
Average Fee	0.95	0.69	0.65

Source: Hewitt Associates, 2005.

fiduciary, gathering all of the plan costs together will allow you to compare apples to apples, one provider to another, in order to select the most cost-effective investments and services for your plan.

Finally, trustee and other costs should be considered. Costs need to be evaluated on their own as well as in relationship to each other. Unfortunately, fee benchmarking can be difficult. The good news is that investment management fees can be compared readily, but other fees such as administration typically are tougher to compare. Plan complexities, such as the number and automation of payrolls, the breadth of Web functionality and communication, and other services, drive cost differences. However, many consulting firms maintain proprietary databases to help plan sponsors both shop services and compare fees.

KEEPING FEES REASONABLE

Keeping fees reasonable is important when designing custom strategies since many of the costs associated with plans are passed on to the plan participants. Thomas Idzorek, chief investment officer at Ibbotson Associates, made these recommendations about fees:

> Any plan sponsor's goal is to produce the best-possible solution at the lowest-possible cost. For mega-plans that means having an independent asset allocator design a custom glide path, which the plan then implements, hopefully, with various low-cost, institutionally priced investment lineup options. Then, as time goes on, if the consultant or plan sponsor has problems with any individual investment sleeve, it can replace any given manager with a new manager with little hassle or communication challenges.[2]

Idzorek points out that many medium-size plans and even plans with assets as low as $25 million, are following the example of the mega-plans and making the move to custom strategies. "Consultants, record keepers and trust companies are building advanced systems and processes to enable plan sponsors to build custom plans at very low asset levels in a cost-effective way."

How do plan sponsors determine whether they are paying reasonable fees? Hurd and Lucas of Callan Associates offered some helpful guidance. First, they said that it is important to itemize those components that make up the total cost. This means figuring out *all* the elements included in fees, and examining "how these stack up individually and as part of a weighted-average expense," which they defined as the total cost of everything related to the plan, divided by the plan's assets. However, they cautioned that since each plan has its own unique complexities, asset allocations, and service provisions, making a "meaningful and fair comparison" to other plans can be challenging. In essence, however, the key factor is not providing the lowest fees but the most reasonable ones in light of the services provided.

> *[T]he DOL [Department of Labor] isn't saying all fees need to be the lowest. If this were the case, plan sponsors might be encouraged to offer a limited selection of index funds such as the S&P [Standard & Poor's] 500. Rather, the fees need to be reasonable for the investment category and strategy. For instance, plan sponsors typically offer actively managed funds as well. The fees for these funds should be compared to the peer group of managers for each strategy.[3]*

They also stated that some investment categories are more expensive to manage and administer than others, justifying a higher fee. For example, "non-traditional investments such as global bonds, real estate and emerging markets may have higher expenses, yet still may be appropriate for a plan and fees can be deemed 'reasonable' given their respective peer groups."

Georgette Gestely, director of the New York City Deferred Compensation Program, agreed that playing it safe by using only index funds is not the way to go, not only in reference to costs but also in terms of styles of management. "Our investment advisors tell us that if we have nothing but index funds we may forfeit something in the upside potential of active management. We want both active and passive management."[4]

Ross Bremen and Rob Fishman of NEPC also commented on the cost effectiveness of nontraditional investment classes. They advised that including alternative strategies in a DC plan lineup could improve the plan's risk-versus-return aspects. Using equity alternatives enable plan managers to

> *include many strategies designed to provide equity-like returns with more bond-like risk levels, which is attractive for a DC plan. Investing in these alternatives gives us a tool to help reduce the traditional equity exposure and improve diversification for participants without sacrificing return potential. We can achieve this particularly well in target-date strategies.[5]*

However, they pointed out that plan sponsors could not simply tell participants to go out and find alternative assets and add them to their portfolios because the number of alternatives available for DC plans is limited and some are very expensive. "But we also see more competitively priced strategies. While we're willing to pay for liquidity, there's a limit to how high the fees can go before the cost outweighs the benefit."

UNBUNDLING CAN KEEP DOWN COSTS

Dan Holupchinski, the retirement plans manager for Deluxe Corporation, points out that by their very nature, custom strategies keep fees lower than the normally more expensive off-the-shelf funds.

> *Since most of our DC assets are in separate accounts, our investment-management fees decline as assets increase. By offering custom strategies, we tap into the lower fees and continue to feed assets to the core, thus further reducing total plan costs over time. Consequently, by using a custom plan, we keep our fee structure down. It's something we've been very keen to accomplish through the years and the reason we established separate accounts, unbundled services, and the entire structure now in place for almost a decade.[6]*

Deluxe has found that not only does unbundling keep fees low, but it creates a good perception in plan participants who appreciate these lower costs. As we saw at the beginning of this chapter, such savings build up over the years, giving participants more money per month in retirement.

Hurd and Lucas pointed out that since unbundling is such an effective strategy, larger plans increasingly are moving in that direction, particularly those plans with assets of $750 million and up. They have observed "a greater desire for flexibility in the investment lineup—and not using record keepers' proprietary funds necessarily." Choosing to incorporate the flexibility of "privately managed funds such as commingled funds (that is, 'collective trusts') or separate accounts, which typically offer lower expenses as assets grow" is also becoming a more prevalent practice.[7] In fact, in her article "Is It Important for 401(k) Fees to Be Equitable?" Lucas points out that this approach "effectively eliminates the problem of uneven fee payments altogether" because

> *Administrative fees in the unbundled situation are then paid through a dollar-based per participant fee (e.g., $100 annually per participant); a percentage-based add-on administrative fee (e.g., a 10 basis-point fee is assessed against every fund in the plan); or some combination of both.*

> *The rationale for the dollar-based fee is that 401(k) administrative costs are largely fixed costs, so all participants should pay the same amount, regardless of the account size. The rationale for the basis-point fee is that it would be unreasonably burdensome for an individual with a $1,000 account balance to pay the same $100 annual fee as someone with a $100,000 account balance.[8]*

Therefore, companies with larger assets are encouraged to look at non–mutual fund structures to see if they can save on costs.

Unbundling provides other benefits to plan sponsors. Besides reducing plan costs overall, it "can allow the plan sponsor to incorporate a broader array of institutional investment managers," which includes those managing the DB plan, and "results in much greater fee and investment flexibility."

If creating lower fees by fully unbundling the plan is not possible,

> *plan sponsors can still consider creating a more even playing field by selectively reducing or eliminating revenue sharing and introducing a small per participant fee to offset administrative expenses. At a minimum, plan sponsors may wish to evaluate their comfort level with how revenue-sharing levels vary by fund within the plan. They may also wish to look into the possibility of greater participant disclosure around this topic.*

CUSTOM STRATEGIES AND THE VALUE OF UNITIZING

As we saw in Chapter 3, some companies with significant defined benefit–plan assets favor unitizing so that they can use the same managers in both their defined contribution and defined benefit (DB) plans. The benefit of this choice is that it allows plan sponsors to bring over to their DC plan the DB managers with whom they are already familiar and comfortable. While there is a certain elegance to this solution, plan sponsors still need to do some research to find out whether they will really be saving money by this move.

Michael Riak, director of savings and affiliate plans at Verizon, spoke about the cost savings the company experienced through taking some of its DB portfolios and unitizing them over to the DC side. Specifically, Verizon has used this strategy in designing its emerging markets equity fund. "One of the issues that we were wrestling with when creating our emerging markets option in the plan was that we were not sure of the amount of assets that would flow into the fund."[9] Since Verizon's goal is always to use more than one manager in a plan, it wanted to avoid having only a single manager running its emerging markets investment option. To solve this dilemma, it selected three managers from its DB plan with whom it was very happy and asked them to manage the emerging markets on the DC side.

> What's critical to this unitized structure is that it benefits both the DB and the DC plans. We believed that we achieved that by providing a high quality multi-manager fund that the savings plans did not have the asset base to create on their own and by providing the DB plans with additional liquidity through contributions from savings plan participants who invested in the fund. Independent fiduciaries monitor and approve the transactions in the unitized fund. Our trustee for the DB plan was very helpful in setting up this structure. They strike a daily net asset value and report it on a timely basis to our DC record keeper; it's worked out very well.

Initially, there may be some work involved in unitizing. However, Hurd and Lucas feel that this transition may not be as difficult as it seems. "Regarding the hassle, in most cases plan sponsors with a DB plan already work with a custodian and so sponsors understand how separate accounts operate. So it's not a great leap to apply the same principals to the DC plan."[10]

The situation may be somewhat different when a plan sponsor offers *only* a DC plan, but Lucas and Hurd point out that commingled funds can be the answer there since they are

> a great middle ground for plan sponsors who have DC plans that are conducive to privately managed funds, but who aren't comfortable with separate accounts. A separate account requires the extra steps of hiring a custodian and understanding that marketplace. By contrast, the investment manager handles the commingled funds, including the trust, custody, and unitizing.

EXPERTS DISCUSS FEE TRANSPARENCY

Professor Richard Thaler of the University of Chicago has studied how behavioral economics has impacted defined contribution plan design and decisions. Thaler stressed that helping participants to understand fees was a behavioral issue and needed to be addressed from that standpoint. "In the past, participants haven't been sensitive to fees as they've chosen plan investments." In other words, participants tend not to realize that everything in a plan comes with a price. Thaler felt that plan sponsors have a responsibility to keep fees as low as possible. "Certainly, if a plan sponsor chooses the default fund and wants to stay out of trouble, it should keep the fees down. Sponsors should be cognizant of fees in the same way they were when they managed a DB plan."[11]

Pam Hess, director of retirement research at Hewitt Associates, points out that with all of the recent litigation and focus in Washington on target retirement-date strategies, making sure fees are reasonable and transparent is now a major concern. (See Chapter 4.) She spoke about how, over the last two decades, Hewitt has been asking employers whether they have ever attempted to calculate the total cost of their plans. Back in the 1990s, they found that "only 20 percent of plans had even tried to calculate . . . the total cost of administration, trustee, communication, and fund expenses." While today that number has risen to 84 percent, "there's still a lot of room for improvement. For those that have calculated it, about a third of employers report having outside help: hiring a consultant or someone to help them understand the fees."[12] While Hewitt has found that some employers are checking prices to see if they can find more competitive fees, one of the biggest changes is that employers are trying

> to understand all aspects of fees. Employers need to understand the whole, as well as the pieces, that comprise the costs. It's about getting comfortable with the fees and the ability to show due diligence. With all the litigation, it's important for employers to document their strategies, processes, and to make certain they understand their fees fully.

Hess also noted that many plan sponsors are surprised when they conduct a total plan-cost analysis for the first time, especially those that use bundled off-the-shelf plans and services, where the prices for individual plan pieces and services are not visible. "Costs depend on the plan's size, assets per participant, and even how long the sponsor has been with a provider. When they break it down, some employers find that they may be paying more than expected or that they should be paying in the marketplace."

When we asked Hurd and Lucas what steps they suggested for evaluating overall fees, they stated that the first step was for plan sponsors to decide how frequently they wished to conduct fee analyses. Their recommendation was that sponsors perform a comprehensive fee analysis every few years and more limited updates annually. The reason behind this frequency is that a "401(k) plan's assets may grow and, to the extent that fees are asset-based, it can produce significant changes in the cost structure. A plan that was priced reasonably when the record-keeping contract first was negotiated may be out of whack a few years later after assets grow." For example, even though the services have remained the same, more of the fees may still be going to the record keeper.

ERISA SECTION 404(C) AND FEE DISCLOSURE

ERISA has mandated that plan sponsors create an annual report that provides all participants with a summary of their plan, an annual report, and individual account statements, all of which are likely to include some type of fee information. In compliance with ERISA Section 404(c), if a plan offers mutual funds, it also provides expense-ratio information. Fund fact sheets listing expense ratios might also be provided. However,

> *it's rare for plan participants to be given fee details such as revenue sharing—or fees credited back to the record keeper that offset administration costs. In part, that's because revenue sharing is difficult to communicate. Plus, of course, revenue sharing is embedded in the expense ratio already. As a result, although the participant may not see revenue-sharing arrangements explicitly, they generally do see via the expense ratio the aggregate fees that include revenue sharing.[13]*

In Table 7.2, you see the types of disclosure documents that are required along with their purpose and how they may provide information on fees.

Lucas and Hurd pointed out that the ERISA Section 404(c) disclosure mandate was having a considerable impact on the amount of detail that plan sponsors felt obligated to disclose to participants, for example, indirect fees such as commissions and float. Fee lawsuits, especially in relation to revenue sharing, had also created a climate of more detailed fee disclosure. "Overall, we're moving to an era of greater transparency—and greater burden of disclosure for providers and plan sponsors alike." They also pointed out that these mandates for more openness were presenting communication challenges.

> *There's high potential for confusion when you try to explain revenue-sharing arrangements to DC participants. We already see plan sponsors attempting to be more proactive in fee disclosure, but many questions remain regarding what sponsors should show and how they should show it. There's a great deal of anticipation about what the regulations will require.*

TABLE 7.2 Required Disclosure Documents to All Participants

Disclosure Document	Disclosure Purpose	Information on Fees
Summary plan description	Explain to participants how the plan operates.	May contain information on how various fees—such as investment, record-keeping, and loan fees—are charged to participants, but is not required by ERISA to do so.
Account statement	Show the participant's account balance.	Typically identifies fees, such as for loans, that are directly attributable to an account during a specific period. Also may show investment and record-keeping fees but is not required by ERISA to do so.
Summary annual report	Discloses the plan's financial condition to participants.	Contains total plan costs incurred by plan participants during the year.

Source: Government Accountability Office analysts.

We asked if communications could become complex when a plan moved from a bundled to an unbundled situation where part or all of the administration fee is not paid via revenue sharing and how they handled this situation. Hurd and Lucas responded that the most sensitive issue here was the switch from basis points to dollar amounts in the fee reporting. "Instead of bundling the administration fee into the overall expense ratio, it now may be a separate dollar amount paid per participant. Investors tend to be more sensitive when fees are expressed in dollar amounts than when they're expressed in basis points—even if the fees are the same."

Another question we asked was whether, in an era of greater fee transparency, fees were equitable across all participant lines. Hurd and Lucas pointed out that this was an issue plan sponsors needed to consider seriously, since fees were *not* equitable across a plan.

For instance, one of the plan funds may charge a higher price to cover administrative costs, while the next fund may cover investment-management fees only. That means a participant who invests in the lower-priced fund may not carry an equal weight of the plan costs. If a plan offers all funds that either share revenue at the same level—that is, pay back a part of the expense to cover plan costs—or more "institutional" investment options—that is, they have lower expenses and don't offer revenue sharing—then participants likely share the same cost burden. Unfortunately, many plans offer a combination of revenue-sharing mutual funds and non-revenue-sharing institutional funds, which leads to uneven cost sharing.

For them, the ideal plan would be one that not only generated the lowest costs for all participants but enabled them to share all costs equally.

COSTS OF IMPLEMENTING AND RUNNING CUSTOM TARGET STRATEGIES

As you consider implementing custom target strategies, you may consider costs in the same way as you have all other plan expenses. You will need to evaluate each component of cost and then tally them together to evaluate the total plan cost relative to alternative approaches. Investment management again will be the majority of cost. Yet there are other costs to add in as well, including these types:

- **Investment consulting or advisory fees.** You may want to retain an investment-consulting firm or other investment advisor to create the target retirement-date asset allocation (i.e., glide path) as well as to monitor and revise the allocation over time. Many investment-consulting firms and investment managers provide this service. Fees may be charged as a one-time project fee, an annual retainer, or based on assets within the target-date strategies. Typically, when the firm acts as an investment advisor overseeing the strategies, a basis-point fee is imposed. Investment advisory fees vary, typically ranging from 3 to 30 bps on assets in the target-date strategies. A flat dollar-project fee or retainer also are commonplace costs for consulting assignments that include fiduciary oversight yet stop short of accepting investment advisor oversight. Clearly, the more responsibility and liability the consultant or advisor accepts, the higher the likely fee. You also may want to consider hiring a consultant for projects such as conducting a record-keeping search or managing the custom strategy implementation.
- **Record-keeping fees.** Your record keeper may charge to add additional investment options to the system. This charge is likely to be the same, regardless of the fund structure (e.g., mutual fund, collective investment trust, or separately managed account). The record keeper and/or trustee also need to establish operations to receive the asset-allocation adjustments and may base fees on the frequency that rebalancing is conducted,

for example, monthly or quarterly. However, major providers with whom we have spoken do not charge to rebalance, since they are required to manage normal cash flows daily anyway. Consequently, they do not consider this work as difficult or as an additional service.

- **Trustee fees.** You also are likely to incur added trustee fees. Typically a trust company charges for each additional fund or strategy. Trust companies charge a lower amount for a mutual fund than for a non–mutual fund, because a non–mutual fund, such as a CIT or separately managed account requires the trust to calculate a daily net asset value. For example, your trustee may charge $2,000 to add a packaged target retirement-date mutual fund and possibly $5,000 to add a custom target retirement-date institutional strategy. Overall, the total cost for adding six custom target-date strategies may be $30,000, compared to adding six packaged funds, which may cost $12,000—a difference of $18,000. Ask your trustee for a quote. As discussed in Chapter 5, not all custom strategies are set up in a trust account. If a model portfolio approach is used, the trust fee may not be applicable.

- **Communication costs.** Whether you create your own custom strategies or use existing mutual funds, you should consider creating integrated materials that address all investment choices rather than simply present new strategies. While it may be attractive to use fund-company materials that address only the company's target strategies, communication professionals suggest that the best practice is a more integrated communication package that shows all investment options. Over time, the cost to create materials for custom funds will not exceed the cost of using materials for packaged mutual funds. Over the long run, as fund managers change, communication experts suggest that the cost of custom communications may even be lower than those of packaged funds. This is because the changes are likely to be more contained (e.g., the asset allocation may shift slightly or some of the core funds may change, rather than target-fund managers changing to a different organization and thus requiring additional communication for the new funds). See Chapter 6 for more in-depth information about facilitating communication with plan participants.

- **Legal fees.** As we saw in Chapter 4, you may require support from legal counsel for a range of services, including a consulting review and document updates (e.g., plan and trust documents, service agreements, or other contracts in compliance with Section 404(c) of ERISA), and communications review.

- **Other costs.** Internal staff time dedicated to the project is also a factor. You may have other incremental costs as well, such as the cost of adding strategies to advice models, preparing Form 5500, and plan audits. Each plan's situation is unique, and costs should be budgeted from that perspective.

Record keepers suggest that fees related to additional target strategies be charged directly to each respective target strategy. To get strategies off the ground, you may wish to accrue expenses over a year or more and apply a basis-point charge.

Plan sponsors also should consider whether they want to encourage plan participants to remain invested in the plan, even after termination. Encouraging retirees to remain in the plan may result in significant additional assets, which in turn can reduce the overall plan cost. At the same time, retirees typically incur a lower investment cost than in the retail market.

IN CLOSING

While there are many components of fees for you to consider in creating custom target strategies, you are likely to find the total cost of offering custom strategies will save your participants money relative to packaged products; this is particularly true for larger plans and as assets grow over time. What is important in evaluating the cost of custom strategies is to take into account all plan costs, including investment management, administration, trust, and other fees, such as communication. While some providers may suggest that certain services, such as administration or communication, are "free," do not be fooled. Costs are being covered somehow, typically through the investment management fees or possibly with the anticipation of a percent of individual retirement account rollover capture, or a combination of the two. It is worth your time to find out how the costs are covered and to make sure that you understand the effective expense your participants will bear. Once you go through this exercise, again, be sure to project how the costs relative to assets will change over time. Particularly for larger plans, you are likely to confirm that a movement to custom strategies makes sense. As discussed earlier, gaining control over plan costs is a primary driver of custom strategies. In the next part of this book, we turn to another significant driver: retaining and increasing control over the investment structure, including the glide path, asset classes, and benchmarking.

Designing and Benchmarking Custom Target-Date Strategies

CHAPTER 8

Glide-Path Design

Now we are entering the heart of target-date strategies, looking at the structure of the asset allocation, or what many refer to as the glide path. What does "glide path" mean? We've provided a brief definition up to this point, yet let's take a closer look. The dictionary defines it as "the path of descent of an aircraft, delineated by a radio beam that directs the pilot in landing the craft." For target-date strategies, we can think of retirement as the plan participant's destination and how money is managed up to the point of retirement as the glide path. Similar to a plane, which begins its descent as it approaches its destination, a target-date glide path seeks to reduce exposure to higher-risk assets as it approaches retirement age. David Fisser, consultant and former chairman of the Southwest Airlines Pilots' Association 401(k) committee, uses this metaphor when he talks about its glide-path strategies:

> The glide path is...like a flight plan. When you fly from Dallas to L.A., you determine a flight plan, the altitude at which you'll fly, how much fuel you need to climb, and how weather may impact the flight. Based on the airplane's weight, it may take 15,000 pounds of fuel. Then you need a certain reserve. You plan it out, but you always build in a little fudge factor, in case things don't transpire as they're supposed to, because many times they don't—the weather's bad, or something happens. Retirement and investing are like the flight plan. You know when you'll start. You have a decent idea where you're headed. You determine how much to save. And you need to plan for turbulence and contingencies along the way.[1]

Selecting and managing a target-date glide path may be one of the most perplexing steps in setting up target-date strategies. Plan sponsors ponder these and other questions: How much equity should be in the glide path at retirement? What about early on, when the participant begins investing? What about other asset classes? These are important decisions, since selecting the appropriate weights of assets for participants at different ages (i.e., designing glide-path structure) will be one of the most significant factors in determining whether plan participants will succeed in reaching their retirement destination. Investment professionals and academics have written for decades about the importance of asset-allocation policy in determining the success of portfolios. For instance, according to Roger G. Ibbotson and Paul D. Kaplan: "about 90 percent of the variability in returns of a typical fund across time is explained by policy"—in other words, the asset allocation for the glide path of target-date strategies.[2]

Unfortunately, while the experts have studied and written extensively about the appropriate asset-allocation structure, there is considerable disagreement on which structure is best. Glide-path experts typically all begin a participant's career with more than 75 percent invested in equity, but they begin to diverge in asset allocations as retirement age approaches and even more so postretirement. At that point, the equity allocation may be less than 20 percent or as much as 60 percent. So, who is right?

As discussed in Chapter 4, even regulators in Washington D.C. are focused on the structure of the glide path and whether it is appropriate for participants. These regulators' particular focus is on the later years as the participant approaches retirement. One significant question is whether the glide path is simply managed to the retirement date or through the retirement date (i.e., to a mortality date). To a large extent, this answer will drive the design of the glide path. Managers who focus through retirement to mortality assume a time horizon for investment that extends another 20 to 30 years. Thus they believe in supporting the ability of the glide path to assume a higher risk level. At PIMCO, we believe it is important to focus on the retirement-income goal as well as risk exposure as you develop a glide path. This focus will help guide the plan sponsor in determining what glide path is most appropriate.

In this chapter we explore the analytic approaches to creating target-date glide paths. First, we look at the common analytic framework taught by academics and how this framework actually is used by professionals. Then we present a way to evaluate glide paths using a retirement-income adequacy framework. Next we suggest that we move beyond efficient frontier modeling and share PIMCO's suggested approach to structuring glide paths, which is based on the identification of the fundamental risk factors that help drive investment returns. Finally, we share the glide-path designs of several plan sponsors and the philosophies behind them.

AN ACADEMIC LOOK AT CREATING OPTIMAL ASSET-ALLOCATION STRATEGIES

To help examine the appropriate asset-allocation strategy and measure its likelihood of success, let us first take a look at the investment analytic approaches taught by finance and business schools. Currently, the most prevalent theory, in terms of the asset-allocation process, is known as Modern Portfolio Theory (MPT). The concept was first proposed by Harry Markowitz (1952) and then expanded by William F. Sharpe et al. (1964).[3] Essentially, MPT provides a working theory of how individuals can help maximize return and mitigate risk when they make investment decisions and how they can use market information to allocate money among competing assets. In essence, MPT may help users to evaluate what they might expect as a return versus the potential risk of various combinations of and allocations to asset classes. Further, it helps investment managers and advisors to create "optimal" portfolios that seek to maximize the level of potential return for each unit of risk taken.

While MPT has advanced our understanding of how asset diversification can have a positive impact on the risk-adjusted return of portfolios, we see a need to improve on it in practice. For instance, when asked to provide a solution for an optimal portfolio using capital-market assumptions, including historical asset correlations, MPT often produces undiversified portfolios that are unlikely to be used by most investors. For example, it may select a portfolio comprised of 80 percent emerging markets and 20 percent precious metals. Such results are due to the sensitivity of the mean-variance framework to input data. As a result, most investment managers and advisors change the outcome by using constraints on how much can be invested in each asset class. In other words, they set a maximum or minimum for each asset class, which we often refer to as caps and floors. People use different methods to set caps and floors, each resulting in considerable changes to the solution derived by the unconstrained MPT.

Of course, one of the greatest concerns with MPT is the approach it takes when capturing risk, return, and correlation assumptions. Typically, we base these inputs on historical observations because that is all we have—so we use this history to project market trends into the future. Yet we all know that history is unlikely to repeat itself. To get around this MPT flaw, practitioners and advisors create their own variations or extensions to the theory, which they apply in order to help create optimal asset-allocation strategies.

Let us take a brief look at the four most popular alternatives and extensions to MPT:

1. Tactical asset allocation (TAA)
2. Black-Litterman model
3. Value at risk (VaR)
4. Monte Carlo simulation

Tactical Asset Allocation

TAA is active management that operates on the asset-class level. Tactical asset allocation basically starts with MPT, looks at the asset allocation it creates—the "strategic asset allocation"—then makes short-term adjustments to it, within established constraints, based on the portfolio manager's outlook on the economic environment. For example, if the equity allocation is 60 percent based on mean-variance optimization, then we might set overweight/underweight constraints of 50 to 70 percent for equity. A commonly held assumption of those who utilize TAA is that markets are fairly efficient and rational, yet they seek opportunities to take advantage of temporary market inefficiencies.

Black-Litterman Model

As a remedy for the undiversified portfolios that often result from mean-variance optimization, Fischer Black and Robert Litterman developed an optimization approach that in practice begins with a benchmark portfolio as the default asset allocation, then invokes a formal procedure that allows the portfolio manager to vary the portfolio's asset weights using his or her forward-looking market views. For example, an equity manager may begin with a well-diversified index as the benchmark (e.g., the MSCI World Index), then adjust it based on views on asset returns that deviate from "equilibrium" returns, which are estimated from the benchmark weights and covariance matrix. If the manager's views are identical to those derived from the benchmark weights, the portfolio will mirror the index in its allocation weights.

Value at Risk

VaR is a popular risk management and measurement tool. It is typically taken as a measure of the potential mark-to-market losses that can occur within a given portfolio for a particular confidence level and time horizon. For example, we might say, "I have 95 percent confidence that I cannot lose more than 1 percent of my portfolio value on any given day, week, or year." VaR can also be utilized within an optimization framework. Here we would ask, "How can we construct a portfolio that disallows any losses greater than the loss we have set as our VaR value?" In DC plans, this question may change to the statement "Our plan cannot produce income replacement rates below 20 percent." Value at risk and its extensions (e.g., conditional value at risk) can be very powerful and flexible tools in the portfolio manager's arsenal if used appropriately. Yet, its limitation may be the use of historical returns, volatilities and correlations.

Monte Carlo Simulation

Monte Carlo simulation is a computer-based tool for asset allocation that allows the user to test a range of possible investment outcomes or what-if scenarios. Employing user-defined capital-market assumptions as inputs (e.g., expected returns, volatilities, and correlations), a Monte Carlo simulation provides a statistical description of asset-allocation outcomes by calculating a multitude of random investment scenarios and information regarding the likelihood of each scenario. For example, we can ask, "How likely is it that an individual will replace 65 percent of his or her income? And how likely is it that 80 percent of plan participants will achieve that success rate?" It is a useful tool for portfolio managers because it provides probabilistic solutions to problems that have proven to be intractable using traditional analytical methods. In fact, it can be considered a statistical counterpoint to analytic techniques. An additional advantage of a Monte Carlo simulation is that it can efficiently handle multiperiod investment problems in a manner that is more efficient than many analytical methodologies, such as mean-variance optimization.

A PRACTITIONER'S LOOK AT CREATING OPTIMAL ASSET-ALLOCATION STRATEGIES

Now that we have discussed the asset-allocation optimization approaches taught in finance programs, let us turn to what investment consultants do when they help clients structure and evaluate the success of their DC plans.

DC investment consulting firms increasingly approach the evaluation of plan success by focusing on the probability of participants attaining sufficient retirement income. In 2008 PIMCO conducted a survey to determine what approaches experts apply in determining the asset allocation for DC plans.[4] We found that the majority of consultants (79 percent) used efficient frontier analysis, as taught in finance programs. Notably, we also found that nearly two-thirds (63 percent) analyzed the probability of meeting retirement-income goals given asset allocation and projected savings over time—some of these firms applied both approaches as they help structure DC investment offerings.

We also asked what software firms use for their modeling, or if they used proprietary software applications. The majority, 62 percent, said they used proprietary approaches.

The others said they use outside analytic software. Of the respondents that use outside efficient frontier-type modeling software, 64 percent named Ibbotson Associates as their provider and 18 percent referred to Zephyr models. For those that create their own proprietary models, half used Microsoft Excel, one used the Monte Carlo simulation of the Oracle Crystal Ball® software, while the remainder used other proprietary approaches.

One of the more critical questions we asked consultants pertains to their capital-market assumptions. The vast majority (86 percent) stated that they created their own assumptions. When we asked on what they based those assumptions, nearly two-thirds (62 percent) said they create future or forward-looking assumptions based on the current levels of risk premiums. For instance, they might use data from the last 5 to 20 years as a basis to extrapolate and then use their own judgment to refine their capital-market projections.

We also wanted to know which "risk-free"[5] asset they use in their models. Not surprisingly, the majority (79 percent) used Treasury bills (T-bills), which is what we all were taught in school. Yet the survey shows that 17 percent of consultants use Treasury Inflation Protected Securities (TIPS). At PIMCO, we believe TIPS are a more appropriate risk-free asset for DC plans since retirees tend to rely on the real or inflation-adjusted value of their savings to pay for goods and services in retirement. By contrast, T-bills do not adjust for inflation, which is one of the key risks for anyone saving for retirement.

Another critical area that our PIMCO survey explored was how consultants think about inflation for DC plans. We asked how important they believe it is to have inflation protection within a DC plan. Two-thirds (66 percent) felt that it is "critical" or "very important," while another 24 percent said it is "somewhat important." Surprisingly, the remaining 10 percent said that it "isn't important at all."

We also asked what type of assets provide the most protection from inflation. Of those surveyed, 62 percent chose TIPS, 17 percent equities, and only 7 percent commodities. Real estate was noted as an important inflation hedge second to TIPS.

We found that all of the firms account for inflation in their modeling but do this in different ways. Just over one-third (36 percent) use a static inflation rate, an equal percentage (36 percent) model inflation as a dynamic variable, over a quarter (28 percent) adjust asset-class returns, and the balance use either a combination or another approach.

Finally, we asked whether consultants believed the concept of liability-driven investing (LDI) has any application within DC plans. (LDI is an investment approach companies often use to manage their DB plans; the approach aims to match the allocation of a plan's assets to its liabilities in a way that seeks to reduce exposure to market risk.) The majority of those queried (66 percent) either said "definitely yes" or "yes, at least in part" that LDI should apply to DC plans as well. That means, they believe that even in a DC plan we should consider the retirement income "liability" as we create asset allocation structures for participants.

DC PLAN SUCCESS REQUIRES A NEW APPROACH

In order for DC plans to fulfill the objective of providing adequate retirement-income levels, we need to broaden the way that we teach and apply finance and navigate to a new destination. We suggest moving beyond the efficient frontier paradigm that deals with assets only and toward a more-comprehensive framework that incorporates DC contribution levels and the probability of meeting retirement-income goals. What is more, we believe it is critical to account for inflation in the analysis. As discussed earlier, the good news is that many consulting firms are evaluating the probability of success using models that incorporate savings, probabilities, and inflation factors.

For plans whose primary objective is adequate retirement income, we suggest this three-step approach which accounts for the key risk factors your participants face including inflation:

1. Use a stochastic or Monte Carlo modeling approach that factors in the plan participants' assumed savings by using the actual contribution levels of employees and employers, the asset allocation of the plan or default vehicle, and reasonable forward-looking capital-market assumptions.
2. Account for inflation as a stochastic variable. This can be achieved by using "real" expected returns and volatilities or by incorporating inflation directly into models that utilize nominal returns and volatilities.
3. Calculate the real replacement-income percentage.

At PIMCO, we calculate the real replacement-income percentage by converting the final projected savings from the Monte Carlo simulations into an assumed real or Consumer Price Index (CPI)–adjusted annuity payout by using an estimate of the amount an insurance company may provide for such an annuity. For instance, currently an insurer may pay a 65-year old $60,000 in CPI-adjusted dollars a year for life on a $1 million account balance for a single-premium annuity. To determine retirement-income replacement, simply take the projected accumulated savings, multiply the real annuity conversion factor (e.g., 6 percent), and divide this amount by the real wage-growth-adjusted future value of savings. To continue our example, let us assume that the worker has a real wage of $100,000 a year at retirement. If the median projected savings is $1 million, then the real annuity would be $60,000 a year. These numbers provide a real replacement rate of 60 percent when dividing $60,000, the real annuity, by $100,000, the final pay.

As with any model, the assumptions we make determine the quality of the output. Here are a number of helpful suggestions about how to make useful and accurate assumptions:

- **Be conservative, or at least realistic.** As you consider savings levels and capital-market assumptions, be careful not to be overly optimistic. We suggest varying the savings rate based on the age of the participant and escalating this amount as she or he grows older. Our model uses the Hewitt Associates participant savings-rate data, which varies by age band. Be particularly careful with capital-market assumptions. Past performance does not predict future results. Rather than taking historic averages, use forward-looking assumptions.
- **Study the probable results.** Run at least 10,000 trials to help produce relatively stable outcomes. Vary the inputs to view how a change in the assumption set can impact the results. For instance, you may see that saving an additional 1 percent of income has far less impact than increasing real returns by 1 percent.
- **Evaluate the risk of unacceptable outcomes ("left tail") and volatility along the way.** Is it possible to retain the median outcome yet reduce the risk of unacceptable outcomes by varying the asset allocation or asset mix? What happens when less-correlated assets, such as commodities, are added to the mix? We know that participants may be frightened away from a highly volatile asset allocation, so it is important to understand the expected volatility over the full time horizon of investing (e.g., 40 years) as well as the volatility along the way (e.g., annual expected volatility for each vintage). We suggest evaluating this volatility and, more important, the expected return relative to the volatility (the risk-adjusted expected return).

EVALUATING THE PROBABILITY OF MEETING DC RETIREMENT-INCOME GOALS

To demonstrate this approach, let us take a look at an application PIMCO developed that evaluates the probability of meeting retirement-income goals. PIMCO YODcA™ (Your Optimal DC Allocation) is an analysis tool PIMCO provides at no cost to consultants and plan sponsors to help project the likelihood of an asset allocation structure of meeting retirement income goals. In the next example, we explain the inputs and then show the sample outputs. We then vary key inputs to demonstrate the impact on the outcomes.

As suggested earlier, you will need to gather three sets of inputs: savings, asset allocation, and capital-market assumptions.

PIMCO YODcA™ Model Inputs

Step 1: Input Projected Savings In order to discover how much participants will save, PIMCO YODcA requests starting salary, real wage growth, and contribution levels. (See Figure 8.1.) Plan sponsors or consultants can

Income:	
Starting Salary:	$50,000
Real Wage Growth:	1%

Savings:	
Starting Balance:	$0

Employee and Employer Contribution Rates:			
Years from Present	Employee Deferral %	Employer Contribution %	Total % Contributed
0–5	6.0%	3.5%	9.5%
6–10	6.0%	3.5%	9.5%
11–15	7.3%	3.5%	10.8%
16–20	7.3%	3.5%	10.8%
21–25	7.9%	3.5%	11.4%
26–30	7.9%	3.5%	11.4%
31–35	9.1%	3.5%	12.6%
36–40	9.1%	3.5%	12.6%
40+	9.8%	3.5%	13.3%

Annual Income at Retirement:	
Ending Salary:	$73,706
Real Annuity Conversion:	6%

Hypothetical example for illustrative purposes only

FIGURE 8.1 Savings Assumptions
Source: PIMCO, Department of Labor, Society of Actuaries 2007.

vary the starting salary based on the organization's population. Salary increases are derived from the rate of real wage growth. (Our model's default rate is 1 percent real, based on historical data reported by the Department of Labor.) Investors tend to save a higher percentage of their salaries as they grow older, so the savings input allows for this variation. The application default is set to the typical saving behavior, as reported by the most current Hewitt Associates in its Universe Benchmarks Survey. We also input a real annuity conversion rate, which is defaulted at 6 percent, given current real annuity rates. The model calculates the real ending salary, assuming the participant works for 40 years.

Step 2: Determine Asset Allocation   How do we allocate our participants' assets? PIMCO YODcA asks for the plan's asset allocation. This may be how the plan assets are currently invested overall, or it may be specific to a target-date, target-risk, or managed-account strategy. As shown in Table 8.1, we input the asset allocation in a table, which is compared separately to a second selected asset allocation.

Step 3: Select Real Capital-Market Assumptions   The performance of the assets depends, in large part, on future expectations. How do you expect each asset class to perform in terms of return, volatility, and relative to each other (asset correlation)? You may input expectations in real rather than nominal numbers. (See Table 8.2 and Figure 8.2.) This means that the real numbers will likely be lower since they represent expected return over inflation. PIMCO YODcA also allows you to model in nominal terms instead by stating returns, wage growth, and the annuity conversion rate, all before inflation. For example, the below-historical data or forward-looking assumptions may be inputs the plan sponsor or client would like to use. Again, the more forward looking the better.

Note: PIMCO no longer uses traditional capital market asset-class assumptions, rather currently we use instead forward-looking risk factors. We discuss this approach later in this chapter. Nonetheless, next we provide an example using the hypothetical capital market assumptions.

PIMCO YODcA Model Results

Once the inputs are set, we are ready to run the model to generate results. The PIMCO YODcA software allows us to run millions of Monte Carlo simulations in a short time frame. In this example, however, we have set the model to run just 10,000 trials, which can be accomplished in fewer than 10 seconds. The software takes the savings, asset-allocation, and capital-market assumptions and randomly projects the future savings for our DC

TABLE 8.1 Asset Allocations of a Diversified and a Typical Stock and Bond Glide Path

	Asset Allocation #1 Diversified Glide Path							
Years from Present	**0–5**	**6–10**	**11–15**	**16–20**	**21–25**	**26–30**	**31–35**	**36–40**
Commodities	15%	15%	13%	13%	10%	8%	5%	3%
REITs	15%	15%	13%	13%	10%	8%	5%	3%
U.S. Intermediate-Term Taxable Bonds	3%	3%	5%	5%	15%	25%	30%	35%
U.S. Diversified Large-Cap Equities	15%	15%	15%	15%	13%	10%	8%	5%
U.S. Small-Cap Equities	15%	15%	15%	15%	13%	8%	5%	3%
Emerging Markets Equities	10%	10%	10%	10%	8%	8%	5%	3%
U.S. Inflation Protected Bonds	8%	8%	10%	10%	18%	25%	30%	35%
Non-U.S. Diversified Equities—Unhedged	15%	15%	15%	15%	13%	10%	8%	5%
U.S. Short-Term Taxable Bonds	0%	0%	0%	0%	0%	0%	5%	10%
U.S. High-Yield Bonds	0%	0%	0%	0%	0%	0%	0%	0%
Long Treasuries	5%	5%	5%	5%	3%	0%	0%	0%
Total	100%	100%	100%	100%	100%	100%	100%	100%

	Asset Allocation #2 Typical Stock and Bond							
Years from Present	**0–5**	**6–10**	**11–15**	**16–20**	**21–25**	**26–30**	**31–35**	**36–40**
Commodities	0%	0%	0%	0%	0%	0%	0%	0%
REITs	0%	0%	0%	0%	0%	0%	0%	0%
U.S. Intermediate-Term Taxable Bonds	10%	10%	10%	13%	21%	29%	36%	42%
U.S. Diversified Large-Cap Equities	72%	72%	72%	69%	63%	57%	51%	44%
U.S. Small-Cap Equities	0%	0%	0%	0%	0%	0%	0%	0%
Emerging Markets Equities	3%	3%	3%	3%	3%	3%	2%	2%
U.S. Inflation-Protected Bonds	0%	0%	0%	0%	0%	0%	0%	4%
Non-U.S. Diversified Equities—Unhedged	15%	15%	15%	14%	13%	12%	11%	9%
U.S. Short-Term Taxable Bonds	0%	0%	0%	0%	0%	0%	0%	0%
U.S. High-Yield Bonds	0%	0%	0%	0%	0%	0%	0%	0%
Long Treasuries	0%	0%	0%	0%	0%	0%	0%	0%
Total	100%	100%	100%	100%	100%	100%	100%	100%

Source: PIMCO. Hypothetical example for illustrative purposes only.

TABLE 8.2   Asset Class Return and Volatility Assumptions

Asset Class	Expected Return	Volatility
Commodities	7.2%	14.4%
REITs	15.5%	14.6%
U.S. Intermediate-Term Taxable Bonds	6.3%	3.6%
U.S. Diversified Large-Cap Equities	7.7%	15.2%
U.S. Small-Cap Equities	9.6%	20.0%
Emerging Markets Equities	8.4%	24.1%
U.S. Inflation-Protected Bonds	6.7%	4.9%
Non-U.S. Diversified Equities—Unhedged	8.6%	15.0%
U.S. Short-Term Taxable Bonds	3.7%	0.5%
U.S. High-Yield Bonds	6.9%	6.7%
Long Treasuries	7.8%	8.4%

Source: Zephyr StyleADVISOR (Historical 10-Year Returns/Volatilities as of March 2007). Hypothetical example for illustrative purposes only.

plan. It then groups into probabilities the range of 10,000 results, so that we have a one-in-10,000 chance to arrive at a certain outcome, or perhaps a 50 percent chance of another outcome. This analysis then allows us to see graphs of the projected real savings the plan may experience as well as the real replacement-income percentage. What is more, we are able to vary the asset allocation or other inputs to compare results.

Example 1: Asset Allocation Comparison   Given the assumption sets provided earlier, let us compare the two asset allocations. At the conclusion of the 10,000 trials, Figure 8.3 shows the model outputs in terms of the projected final DC account value.

By running simulations, we can see that the range of probable and possible outcomes is quite broad and differs based on the asset allocation. This finding underscores the importance of viewing data in this probability format rather than simply evaluating a DC asset allocation in an efficient frontier framework or by projecting future account values using a straight-line or deterministic approach. In other words, we cannot simply say, "To determine the amount a participant is likely to have for retirement, let's assume he or she saves for 40 years and earns an average return of 8 percent."

Modeling stochastically allows the plan sponsor or consultant to evaluate the impact of various asset classes and mixes. Plan sponsors should evaluate the range of potential outcomes for participants as no one knows the specific outcome that the future may deliver. In the first example, Asset

	Commodities	REITs	U.S. Intermediate Term Taxable Bonds	U.S. Diversified Large Cap Equities	U.S. Small-Cap Equities	Emerging Markets Equities	U.S. Inflation Protected Bonds	Non-U.S. Diversified Equities—Unhedged	U.S. Short-Term Taxable Bonds	U.S. High-Yield Bonds	Long Treasuries
Commodities	1	0.08	0.04	0.08	0.19	0.27	0.19	0.2	−0.12	0.07	0.04
REITs	0.08	1	0.04	0.29	0.44	0.36	0.12	0.29	−0.08	0.29	0.01
U.S. Intermediate-Term Taxable Bonds	0.04	0.04	1	−0.11	−0.12	−0.18	0.77	−0.15	0.11	0.15	0.95
U.S. Diversified Large Cap Equities	0.08	0.29	−0.11	1	0.72	0.71	−0.18	0.81	0.03	0.48	−0.18
U.S. Small-Cap Equities	0.19	0.44	−0.12	0.72	1	0.73	−0.16	0.72	−0.05	0.54	−0.18
Emerging Markets Equities	0.27	0.36	−0.18	0.71	0.73	1	−0.11	0.78	−0.18	0.51	−0.24
U.S. Inflation Protected Bonds	0.19	0.12	0.77	−0.18	−0.16	−0.11	1	−0.16	−0.05	0.06	0.79
Non-U.S. Diversified Equities—Unhedged	0.2	0.29	−0.15	0.81	0.72	0.78	−0.16	1	−0.08	0.47	−0.2
U.S. Short-Term Taxable Bonds	−0.12	−0.08	0.11	0.03	−0.05	−0.18	−0.05	−0.08	1	−0.12	0.05
U.S. High-Yield Bonds	0.07	0.29	0.15	0.48	0.54	0.51	0.06	0.47	−0.12	1	0.07
Long Treasuries	0.04	0.01	0.95	−0.18	−0.18	−0.24	0.79	−0.2	0.05	0.07	1

FIGURE 8.2 Correlation of Asset Classes (July 1999–June 2009)
Source: PIMCO.

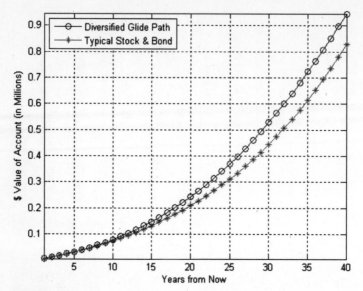

FIGURE 8.3 Expected Value Projected Glide Path
Source: PIMCO YODcA™. Hypothetical example for illustrative purposes only.

Allocation #1 (Diversified Glide Path) is far more diversified than Asset Allocation #2 (Typical Stock & Bond Glide Path) as shown in Figure 8.1. Figure 8.4 graphs the probability of receiving various final account values. You see the typical glidepath shows a much "fatter tail" (i.e., less fortunate final account values) compared to a more diversified glidepath. Figure 8.5 provide a numeric comparison of the two asset allocations. The result of these added asset allocations on the probable results is notable, particularly when we look at the volatility of returns. Not only is the mean real-replacement income amount higher for the more diversified portfolio—76 percent rather than 67 percent of final pay—the standard deviation or volatility of the more diversified portfolio is significantly lower—24 percent versus 32 percent. This means that, at 1 standard deviation, which accounts for 68 percent of the observations, this higher average expected replacement rate of 76 percent actually may be as high as 100 percent or as low as 52 percent. By comparison, Asset Allocation #2 may have a replacement rate as high as 99 percent or as low as 35 percent.

We may conclude from this series of figures that a more diversified asset allocation has the potential to both reduce volatility and improve risk-adjusted returns. Importantly, we may want to view this analysis in a VaR

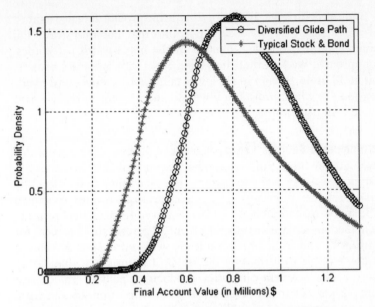

FIGURE 8.4 Probability Distribution of Final Account Values
Source: PIMCO YODcA™. Hypothetical example for illustrative purposes only.

Asset Allocation	Account Value		Replacement %	
	Diversified Guide Path	Typical Stock & Bond	Diversified Guide Path	Typical Stock & Bond
Median	$893,810	$737,192	72%	59%
Mean	$945,964	$827,917	76%	67%
Std Dev	$297,939	$394,113	24%	32%
Percentiles: 1%	$475,041	$299,898	38%	24%
5%	$566,578	$385,512	46%	31%
25%	$732,738	$558,041	59%	45%
50%	$893,810	$737,192	72%	59%
75%	$1,098,825	$997,715	89%	80%
95%	$1,508,488	$1,568,986	122%	126%
99%	$1,887,946	$2,188,641	152%	176%

FIGURE 8.5 Asset Allocation
Source: PIMCO YODcA™. Hypothetical example for illustrative purposes only.

framework and select an asset allocation that helps provide a hedge against downside risk. In that case, we seek a portfolio that minimizes the "tail risk," or unacceptable probable outcomes in the first or fifth percentiles. Given this approach, we find that diversified Asset Allocation #1 projects replacement at 38 or 46 percent in the lower tail, versus a stocks and bonds Asset Allocation #2, which projects a lower 24 and 31 percent replacement at the first and fifth percentiles.

Example 2: Increased Savings versus Increased Return   We can use this model to evaluate the impact of various changes on probable outcomes.

For instance, we may want to increase the plan contribution level by adding employer money or encouraging employees to save more. As shown in Table 8.3, an increase in savings of 1 percent over 40 years may result in an increase in median replacement income from 72 percent to 78 percent for Asset Allocation #1 and from 59 percent to 64 percent for Asset Allocation #2. This is comparable to increasing the series of returns in Table 8.4 by 1 percent across all investment categories, producing a median replacement income from 72 percent to 73 percent for Asset Allocation #1 and from 59 percent to 60 percent for Asset Allocation #2.

As plan sponsors and consultants consider various asset-allocation structures, it is vital to understand the impact of assumption sets. Increasing the savings rate has the greater impact on improving expected outcomes, plus

TABLE 8.3 Increased Savings Rate by 1%

Asset Allocation	Account Value		Replacement %	
	Diversified Glide Path	Typical Stock and Bond	Diversified Glide Path	Typical Stock and Bond
Median	$971,351	$800,210	78%	64%
Mean	$1,028,229	$899,245	83%	72%
Std Dev	$325,021	$429,472	26%	35%
Percentiles				
1%	$515,103	$325,148	42%	26%
5%	$614,739	$417,491	50%	34%
25%	$795,526	$605,267	64%	49%
50%	$971,351	$800,210	78%	64%
75%	$1,194,546	$1,083,278	96%	87%
95%	$1,641,603	$1,707,143	132%	138%
99%	$2,056,788	$2,383,519	166%	192%

Source: PIMCO. Hypothetical example for illustrative purposes only.

TABLE 8.4 Increased Returns by 1%

	Account Value		Replacement %	
Asset Allocation	Diversified Glide Path	Typical Stock and Bond	Diversified Glide Path	Typical Stock and Bond
Median	$897,102	$740,511	73%	60%
Mean	$949,240	$831,917	77%	68%
Std Dev	$297,980	$394,247	24%	32%
Percentiles				
1%	$478,161	$303,009	39%	25%
5%	$569,723	$388,569	46%	32%
25%	$735,920	$561,422	60%	46%
50%	$897,102	$740,511	73%	60%
75%	$1,102,126	$1,000,940	90%	81%
95%	$1,511,802	$1,572,628	123%	128%
99%	$1,891,263	$2,192,168	154%	178%

Source: PIMCO. Hypothetical example for illustrative purposes only.

is more reliable that hoping the future market returns deliver the desired retirement income. Clearly, it is critical to seek investment managers who can help enhance expected returns yet also not overstate return expectations. We encourage DC plan sponsors, consultants, and other experts to study the impact of various assumption sets, whether it is a change in the savings, asset-allocation, or capital-market assumptions.

PIMCO Approach to Asset Allocation: Looking Forward and Considering Risks

At PIMCO, we believe that defined contribution assets should be managed to help *each* participant in a plan meet a reasonable *real* retirement income goal. As human beings, with careers that average only 30 to 40 years, participants only have *one chance* to accumulate sufficient wealth in their DC plans to replace their salary in retirement. Therefore, we focus on maximizing the probability that the plan will reach a reasonable retirement-income replacement level (e.g., 50 percent of final pay replaced throughout retirement) at the *median* probability level versus the mean or average expected outcome. To achieve this target, we seek to minimize the risk of unacceptably low income-replacement levels (e.g., replacing less than 30 percent of pay) by giving up the probability of reaching extraordinarily favorable outcomes (e.g., 150 percent replacement). In essence, we'll trade off the extreme winners to help provide a hedge against the risk of producing extreme losers.

Plan sponsors need to consider the importance of this approach as participants do not have time to rebuild if their retirement savings is insufficient. In statistical terms, that means that we focus on minimizing fat left-hand tails (i.e., the unexpected yet highly undesirable expected outcomes in the distribution of probable retirement income outcomes).

Further, we underscore the importance of targeting income replacement in "real" (i.e., inflation-adjusted) terms. Participants' savings levels need to keep ahead of inflation not only as they accumulate DC assets during their working years but also, more important, during their retirement years when their spending power must keep up with the price of goods and services. Another way that we think about the retirees' need for sustainable real income is to model the income replacement as a *liability* and then consider the asset that is most like this inflation-sensitive liability: TIPS. We believe TIPS best match the retiree liability with minimal risk, as they are a government credit that keeps pace with inflation via CPI adjustments. TIPS provide a proxy for retirement-income liability and then enable us to create a glide path that meets this liability with the least amount of tracking error.

This approach allows PIMCO to place DC glide-path construction in the framework of liability-driven investing, which is an investment approach frequently used in defined benefit plans. We define liability as the real replacement income percent (e.g., 50 percent of final pay), knowing that this is the money that retirees must have to cover the escalating costs of goods and services throughout retirement.

Given this objective, we design the glide path to reach the goal in this way. In the early "vintages" or portfolios (e.g., 2050 and 2040) of the glide path, when the participant has the greatest amount of time prior to retirement, the optimal asset allocation includes a heavy allocation to higher-risk assets such as equities, commodities, real estate, and long-duration nominal bonds. We believe when participants are younger they have the ability to tolerate a higher risk level; moreover, account balances in the early years are meager—not much is at stake. In vintages that are closer to the retirement date, the risk is dialed down significantly and more weight is added to TIPS, nominal bonds, and cash. Older participants no longer have the ability to tolerate a high level of market risk as they are likely to have too much at stake.

The actual asset allocation for each vintage is determined using our forward-looking views and risk-factor framework. First, we use a *forward-looking view* to create and update the inputs that drive our glide paths, which allows PIMCO to position participant assets more strategically for the future. These assumptions are drawn from our secular and cyclical views, which are at the core of PIMCO's goal of achieving a consistent track record in delivering above-benchmark returns. Then, we employ a risk-factor

TABLE 8.5 PIMCO Glide Path Development Process

Step 1: Determine DC Plan Liability	Step 2: Determine Optimal Risk-Factor Exposures	Step 3: Determine Asset Allocation or Glide Path
Generate income replacement target (e.g., 60%) using: Average starting salary Savings rates Company match	*Generate optimal risk factor weights by:* Taking risk-factor weights in PIMCO benchmark glide path and calibrating to reach plan income-replacement target at median based on PIMCO outlook	*Map risk factors onto plan fund menu and enhance allocation with alpha opportunities and tail-risk management using:* Existing plan options Additional stand-alone investments Completion strategies Global tactical asset allocation Tail-risk hedging

Source: PIMCO.

framework that digs deeper than the traditional asset-class-level analysis, in an effort to produce well-diversified portfolios that are attuned to the true drivers of investment performance. "Risk factors" can be described as the underlying exposures within asset classes that merit a return premium and are the prime determinants of the variation in asset class returns.

We apply our views and framework in developing glide paths. As Table 8.5 shows, PIMCO follows a three-step process in creating the custom glide path for the clients:

1. **Define the retirement income target for the strategies.** PIMCO will identify the percent of income the plan sponsor seeks to replace with the DC plan in light of an acceptable level of risk. Then PIMCO will determine the probability of meeting the retirement-income replacement level, given plan demographics (e.g., savings rates, employer match, starting and retirement ages) and risk tolerance. Typically, based on an initial evaluation, the plan sponsor may desire to modify the replacement income goal or perhaps the plan design (e.g., match rate).
2. **Optimize risk factor weights for each target portfolio.** Based on the income replacement or inflation targets and acceptable risk level for each of the vintages, the risk factors will be optimized to determine the desirable set of risk exposures for each portfolio. Views on risk factors

derive from PIMCO's Investment Committee and PIMCO's cyclical and secular outlook.

"Risk factors" are underlying risk exposures that explain the variation in asset-class returns and demand a risk premium. For example, returns on equities can be explained in terms of key risk factors such as momentum, size, value, volatility, and liquidity as well as other factors such as country, industry, and currency. Returns on bonds can be explained in terms of basic risk factors such as interest rate duration, inflation, credit spreads, and yield curve slope, among others. Risk factors are utilized as the primary building blocks of PIMCO's asset-allocation process because, relative to asset classes, they provide a clearer picture of the sources of potential returns, they are typically less correlated with each other, and they exhibit stable covariances over time.

3. **Identify asset allocation for each target portfolio, based on a mapping to risk-factor weights.** Given the set of core investment offerings plus any additional investments the plan sponsor would like to add to the target strategies, PIMCO will map the determined risk factor weights to specific asset classes to create the optimal asset allocation. PIMCO utilizes the index for each of the investment offerings (as opposed to using the offerings themselves) to determine the asset allocation rather than evaluating or considering the management or actual returns of the investment offerings.

EVALUATING RISK-FACTOR EXPOSURES IN TARGET-DATE GLIDE PATHS

At PIMCO, our risk-factor approach to asset allocation steps beyond the traditional asset-class framework and use of capital markets assumptions, which often are based solely on historical data and do not fully account for the underlying drivers of risk/return for various asset classes. We believe that using a risk-factor framework helps create more broadly diversified target-date strategies than can be achieved using asset classes alone.

One reason is that correlations among risk factors have tended to be more stable and consistent over time as opposed to correlations among asset classes. Look at Figure 8.6, which shows the correlation of key risk factors relative to the level of interest rates. Then compare that information to the correlation of asset class returns relative to the Standard & Poor's (S&P) 500 Index in Figure 8.7.

We return to look at risk in greater detail in Chapter 10 on helping protect DC assets. For now, we believe it is important for plan sponsors to

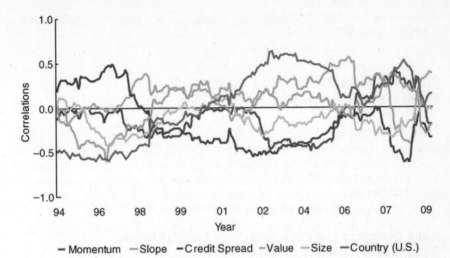

Country, Momentum, Slope, Value, and Size risk factors are calculated and distributed by MSCI-BARRA as part of the Global Equity Model (GEM) by MSCI-BARRA©. The credit spread factor is defined as the average option adjusted spread on the Barclays Capital U.S Aggregate Index. The level of interest rates is represented by 10-year U.S. government bond rate. The country risk factor is for the United States.

FIGURE 8.6 Rolling 36-Months Correlation versus Level of Interest Rates (December 1994–September 2009)
Source: MSCI-BARRA, Zephyr StyleADVISOR.

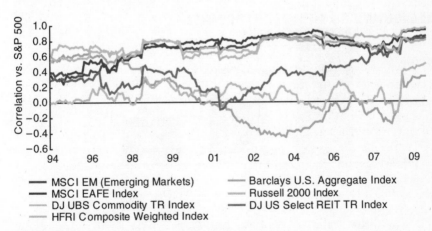

FIGURE 8.7 Rolling 36-Month Correlation versus U.S. Large Cap (S&P 500) (December 1994–September 2009)
Source: MSCI-BARRA, Zephyr StyleADVISOR.

consider the exposure to various risk factors in the target-date glide path being considered.

PLAN SPONSOR APPROACHES TO CUSTOM TARGET-DATE STRATEGIES

Glide-path structures vary notably from one organization to the next. Often retirement-income targets drive the way the various glide paths are constructed. Let us take a look at how several consultants and plan sponsors have structured their glide paths and their philosophies about how to provide adequate retirement income and inflation protection to participants.

When Designing the Glide Path, It Is Critical to Use More than One Metric

Chris Raham, the senior actuarial advisor and retirement income practice leader at Ernst & Young, discussed how companies can evaluate risk when reviewing or considering investment offerings for their glide path. As a solution, Raham recommended that plan sponsors "should perform an analysis that considers not only the mean or simple average of the results, but also the distribution median and tails. This requires a stochastic or Monte Carlo run of probable outcomes from the plan's asset allocation."[6] (See Figure 8.8.)

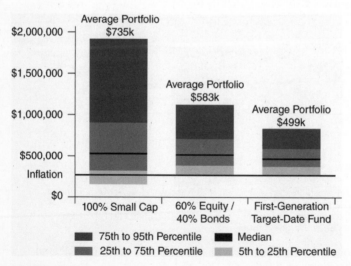

FIGURE 8.8 Dispersion of Ending Portfolio Values
Source: Ernst & Young.

Raham warned "that you can have a significant number of winners and losers if you consider only one metric. Why? When you measure only one variable—say, the mean or its probability of success related to meeting a target number—you lose the distribution of the result." As we pointed out earlier, success depends on having plan participants retire with adequate savings while minimizing the potential for catastrophic outcomes. Therefore, plan sponsors should always consider more than one component when projecting the success of their glide paths. Raham stressed that "if you're not able to communicate the trade-offs involving other important metrics like dispersion of results, then your analysis shortchanges plan participants and sponsors."

Helping Protect against Inflation and Considering Human Capital in Glide Path Construction

We asked Charles Claudio, pension manager at Ahold USA, Inc., if the company started with a retirement income-replacement target when designing their glide path. His answer was both yes and no. The income-replacement ratios in their pension plan vary broadly, depending on whether one is looking at a salaried worker or one who receives an hourly wage. A study Ahold conducted clearly showed that its deferral rates were too low. "Given the lower deferral rates, the expected investment return rates going forward, as well as the anticipated drawdown in post-retirement years, we found that people would come up short—they would not have enough money to make it through their expected retirement years."[7] After this study, Ahold decided to orient its glide path more heavily toward equities than other glide paths out there. It also took inflation into consideration when building target-date strategies and decided to employ TIPS in strategies designed for participants with less than 15 years until retirement. "The closer you get to your target retirement date, the greater the allocation to TIPS."

Thomas Idzorek, chief investment officer of Ibbotson, shared his ideas of what he felt was an appropriate asset allocation in his DC plan in terms of the weight of equity to other assets. Idzorek used an example of a 20-year-old employee with very little financial capital but years of work ahead of him. He pointed out that, theoretically, this individual has a long-term investment horizon, which Idzorek would view as a heavy investment in "human capital." Therefore,

> *in order to achieve a balanced overall total economic-worth portfolio, they need to invest 100 percent of their assets in equities. However, in practice and in order to abide by the current QDIA (Qualified Default Investment Alternatives) regulation, people aren't*

doing that. In a typical glide path most people start out some-
where above 90 percent in equities and hold to it those first 10 or
15 years. At that point the typical glide path begins to become more
conservative. In most cases it's a fairly linear drop from, say, 90 per-
cent equities at age 30 toward about 40 percent equity exposure at
age 65. After age 65 those allocations don't change much.[8]

Most target-date retirement strategies do not dynamically change after
retirement at age 65 but rather go into "income mode." However, Idzorek
illustrates that there is "a sizable number of funds that continue to evolve
beyond age 65." (See Figure 8.9.)

So, we asked, if a person remains in the plan beyond 65—up to age
75 or 85—how far down does that take equity exposure? Idzorek explained
that that depended on the ability of the plan to tolerate risk. "With a rich
DB plan, the amount may not drop below 50 percent. For those without a
DB plan, low risk capacity or low risk tolerance, the equity percentage may
go down close to 20 percent."

Inflation and retirement expenses are another factor that Ibbotson considers when designing glide paths. During one's working years, salaries

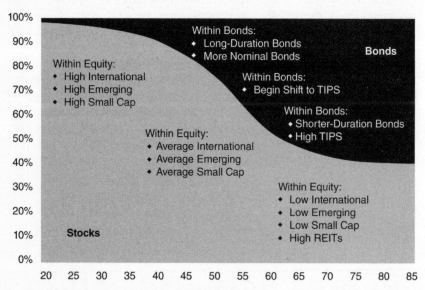

*High, Average, and Low are estimated relative to typical U.S. risk-based asset
allocations with the same stock-bond split

FIGURE 8.9   Characteristics of Ibbotson Glide Path
Source: Ibbotson Associates.

keep pace with inflation. But when we shift into retirement, there are no guarantees that our retirement portfolios will do so. For this reason, asset classes that stand a chance of keeping pace with inflation become essential.

> *In retirement, most of us seek an inflation-adjusted, ongoing series of payments or income so that we can maintain our living standard throughout retirement. Any time a portfolio exists in order to pay for a liability, an optimization framework exists that surpasses the traditional mean-variance framework. In the DB pension space they refer to this as surplus optimization or, as I call it, liability-relative optimization.... Unfortunately, on the negative side the balance sheet includes a liability, an outgoing series of inflation-adjusted payments retirees must make. When we use this liability, this relative-optimization framework, over time it tilts our portfolio toward asset classes that provide a better inflation hedge ... TIPS, real estate and commodities.*

Idzorek suggests tilting participants' portfolios toward long-duration nominal bonds when people are younger. But as participants reach age 30, there is a gradual transition toward "inflation-linked bonds relative to nominal bonds. When TIPS first appear in the glide path, we prefer long-duration TIPS; however, moving closer to retirement and into retirement the duration of the portfolio should gradually decrease." (See Figure 8.10.)

Adopting a More Conservative Approach to Glide-Path Design

Barbara Kontje, director of retirement plan investments at American Express, explained that one philosophy in managing its retirement plan was to make its features and investment options easy for participants to understand. When we asked her if the plan uses a retirement income-adequacy calculation and if Amex set a target income-replacement rate, she explained that its goal for custom retirement-date strategies was "a 35 percent income-replacement ratio, excluding Social Security. [This assumes a participant starts at age 25 and continues in the plan until age 65.]"[9] (See Figure 8.11.)

American Express (Amex) updates its glide path once each year, in January. At that time, Kontje said that while "not all of the strategies change, those with closer maturity dates do." In light of the current market environment, Kontje pointed out that some of Amex's participants

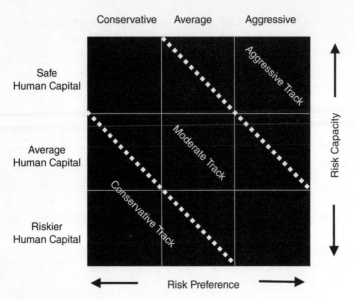

FIGURE 8.10 Target-Maturity Glide-Path Style Box
Source: Ibbotson Associates.

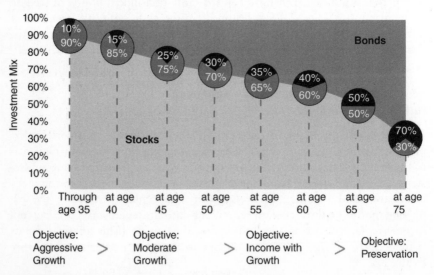

FIGURE 8.11 Retirement Funds Glide Path
Source: American Express.

have become more conservative concerning their asset allocations. Kontje noted that:

> [A]s other asset classes are added, the glidepath will likely change as well. For example, we might change the fixed-income allocation if we decide to add TIPS. Also, the allocation continues to change for ten years after the maturity date, for example, the 2005 Fund continues to decrease its equity allocation until 2015.

Charlene Mims, vice president of benefits, HRIS, and payroll at Dole Food Company, also talked about moving toward a more conservative asset allocation. (See Figure 8.12.)

Dole has hired an investment manager who works closely with its record keeper, advising it when to modify the allocations or adjust the glide path. While the glide path currently is set up to modify investments until age 65, Dole is considering eventually adding strategies for people who have retired. Overall, Mims believes Dole's strategies tend to be conservative: "We'd rather be ultraconservative. If you look at most of the funds we offer, we tend to include ones that do better in a down market rather than include the market superstars."[10]

Mims stated that Dole is also "taking a harder look at protecting assets from inflation, especially since the bulk of our population is approaching retirement. For instance, we're thinking about adding Treasury

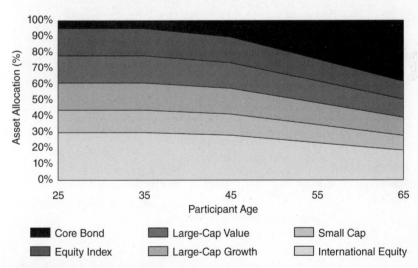

FIGURE 8.12 Dole Target-Date Glide Path
Source: Dole Food Company.

Inflation-Protected Securities (TIPS). In the current economic environment TIPS are attracting more interest, and they may make sense."

Designing the Glide Path in Five-Year Increments

Dan Holupchinski, retirement plans manager at Deluxe Corporation, explained why Deluxe uses 5-year increments in its glide-path design rather than the usual 10-year increments. It stems from the unusual demographic makeup of the company's population, which includes over 50 percent former employees and a significant number of participants approaching retirement. As Deluxe created its glide path, it realized that those were the years when asset allocations begin to shift from equities into fixed income. "We felt that, with the 10-year increments, the deviances between the fund asset mixes were too great. So we decided to set up the five-year increments to make the changes more gradual and more appropriate for our population."[11]

For its glide-path design, Deluxe relied greatly on its outside investment consultants to lead the analysis and explore the appropriateness of different opportunities and to see whether the company needed to change or add to any part of its investment lineups. (See Figure 8.13.)

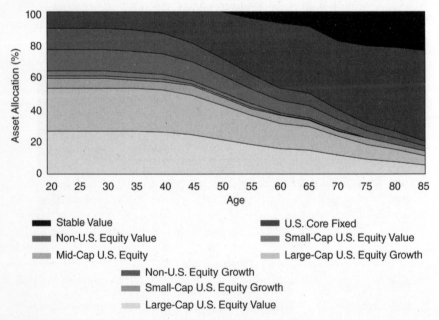

FIGURE 8.13   Deluxe Corporation Glide Path
Source: Deluxe Corporation.

We also stepped back to look at the most appropriate target-date-fund investment vehicles—custom-built or proprietary (developed and managed by an investment firm)—and all the issues around that. Ultimately we decided to do custom and look at creating our own glide path. Our consultants used our demographics and contribution rates in the development. Our 90-percent income-replacement goal for full 30-plus-year career employees set the tone for how aggressive the glide path needs to be.

Using Monte Carlo simulations, consultants ran several different scenarios, projecting different kinds of glide paths, and then presented Deluxe with the six most promising results. "We considered life expectancy to help determine the probability that our retirees would still have a balance up through the average life expectancy, which ended up being around 84 or 85 years. We didn't want to get too conservative or too aggressive as, either way, the risk concerned us."

Of course, a glide path needs to be evaluated and rebalanced periodically. Deluxe conducts this evaluation of the asset allocation and core option lineup every year or two to see if changes or adjustments are necessary.

As time progresses, Holupchinski added, Deluxe projects that new investment vehicles will emerge that can be added to the glide path to "improve the expected outcomes for participants." In closing, he stated that there is "never a right or wrong answer. You get to a level with which you can be comfortable ultimately, but there are many different answers. You just do the best you can with your demographics and plan information, and build from there."

IN CLOSING

Designing the glide path is one of the most important decisions plan sponsors will make as they set up their strategies. We know that control over structuring the glide path is one of the most attractive aspects of custom strategies. Since no organization or population is exactly the same, glide-path structures are likely to vary to fit the unique characteristics of each participant base. For instance, whether a plan sponsor offers a defined benefit plan has bearing on how much risk it may want to introduce in the glide path. One thing is certain, as Holupchinski stated: There is no single right answer when it comes to designing a glide path.

What is important is to have a goal for your target-date strategies. For most organizations, a goal of a certain level of replacement income may be appropriate. At PIMCO, we believe glide paths will vary primarily based on the retirement income-replacement target and the acceptable risk level that the plan is willing to take. We suggest setting a target replacement and then generating a glide path that is most likely to meet that target. Further, we suggest evaluating the risk that the participants will be facing in that glide path and determining whether the risk is acceptable. This glide path should then be revisited at least once a year and adjusted based on changes in your organization or outlook. In the next chapter, we take a look at the various asset classes that you may want to include within your target-date strategies.

CHAPTER 9

Asset Classes and Alternatives

Determining the appropriate number and array of investment choices for your plan is perhaps the most important action of the plan sponsor. This is true not only from an investment perspective but from a behavioral economics standpoint as well. In the award-winning book *Nudge: Improving Decisions about Health, Wealth, and Happiness*, Richard Thaler and Cass Sunstein refer to plan sponsors as "choice architects" who have the "responsibility for organizing the context in which people make decisions." They point out that "through better choice architecture, plans can help their participants on many dimensions."[1] Behavioral scientists have documented this fact by determining that, in some cases, the best-choice architecture is to place participants on the path of least resistance and do what is in their best interests by default, so in essence they do not have to make a choice if they do not want to. This approach has been very successful in raising participation rates and contribution levels via auto-enrollment often coupled with auto-increase. The effectiveness of using defaults seems self-evident today, and is fully supported by the Pension Protection Act, yet 10 years ago the industry was generally unaware of the impact of this type of choice architecture—more specifically, understanding and harnessing the power of inertia for the participant's benefit.

While we have made progress in many areas, we still have work to do with defined contribution (DC) investment lineups. Thaler and Sunstein comment that "attention to choice architecture has become increasingly important over the years because plans have greatly increased the number of options they offer, making it even harder for people to choose well." Both the array and the number of choices offered to plan participants may well impact their ultimate investment structure and retirement-income replacement. While we may think we are simply providing a menu, what is on that menu and how it is presented makes a difference that we need to consider.

There are many philosophies on the appropriate number and types of assets to offer to participants. What is important is that the offerings provide sufficient choice for participants to create a mix that meets their unique investment objectives, whether they are ultra-conservative or more aggressive. Further, the array needs to be sufficient to support the lineup in custom target-date strategies. To meet these objectives, we suggest that you seek an investment lineup that offers global market coverage and the ability to maximize diversification yet at the same time delivers the choices in a simple design.

In Chapter 2 we examined the intricacies of DC plan design, including the number and types of investments in plans as well as potentially effective ways to present these strategies to participants. For a participant to understand and not be overwhelmed by a lineup, we introduced a three-tier structure: Tier I for target-date strategies, Tier II for the core investment offerings, and possibly a Tier III for a brokerage window. Plus, we mentioned that more recently some plan sponsors are adding a tier for index strategies, such as the Standard & Poor's (S&P) 500. Offering tiers makes sense from a communication perspective, allowing plan sponsors to keep it simple yet offer participants investment choices.

As we have seen, target-date strategies in Tier I are aimed at participants who want a professional to manage their money for them over time. While on the surface it may appear that target-date strategies are attractive only to less sophisticated participants, in reality they may be highly attractive to even the most advanced investors since they can be designed using state-of-the-art investment analytics and the breadth of diversifying investment strategies. Ideally, these strategies are designed to tap into a broad range of the best-in-class managers offered in Tier II as the core investment offerings, plus possibly some additional diversifying strategies that may be excluded from the core lineup (e.g., higher-volatility investments such as emerging markets). Finally, Tier III allows participants access to a full or mutual fund–only brokerage window. You also may want to consider an index or passive management tier, although we suggest that the index strategies be included along with other core investment options. Our suggestion is that you build Tier II, your core options, by beginning with the asset class and then deciding whether to use an active or passive strategy for each class.

In this chapter we focus on what we consider the most appropriate investment offerings to include in the core lineup as well as ones beyond the core to consider for inclusion in custom target strategies. We share what other plan sponsors are offering within their core lineup—and why. In addition, we briefly discuss the investment structures that you may want to consider. Before we launch into the discussion of core investment options, let us briefly address brokerage windows.

CLEARING THE DECKS: OFFERING A BROKERAGE WINDOW TO PARTICIPANTS

Often plan sponsors are worried about making any changes to their core investment lineup as it may upset participants, especially if they have invested in a favorite brand-name mutual fund for many years. Plus, plan sponsors fear that if they remove a poorly performing fund from the lineup, once it is no longer offered it will rise like a phoenix, outshining the laggard that the sponsor has selected to take its place. There must be a Murphy's Law of sorts for investment selection oversight that goes something like this: Any fund that is removed from the plan will likely perform better than any fund that replaces it. While I have no proof regarding how frequently this happens, I have heard anecdotes from plan sponsors about participants who have tracked the removed funds for years and told the sponsor about its lack of wisdom in removing them.

As the saying goes: You're not paranoid if people actually are out to get you. And some participants just may be out to get you, or at least to point out where they think you have made a mistake. For that reason, brokerage may be a great way to keep those people happy. They can have their favorite name-brand funds and, at the same time, free you from worrying about being second-guessed. This freedom allows you to refocus the core lineup institutionally with a limited yet well-diversified selection of investments. Brokerage windows may quiet the squeaky wheel.

For this and other reasons, we suggest that plan sponsors seriously consider brokerage for their plan. What is more, we encourage you to consider full brokerage, which includes not only mutual funds but also bonds, stocks, and exchange-traded funds. This full range of investment flexibility allows participants to craft their retirement account to their specific objectives, whether they are working on their own or with a financial advisor.

While only a small percentage of participants tend to invest via brokerage, those who do tend to be the higher-balanced, longer-tenured older participants who often are working with an outside financial advisor to design a holistic investment strategy. Providing these participants the flexibility to meet their individual investment needs as they approach retirement is a good reason to make full brokerage available. Plus, as mentioned earlier, offering this option may increase overall plan satisfaction, even for participants who decide not to invest via the window. While some may argue that participants could invest unwisely using the brokerage window (e.g., invest 100 percent in a single security), often participants may face considerable risk of loss even within the core lineup, especially when company stock—a single undiversified security—is among the core investment offerings.

Most record keepers offer access to proprietary brokerage capabilities, which typically are well integrated into their plan servicing operations, or they may connect to an outside brokerage platform to provide participants a window to full brokerage. What is important to know is that most of the brokerage platforms allow the plan sponsor to decide whether to offer full brokerage or just mutual funds. These platforms also may enable you to exclude certain types of investments, such as bulletin board or penny stocks, securities that tend to be more volatile and may present a greater risk of loss for participants.

As a plan fiduciary, when selecting a brokerage provider or evaluating the integrated brokerage services offered by your record keeper, you will want to understand the breadth of products available and the pricing relative to others in the market. To do this, you must not only look at the pricing of stock trades but also examine the cost of trading bonds and whether they carry a markup in price. You may also want to consider the expense of the money market sweep or the interest paid on cash balances held in the brokerage window. Your consultant may be able to help you evaluate brokerage window providers and confirm the competitiveness of your platform.

From a liability perspective, if you are worried that plan participants may invest inappropriately through a brokerage window and then turn around and blame your organization for making the offering available, some legal experts have suggested that plan sponsors add a waiver to their DC Web site that requires participants to acknowledge and accept the risk of investing via the brokerage window prior to being allowed to open an account. Clearly, participants need to be warned that investing on their own carries both responsibility and risk, which they need to accept. Otherwise, they should remain in the core or target-date strategies, which offer professional oversight. Let us turn to the core offerings now.

TYPICAL DC CORE INVESTMENT OFFERINGS

As illustrated in Chapter 2, a typical DC plan may offer many core investments, including one or more in these asset categories:

- Money market or stable value
- Core bond
- Balanced
- Large-cap U.S. equity (often S&P 500 Index)
- Small/mid-cap U.S. equity
- Non-U.S. equity (developed and emerging markets)

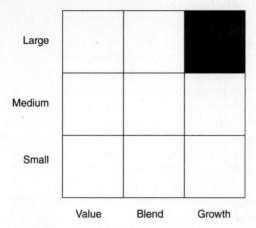

FIGURE 9.1 Equity-Style Box
Source: Morningstar.

Plans often offer multiple choices among the equity funds, including possibly covering the equity-style box (e.g., a large-cap growth strategy) as presented by the Morningstar chart in Figure 9.1.

Many plans have evolved to offer at least one investment choice within each of the listed style boxes, such as large-cap value, large-cap blend, large-cap growth, and so forth. What is troubling about this approach is that it may provide the illusion of diversification, yet often these investment styles run together. In other words, they correlate closely to one another, as shown in Table 9.1. Yet returns may differ sufficiently for participants to be tempted to buy the equity strategy that is going up or to sell out of the one that is going down, creating a seesaw of buying and selling at just the wrong time.

A plan sponsor offering this lineup may have good intentions of providing choices that cover a broad range of possible investments, however most participants do not understand the difference between equity styles such as value and growth. By offering a blend of strategies, such as combining large-cap value and growth styles into a single fund, the volatility of the investment offering should be lower, meaning that the returns are less likely to trigger chasing or fleeing behavior among participants.

Another concern with offering equity choices that cover the style boxes is that participants may become confused and do nothing or perhaps even make naive choices. One naive approach they might take is to simply spread their assets evenly across all of the investment options in the plan. Schlomo Bernartzi and Richard Thaler refer to this approach as a *1/n heuristic:* "When

TABLE 9.1 Correlation Matrix (September 1999–June 2009)

	Wilshire 5000 Index	Russell 1000 Value Index	Russell 1000 Growth Index	Russell 1000 Index	Russell 2000 Index	Russell 2000 Growth Index	Russell 2000 Value Index	Russell Midcap Index	Russell Midcap Growth Index	Russell Midcap Value Index	S&P 500 Index
Wilshire 5000 Index	1										
Russell 1000 Value Index	0.88	1									
Russell 1000 Growth Index	0.96	0.73	1								
Russell 1000 Index	0.99	0.91	0.95	1							
Russell 2000 Index	0.87	0.69	0.80	0.82	1						
Russell 2000 Growth Index	0.85	0.58	0.85	0.79	0.97	1					
Russell 2000 Value Index	0.81	0.81	0.65	0.78	0.92	0.79	1				
Russell Midcap Index	0.96	0.85	0.89	0.94	0.92	0.88	0.87	1			
Russell Midcap Growth Index	0.90	0.63	0.93	0.86	0.89	0.95	0.70	0.91	1		
Russell Midcap Value Index	0.85	0.95	0.70	0.87	0.76	0.63	0.89	0.90	0.65	1	
S&P 500 Index	0.99	0.92	0.94	1	0.79	0.76	0.77	0.92	0.83	0.87	1

Source: Zephyr StyleADVISOR.

faced with 'n' options, [participants] divide assets evenly across the options."[2] In other words, participants, not knowing what else to do, put an equal percentage of their allocation into each of the investment strategies offered (e.g., if there are 10 choices, then 10 percent is invested in each). What would your participants' asset allocation look like if they invested in a 1/*n* approach? For most plans, the resulting allocation likely would have at least 70 percent in equity and the remainder in core bond and stable value. Is it possible that most participants have been given an unintended suggestion to invest over 70 percent in equity? While most plan sponsors do not intend that participants select this allocation, the investment lineup or plan design may lead participants down this path inadvertently.

SIMPLIFY, SIMPLIFY, SIMPLIFY

Most plan sponsors and other experts agree that in order to help participants make wiser—and less risky—investment decisions, we must simplify the lineups in our plan. Charles Claudio said it best when he described the redesign of Ahold's defined benefit (DB) plan into a custom target-date DC plan as a way to "simplify our investment menu" and "weed out the underlying risks in our different funds."[3] In early 2009, Ahold moved to a three-tier design in which Tier I is the custom target, Tier II is the core lineup, and Tier III is a full brokerage window for those who like to manage their own investments. Ahold reduced its core lineup from 15 funds to 6, including "money market, core bond, two large-cap stock, small/mid-cap stock and international equity," making communicating options to participants a much easier undertaking.

Academics support Claudio's suggestion to keep the lineup simple. For instance, Sheena Iyengar of Columbia University, one of the leading experts on the psychology of choice, conducted her now-famous Jam Study, which demonstrated that too much choice can confuse and create inertia, hampering people's ability to make decisions.

While freedom of choice is an American ideal, Iyengar proved that too much choice is counterproductive—and even detrimental to sound decision making. Iyengar's field study, conducted at Draeger's Market in Menlo Park, was simple: set up two tasting booths at which customers could sample a variety of jams. However, one booth offered only 6 jars of jam while the other offered 24 selections. The results were thought provoking. Of the 20 people who sampled jam at the smaller tasting booth, 6 actually bought jars of jam. However, at the booth offering 24 tasting jars, while 30 people (10 more than the first booth) sampled the jam, only 1 actually bought any.

Iyengar concludes that too much choice was just overwhelming, resulting in inertia, the inability to choose anything.[4]

In another study conducted by Sheena Iyengar, Wei Jiang and Gur Huberman, they found that " . . . if a plan offered more funds, this depressed [the] probability of employee 401(k) participation . . . If there were only two funds offered, participation rates peaked at 75 percent, but when there were 59 funds offered, participation rates dipped to a low of approximately 60 percent."[5]

In fact, other studies have shown that our memory span may be limited to only seven items (plus or minus two)—sometimes referred to as the "magic number 7."[6] In light of this, it may not be surprising that, historically, phone numbers in the United States are composed of just seven numbers. As a result, plan sponsors focus on reducing the number of core options so that, from a behavioral standpoint, people can deal more effectively with the number of choices offered.

SIMPLIFY YET DIVERSIFY

As plan sponsors try to reduce the number of core offerings, they do not necessarily reduce asset diversification necessarily. Rather, they maintain diversification and often add to it by combining various asset classes together into single core investment options. For example, they may blend value and growth styles together or combine developing and emerging international strategies, and so on.

We believe blending styles and offering a far more simplified core lineup makes sense for multiple reasons:

> **Reason 1. Communication of the investment options may be simplified** as the number is limited and the need to understand styles is lessened. Barbara Kontje, director of retirement plan investments at American Express, explains how Amex simplified its lineup as early as 2006 in order to "remove some of the worry for participants." Along with a stock fund and a brokerage window, which participants manage for themselves, the company has only five core options, which it then taps into in its custom target-date strategies. These include a stable value, plus
>
> > *diversified bond fund, large-cap U.S. equity, small/mid-cap U.S. equity, and international equity. We created all the core investment options by selecting and blending managers, including both active and passive approaches. We*

> *manage the choices behind the scenes so that participants don't have to worry about selecting between value and growth, for instance. Rather, we help balance styles and managers for them.*[7]

Reason 2. It helps reduce volatility in the core options, thus potentially decreasing the behavior of chasing or fleeing investment outcomes. The method also seeks to reduce the risk that a participant may invest too heavily in one style (e.g., small-cap growth) and get hurt in an unfortunate market, such as we saw in March 2000, when the tech bubble broke and those stocks crashed, or in 2002, when small-cap funds lost 30.26 percent.

Reason 3. It opens the door for more diversifying assets (which perhaps carry too much volatility to be presented as stand-alone core options). These assets can be blended into the investment choices in the lineup, which may help further reduce volatility. For example, a plan sponsor may want to add commodities or real-estate investment trusts into an inflation-protection or equity-blended strategy. Deena Katz, associate professor at Texas Tech University, Personal Financial Planning Division, shares her ideas on effective diversification of assets. While Katz admits that "there is no such thing as a riskless investment . . . merely different kinds of risk," she feels that "certain investments seem less risky than others" and that diversification certainly plays a part in creating less risky portfolios.[8] To achieve an appropriate level of diversification, Katz recommends "some kind of equity holdings along with fixed income, and other asset classes." Using what she calls a "core-and-satellite approach," retirees can be given "access to broad asset classes such as U.S. stocks and bonds, as well as other kinds of investments or 'satellites' that add alpha to the portfolio."

Given that the correlations of some of the equity markets are coming closer together, we asked Katz how she suggests diversifying portfolios to help preserve investor assets. She replied that she believes it is important to

> *diversify the equity as much as possible, including domestic and international holdings as well as developed and emerging, value and growth, and so on. As mentioned, we may also include less-correlated assets in the equity allocation in a portfolio— commodities or natural resources, and also real estate. These types of assets can take up part of the equity allocation.*

SUGGESTED CORE INVESTMENT LINEUP

At PIMCO, we too believe that a DC plan should offer a simplified yet broadly diversified lineup of core investment offerings. We suggest five categories for inclusion:

1. Capital preservation (stable value or money market)
2. Global fixed income (including U.S. and non-U.S. bonds, emerging market, and high yield)
3. Inflation protection (including Treasury Inflation Protected Securities [TIPS], commodities, and real estate)
4. Global tactical asset allocation (including "tail-risk" hedging)
5. Global equity (including U.S. large, mid, small, non-U.S. developed and emerging)

Compared to today's typical lineup of investment offerings, these categories offer much broader asset and risk diversification to plan participants. This lineup provides access to all of the major asset classes, including real assets that tend to perform well and help protect assets in inflationary environments. We discuss the topic of inflation protection assets in Chapter 10. For now, let us take a look at each of these asset classes.

Capital Preservation

Plan sponsors typically select between stable value and a money market fund as the lowest-risk investment option for the plan. When we say "lowest risk," we are referring to the market volatility rather than other risks, such as protection from inflation.

Stable-value funds have tended to be more prevalent than money market strategies, particularly among larger plans. Over three-quarters (76 percent) of plans with 5,000 or more participants offer a stable-value fund, whereas just 32 percent of the smallest plans (under 50 participants) offer this investment choice. Those sponsors who do not offer stable value tend to offer a money market fund instead. When we consider the return differences between stable value and money market strategies, it is easy to understand why stable-value has been attractive for many plan sponsors. (See Table 9.2.)

Yet stable value strategies present complexities and risks that the market has struggled with over time. In 2008 and 2009, with the credit crisis and losses in many bond strategies, several issues with stable value strategies came to light. Plan sponsors often were forced to work with their stable value providers to make sure they continued to wrap the underlying assets, given market value losses masked behind the stable value wrapper. As a

TABLE 9.2 Comparison of Capital Preservation Investment Returns (as of 9/30/09)

	1 Year	3 Years	5 Years
Crane Treasury Institutional Mutual Fund Index	0.10%	2.32%	2.76%
Crane Government Institutional Mutual Fund Index	0.35	2.69	3.04
Crane Prime Institutional Mutual Fund Index	0.69	3.05	3.29
Hueler Stable Value Index	4.58	4.76	4.60

Source: Bloomberg and Hueler Companies.

result of concerns with stable value, as well as the overwhelming concern of plan sponsors to offer the least-risky investments possible to their participants, some sponsors added a money market fund to their plan—often a government-only fund; a few went so far as to add a pure Treasury money market strategy. Given the restrictions by stable value wrap providers on offering competing funds, it is rare for a plan sponsor to offer a money market fund in addition to stable value. Let us take a closer look at stable value.

Stable Value It was not long ago that the majority of plans selected the capital preservation option as the default for participants who failed to elect an investment or who were automatically enrolled in the plan. Years ago stable value funds were made up primarily of guaranteed investment contracts (GICs). These contracts from insurance companies guaranteed DC plan participants a fixed rate of return. However, GICs fell by the wayside during the early 1980s, when several insurers financed by low-quality debt became insolvent. Today, it is typical for stable value strategies to be invested primarily in synthetic GICs, which really are bond funds that have a book value wrap from an insurance company. By wrapping a bond fund, the participant gains the returns from the bonds yet has the comfort of the insurance wrap that helps maintain a relatively stable return, regardless of what happens in the bond market.

To achieve this smoothing effect, the stable value fund will increase or decrease its interest crediting rate to reflect actual underlying bond fund market performance, in some cases paying participants more than the bond fund earned and in other cases paying them less to cover past losses. Participants rarely are aware of what is happening behind the scenes with their stable value fund. Generally, they believe they are investing in stable value to hedge against market risk. It is important, however, for plan sponsors to understand what is going on behind the curtain of stable value. They need to understand, for instance, what the market-to-book ratio is within their stable value fund. This number will reveal whether the fund is carrying a

TABLE 9.3 Hueler Analytics Pooled Fund Universe Market Value/Book Value Percentiles (as of 9/30/09)

Percentile	Synthetics	Entire Fund
10%	103.43%	103.10%
25%	101.55%	101.52%
50% (median)	100.34%	100.29%
Straight average	99.97%	99.99%
75%	98.96%	98.96%
90%	93.83%	94.74%

Source: Hueler Companies.

loss. In other words, is the market value of the securities within the funds actually less than the value that is booked to the participants? For instance, in 2008, as some fixed-income managers were losing significant value in the bond funds that underlie stable value, the average market-to-book ratio fell to 92 percent, according to Hueler Companies, a leading tracker of stable value funds. This means that the underlying bond portfolio lost 8 percent on average, a loss that would need to be amortized by reducing the future interest crediting rate of those participating in the funds. By the fall of 2009, the market-to-book on average had risen to over 99 percent, yet the bottom 10 percent of managers were still below par at 93.8 percent, meaning that over 6 percent of loss remained to be amortized via future crediting holdbacks. (See Table 9.3.)

As Steve Ferber and Bret Estep of PIMCO state in a 2009 PIMCO *Viewpoint*, as many plan sponsors began to "look 'behind the curtain' or within the book value wrapper," they discovered that the poor investment performance of certain managers was to blame for these "market-to-book ratios in the low 90's and even much lower."[9] With the challenges in the market during 2008, many plan sponsors began to worry whether stable value was worth the trouble. Insurance company "wrap capacity" all but dried up as insurers reassessed the potential liability in wrapping stable value. They no doubt did not anticipate the level of bond fund losses experienced in 2008 and fretted about closing the gap between market and book values. Ferber and Estep point out that during this time: "Few issuers were writing new wraps and some issuers even declined new deposits to existing contracts as the providers dealt with the surprise of the very low market-to-book ratio's and the overall financial crisis. Obviously, stable value is dependent on wraps, so the lack of capacity is a significant concern."

As a result, more insurers required that no "competing investment choices" be allowed to be added to the plan. "Competing" choices included investment offerings such as a money market or short-term bond fund, yet some wrap providers included other investments, such as a TIPS bond fund and even a brokerage window. Plan sponsors who added such strategies would be required to add a 90-day equity wash to the plan. This provision requires that participants currently in a stable value fund are not allowed to transfer their assets to a competing fund. Alternately, those already in a competing fund are not allowed to transfer their assets directly into the stable value fund. The only exception to these rules requires that participants transferring in or out of stable value spend at least 90 days exposed to the risk inherent in the stock market, meaning that any money they moved out of the stable value fund would need to go to an equity strategy for 90 days before it could go to a competing fund (e.g., money market). However, plan sponsors feared that adding a competing fund could jeopardize the wrap altogether or at least hinder their ability to add more wrap coverage as their stable value assets grew. It became commonplace for stable value funds to lack sufficient wrap coverage for the entire amount invested, resulting in a percentage of the fund being invested in cash rather than bonds. As a result, cash buildups dampened the overall return of many stable value strategies.

A small number of plan sponsors became frustrated with the limitations imposed by their wrap providers and decided to move out of stable value altogether. For example, Charles Claudio, pension manager for Ahold USA, Inc., explained why the company currently is in the process of slowly phasing out its stable value fund. Even though the yield typically had been higher than a money market fund, in 2008 Ahold identified two concerns:

Number one: Stable value doesn't necessarily mean "no risk," which is a common misconception. One redesign goal was to weed out the underlying risks in our different funds. Number two: Our stable-value fund was an encumbrance to overall plan redesign because of equity-wash rules around which we had to maneuver. We want our participants to be able to move in and out of any fund without any restrictions. If we'd simply liquidated the stable-value fund, we would've been subject to market pricing, and would've taken too much of a loss. So we'll phase it out over time.[10]

While some may choose to move away from stable value, other plan sponsors have moved into it as they seek higher returns than are available from the capital preservation alternative—money market funds. Kevin Vandolder, CFA, principal at Ennis, Knupp & Associates commented:

At this point [2009], we do not see a groundswell of movement away from stable value in favor of money market funds because the stable value continues to deliver extremely well on its overall

promise. And we're hopeful that in the wrap provider marketplace
that there will be a number of new insurance providers within the
next 12 to 18 months. We anticipate wrap fees to increase. This
is likely to encourage folks to step up to the plate and become
the service provider in that space, providing new competition and
additional flexibility within the guidelines.[11]

Money Market Funds   Money market funds are generally open-ended mutual funds that invest in short-term (one day to one year) debt obligations
such as Treasury bills, certificates of deposit, and commercial paper. The
net asset value of nearly all of these funds remains constant, typically $1 per
share; however, the interest rate does fluctuate. While money market funds
are invested for capital preservation and must meet certain requirements to
be labeled as such, the holdings within them may vary. For instance, plan
sponsors may be interested in a money market fund that invests 100 percent in Treasury securities, such as Treasury bills, or entirely in government
securities, which may include agency short-term paper.

As mentioned, in 2008 and 2009 some plan sponsors decided to add
a money market fund in addition to stable value or to add a more conservative money market fund, such as one holding only government paper.
Some may consider adding a government-only money market fund overly
conservative, resulting in too much of a give up in return. However, for
the most conservative plan sponsors, it is something to consider. Most plan
sponsors will likely continue to select either stable value or a general money
market fund.

Global Fixed Income

Fixed income is the second investment offering that we believe is necessary
within a DC plan. Typically, the fixed income offered within a plan is
limited to a core bond fund that tracks the Barclay's Capital U.S. Aggregate
Index. Table 9.4 shows the types of securities to which this index provides
exposure.

While this exposure is broad, we believe other parts of the bond market
should be better represented, including high-yield bonds and non-U.S. bonds
(both developed and emerging markets). Yet as a plan sponsor, offering
access to certain parts of the bond market may carry an unacceptably high
level of volatility; therefore, we suggest that the bond approaches be blended
together to help reduce volatility, just as suggested for the equity markets.
As you can see in Table 9.5, the volatility (measured by a 10-year standard
deviation) of high-yield as well as emerging market debt exceeds other types
of fixed-income securities. As a result, offering these funds as stand-alone

TABLE 9.4 Barclay's Capital U.S. Aggregate Index
(Market Value%) (as of 6/ 30/09)

Government related	39.4
Mortgage	41.5
Investment grade	19.1
High-yield credit	0
Non-U.S. developed	0
Emerging markets	0
	100

Source: Zephyr StyleADVISOR.

funds for the core investment lineup may be inappropriate. Yet given the
low correlation of high-yield and emerging markets debt to aggregate bond,
by blending them within a broader global bond strategy, participants may
benefit from added diversification without experiencing the level of volatility
likely in these individual asset classes. (See Table 9.6.)

TABLE 9.5 Bond Returns and Volatility as of June 2009 (not annualized if less
than one year)

	Returns				Volatility
	1 year	3 years	5 years	10 years	10 years
Barclays Capital U.S. Aggregate Index	6.06%	6.43%	5.02%	5.98%	3.78%
Barclays Capital U.S. Treasury Index: U.S. TIPS	−1.11	5.77	4.94	7.23	6.65
BofA Merrill Lynch High Yield Master Index	−3.63	1.77	4.06	4.72	10.75
Barclays Capital U.S. Investment Grade Corporate Index	3.84	4.49	3.82	5.64	6.18
Citigroup Mortgage Master Index	9.38	7.87	6.03	6.32	2.99
Barclays Capital Emerging Markets Index	−18.71	1.04	8.64	11.36	14.03
Barclays Capital U.S. Government Index: Intermediate	6.43	6.99	5.00	5.62	3.28
Citigroup World Government Bond Index	4.00	7.77	6.06	6.53	7.38

Source: Zephyr StyleADVISOR.

TABLE 9.6 Correlation Matrix (July 1999–June 2009)

	Barclays Capital U.S. Aggregate Index	Barclays Capital U.S. Treasury Index: U.S. TIPS	BofA Merrill Lynch High Yield Master Index	Barclays Capital U.S. Investment Grade Corporate Index	Citigroup Mortgage Master Index	Barclays Capital Emerging Markets Index	Barclays Capital U.S. Government Index: Intermediate	Citigroup World Government Bond Index
Barclays Capital U.S. Aggregate Index	1							
Barclays Capital U.S. Treasury Index: U.S. TIPS	0.78	1						
BofA Merrill Lynch High Yield Master Index	0.21	0.32	1					
Barclays Capital U.S. Investment Grade Corporate Index	0.84	0.71	0.57	1				
Citigroup Mortgage Master Index	0.89	0.61	0.02	0.61	1			
Barclays Capital Emerging Markets Index	0.06	0.18	0.64	0.35	-0.08	1		
Barclays Capital U.S. Government Index: Intermediate	0.89	0.64	-0.19	0.54	0.86	-0.23	1	
Citigroup World Government Bond Index	0.66	0.59	0.11	0.54	0.53	0.06	0.64	1

Source: Zephyr StyleADVISOR.

As a plan sponsor, you may want to select different managers for each of the bond sleeves, or you may prefer to select a single manager who can move the money within the allocation to seek additional returns or alpha (i.e., a return higher than expected, given the level of risk taken). This is the primary advantage of using a single global fixed-income manager. According to David Fisher, PIMCO global product manager and executive vice president:

> *Investments in global fixed income provide diversification, an expanded opportunity set, and potential hedge against a loss of purchasing power. Particularly with the world entering a period characterized by profound secular change, global bonds should now more than ever be considered an integral part of a diversified investment portfolio.*[12]

Whether choosing a single manager or multiple managers, the plan sponsor may want to consider representing these regions in the global fixed-income option:

- North America
- Eurozone
- Other industrialized nations
- Japan
- Emerging markets

As appropriate, exposure to government, investment-grade corporate, and high-yield securities within the various regions should be designed into the global fixed-income offering. By investing in a broad array of fixed-income instruments, many bond risks (single country, single currency, limited selection) can be mitigated.

Depending on how many investment choices you would like to offer on the equity side, you may want to balance the number of choices within the bond category. While we suggest a single, globally diversified bond fund, some plan sponsors may wish to offer slices of the bond market. Here are some to consider.

If you do not offer one already, you may want to consider providing a fund that is benchmarked to the Barclays Capital U.S. Aggregate Index. As an alternative, you may offer an investment-grade bond fund that tends to have a lower volatility than the Barclay Capital U.S. Aggregate Index. In addition, you may wish to offer a core-plus bond fund that often has the majority of assets invested in investment-grade bonds and the remaining assets in "plus" sectors, such as high-yield and emerging market debt. Further, you may consider offering an intermediate or possibly longer-duration government bond fund that offers securities backed by the full faith and credit of the U.S. government. We do not suggest offering high yield or emerging markets as stand-alone choices, given the high volatility of these investment types.

Inflation Protection

Participants should be provided with a specific investment option that is intended to help protect their assets from inflation. There are many ways to gain this inflation protection in DC plans. What is critical to understand is that equity strategies do not provide sufficient inflation protection, as we discuss in detail in Chapter 10. Investments that *do* tend to provide protection in inflationary times include TIPS, commodities, and real estate.

Next we present a description of each type of inflation-hedging strategy, a rationale for using each one, and implementation considerations for including each in a defined contribution plan.

Asset Class 1: Treasury Inflation Protected Securities   Treasury Inflation Protected Securities are government bonds that are designed to provide a return linked to the rate of U.S. inflation (as measured by the Consumer Price Index (CPI). If held to maturity, TIPS are unique in that they provide a government-guaranteed return in excess of inflation, regardless of the level of future inflation. This is called a "real return," which represents an increase in an investor's purchasing power. TIPS currently represent approximately 10 percent of the outstanding marketable debt of the U.S. government. U.S. TIPS represent about 40 percent of the global inflation-linked bond market.

An allocation to TIPS helps investors preserve and enhance the purchasing power of their investment through exposure to government-guaranteed bonds (Treasuries) that have returns indexed to inflation. TIPS are designed to provide investors protection against the risk of rising inflation and can also improve a portfolio's diversification because other financial assets, such as stocks or bonds, may underperform in periods of higher inflation.

Other potential benefits of TIPS include:

- Predictable real return (return above inflation)
- Low volatility
- Diversification relative to other financial assets

Recently TIPS have experienced increased investor interest due to massive government-sponsored fiscal and monetary stimulus to foster economic growth. Since this could result in significantly higher inflation over the longer term, TIPS currently offer inflation protection at very attractive levels.

Paul Solman, business and economics correspondent for the *PBS NewsHour with Jim Lehrer*, believes that it is "critical" to educate plan participants on the value of TIPS because there is no way to predict whether the economy is headed for inflationary periods in the future "a fundamental way to protect your savings from inflation is to buy Treasury Inflation Protected Securities (TIPS)."[13] When held from issuance to maturity, TIPS investors receive not only actual inflation over the life of the bond – via an explicit accrual linked to the US CPI – but also an incremental rate of return, called the real yield. In this way, TIPS investors have a government guaranteed way of hedging inflation risk and also enhancing their purchasing power, regardless of the path of inflation. In addition, TIPS have the added benefit of protecting the investor against cumulative deflation over the life of the bond, since upon maturity, TIPS pay back the greater of the inflation-adjusted principal value, or the original principal value (par). As such, hold-to-maturity investors in TIPS are hedged with respect to inflation and deflation, even though investors typically view TIPS as being exclusively an inflation hedge. Of course, returns to investors who trade TIPS prior to maturity also bear price risk (positive or negative) based on the change in real yields over their holding horizon.

Asset Class 2: Commodities Commodity investing provides exposure across various sectors, including energy, industrial and precious metals, livestock, and agriculture. Commodity exposure typically is achieved through investing in commodity futures with full portfolio collateralization and is typically managed against the Dow Jones UBS Commodity Index, although other indexes are available for benchmarking.

Potential benefits of commodity exposure include:

- Diversification from traditional asset classes
- Inflation protection
- Long-term return potential

Historically, commodity returns and their risk profile have been comparable to the returns and risk profile of the equity market. However, commodity index returns respond to different economic and market factors from equity returns, potentially providing important diversification benefits. Also, because commodities are hard assets, they represent an important inflation hedge, helping to mitigate the effects of rising food, energy, or industrial metal prices or the effects of a depreciating U.S. dollar.

Holding commodities may also provide a way to invest in the strong growth outlook for developing countries such as China and Brazil, which can drive demand for physical commodities higher, potentially resulting in higher inflation.

Robert Greer, real asset product manager and executive vice president at PIMCO, commented on a study conducted by Ibbotson Associates on the role of commodities in a strategic asset allocation (Strategic Asset Allocation and Commodities March 2006):

Because commodities produced high returns with low correlations to other assets, the Ibbotson study found that including commodities in a strategic asset allocation opportunity set produced returns that were significantly higher at any given level of risk relative to returns when commodities were excluded from the opportunity set. Over the common range of portfolio risk, a standard deviation range of approximately 2.4 percent to 19.8 percent, the average improvement in historical return at each risk level was approximately 133 basis points, and the maximum improvement was 188 basis points.

Finally, the study found that commodities were positively correlated to both the rate of inflation and to changes in the rate of inflation, supporting the notion that commodities can provide a hedge against inflation and can provide real purchasing power. In fact, during the period of the study when inflation was high, from 1970 to 1981, commodities far outperformed other asset classes.[14]

Asset Class 3: Real Estate   Numerous investment experts, including those in the academic community, view commercial real estate as a fundamental asset class that should be used in all investment portfolios in addition to equities, bonds, and cash. Many defined benefit pension plans already invest in real estate for purposes such as diversification and inflation protection. In DC plans, in most cases, real estate investing is performed through the use of publicly traded real estate investment trusts (REITs). These REITs typically own and operate income-producing commercial property, such as malls, office buildings, hotels, and apartment buildings, and are traded on various exchanges, particularly the New York Stock Exchange.

Within the past few years, the DC market has seen a dramatic increase in the use of real estate within asset allocation products such as target-date and target-risk funds for diversification and inflation protection. Evidence of this trend may be found in industry data such as Callan Associates' 2009 survey, which found that 73 percent of the target-date fund managers it surveyed had a dedicated real estate allocation in their offerings.[15] As recently as 2005, a minority of target-date fund managers were investing in real estate. While some asset allocation products invest in private real estate, typically, providing real estate exposure within target-date and target-risk funds is accomplished through the use of publicly traded REITs, largely because of the liquidity these REITs provide for purposes such as making benefit payments.

According to Norman Boone, founder and president of Mosaic Financial Partners, Inc., adding REITS as well as TIPS and commodities to a portfolio to be among the best choices a plan sponsor can make to help protect participants' assets from the two main uncertainties of DC plans: rate of returns and inflation.

> *In general, we deal with uncertainty by suggesting that an investor's portfolio be well diversified. What that means is that they have some assets that will succeed under pretty much any scenario. For instance, we hold a fair amount of TIPS and commodities in our portfolios to add diversification as well as to help protect asset values in an inflationary environment. We also hold real estate investment trusts (REITs), which traditionally do pretty well in an inflationary world.*[16]

Many plan sponsors decide to add TIPS only (rather than commodities and REITs as well) to their plan. We encourage a more diversified approach that blends together multiple strategies for added diversification and return. By blending TIPS with commodities and REITS, participants may expect a potential higher return than TIPS alone, yet with lower volatility than investing in commodities or REITs as a stand-alone investment option.

Another approach to inflation protection is to offer a strategy designed to protect assets from inflation, for instance, one designed to beat CPI by 5 percentage points. An example of this type of approach is an all-asset strategy such as the one managed by Rob Arnott at Research Affiliates, LLC. This strategy is designed to allow the manager to tactically move assets among stocks, bonds, and real assets around the globe in pursuit of a total return that may outperform not only a 60/40 equity bond primary benchmark but a secondary benchmark such as CPI plus 5 percentage points as well. Tactical asset allocation managers may also move assets defensively to stay out of harm's way in tough markets, thus helping dampen volatility and potentially offering downside risk hedges against market shocks. Tactical asset allocation strategies may perform well for participants because they not only seek to provide alpha relative to TIPS alone but also help produce lower volatility as illustrated by the CPI + 5 percent shown in Table 9.7.

Global Tactical Asset Allocation

Similar to the argument for offering a tactical inflation protection strategy, plan sponsors may want to consider adding a global tactical asset allocation

TABLE 9.7 Comparison of TIPS, Inflation and Balanced Returns (as of June 30, 2009) (not annualized if less than one year)

	Returns				Volatility
	1 year	3 years	5 years	10 years	10 years
Barclays Capital U.S. Treasury Index: U.S. TIPS	−1.11	5.77	4.94	7.23	6.65
CPI + 5%	3.62	7.27	7.84	7.88	1.51
60/40 Mix (60% S&P 500 Index/40% Barclays Capital U.S. Aggregate Index)	−13.90	−2.20	0.90	1.33	9.63

Source: Zephyr StyleADVISOR.

(GTAA) strategy to their plan. This investment option can be presented as a global balanced strategy in participant communication. With the recognition that today's global investment markets are more challenging to navigate than in the past, this type of option allows a skilled investment professional to actively manage assets on a daily basis. The manager may shift the allocation opportunistically to gain alpha in different markets or securities. In addition, this type of strategy may provide downside protection using tail-risk hedging (i.e., investment strategies such as S&P 500 helps cushion the blow from rare and unexpected market shocks). Many feel that this type of offering can be run much like an endowment, because it is designed to allow a manager to move money around the globe in search of alpha and helps add portfolio protection for risks seen on the horizon.

Rob Arnott believes that the one of the easiest ways to add TIPS and other missing diversifying assets into a plan is by adding global asset allocation strategies. He has stated:

> *DC participants can use these in a very effective and straightforward way, that is, by recognizing that they need to deploy some money into assets that can protect them against inflation, assets that can help diversify them into complementary markets, assets that may serve them well when stocks struggle and won't necessarily soar when stocks soar. In so doing, they can help ramp down the volatility of their returns and allow the manager to have more money invested in seemingly riskier markets.*[17]

At PIMCO, our chief executive and co-chief investment officer Mohamed El-Erian manages a global multi-asset strategy that fits within this category. After spending seven years at PIMCO, El-Erian took a two-year break from PIMCO to manage the assets at the Harvard Management Company, Inc., the largest university endowment in the United States. When he returned to PIMCO in 2007, El-Erian established more comprehensive asset allocation strategies within the company. In an October 2008 interview, El-Erian explained that a global multi-asset strategy

> *seeks to enhance investors' ability to tap investment opportunities and manage risk. What does this mean practically? The strategy involves three distinct, though interrelated, steps. First, a forward-looking asset allocation aimed at maximizing the value offered by markets across different risk factors; second, additional relative value positioning to enhance return potential; and third, proactive risk management, including an inherent focus on "tail risks." We believe that these three factors are crucial to navigating the structural transformation in the global economy, present and future.*[18]

PIMCO's packaged target-date strategies bring much of the same approach to asset allocation. They allow tactical asset allocation around the stated glide path and employ tail-risk hedging to help mitigate the risk of a significant loss in value during a market shock.

Offering a global tactical asset allocation strategy may be attractive to participants as a single balanced-type fund where they do not need to make decisions regarding when to reallocate their money. It also helps provide a diversifying component for a custom target-date strategy. By adding an allocation to a GTAA within a target-date strategy, the custom strategy gains the value of tactical asset allocation as well as tail-risk hedging. Within a custom strategy, you may allocate a smaller static percent of assets to the core investments, such as bonds and equity, to allow for the addition of GTAA, which can then add the opportunistic and defensive positioning for the strategy on a daily basis.

David Fisser, consultant and former chairman of Southwest Airlines Pilots' Association 401(k) committee, agreed that "global diversification and inflation protection are important" to designing a successful target date lineup, especially in light of the need to help protect plan participants from future market downswings.[19] He said: "To compensate for these huge swings and these bad market cycles, we need more asset-strategy-type funds in the models so we can mitigate the impact of the big, bad market swings. We need to help preserve participant assets. We all believed a 1930s scenario couldn't happen again, but it did basically."

TABLE 9.8 Global Equity Correlation Matrix (July 1999–June 2009)

	MSCI EAFE Index	Barclays Capital Emerging Markets Index	Wilshire 5000 Index	Russell 1000 Index	Russell 2000 Index	S&P 500 Index
MSCI EAFE Index	1.00					
Barclays Capital Emerging Markets Index	0.82	1.00				
Wilshire 5000 Index	0.88	0.79	1.00			
Russell 1000 Index	0.87	0.76	0.99	1.00		
Russell 2000 Index	0.79	0.72	0.87	0.82	1.00	
S&P 500 Index	0.87	0.75	0.99	1.00	0.79	1.00

Source: Zephyr StyleADVISOR.

Global Equity

Finally, we would suggest a single global equity offering for the core lineup. This may seem like too big of a step to many plan sponsors, considering that today most plans offer seven or more equity funds. Yet we believe that a single offering would help reduce confusion about which equity strategy to select. As you can see in Tables 9.8 and 9.9, the equity markets both in the United States and abroad correlate relatively tightly to one another. Thus, blending them together in a single investment option (as opposed to offering multiple investment options) may make sense.

TABLE 9.9 Global Equity Return and Risk (as of June 30, 2009) (not annualized if less than 1 year)

	Returns				Volatility
	1 year	3 years	5 years	10 years	10 years
MSCI EAFE Index	−30.96%	−7.51%	2.79%	1.59%	17.80%
Barclays Capital Emerging Markets Index	−18.71	1.04	8.64	11.36	14.03
Wilshire 5000 Index	−26.40	−8.13	−1.60	−1.32	16.53
Russell 1000 Index	−26.69	−8.20	−1.85	−1.75	16.28
Russell 2000 Index	−25.01	−9.89	−1.71	2.38	21.40
S&P 500 Index	−26.21	−8.22	−2.24	−2.22	16.03

Source: Zephyr StyleADVISOR.

If this is too big a step to take, a first step may be to offer a single U.S. equity strategy and a separate non-U.S. equity fund combining emerging and developed markets. Further, if you feel compelled to add more choice, then you may want to add a large-cap blend and a small/midcap blend. Often the large-cap blend is provided as an S&P 500 Index. Offering a small set of equity strategies may still be an improvement over the long and overlapping list that many plans have today. To transition to a shorter, more institutional set of offerings, again think of making the long list available within a brokerage window. Keep in mind that our suggestion is to balance the number of equity offerings with a similar quantity of fixed-income offerings.

ADDING ALTERNATIVES TO TARGET-DATE STRATEGIES

At P&I's 2009 Target Date Strategies Summit, Ross Bremen, a partner with NEPC, stated that he and his fellow panelists believed that "the best way to incorporate alternatives or non-traditional strategies has been in custom target-date options. We have several clients that actually do it today."[20] He also pointed out that many clients who were not yet using custom strategies in their target dates had added them to the core options because they planned to incorporate alternatives into the target-date glide path at a later date.

He admitted that some of these alternatives have a shorter history and a briefer track record than other investments because they are newer and more on the cutting edge of investment strategies. However, he also pointed out that in 2008, "when the equity markets were down significantly...these other asset classes, have done relatively well." He felt this was due to the fact that "these custom target-date funds that incorporate strategies are not perfectly correlated with the equity markets" and that, therefore, "less than perfect correlation has led to what have been very good results in what has been a very difficult market environment."

For these reasons and others, plan sponsors, in addition to their core investment lineup, may well want to consider adding other alternatives and diversifying assets to their plan. Increased exposure to different types of returns may help ensure that plan participants are not locked into a single market and not overexposed to that market's risk factors. Through global and multiasset diversification, risk factors may be controlled and assets can be spread out to help produce well-constructed returns on a consistent basis. Alternative assets may include:

- Global REITs
- Emerging market debt and equity
- Absolute return

- Private real estate
- Private equity
- Hedge funds/fund of funds

Exposure to many of these alternatives may best be accomplished via an inflation-protection or a global tactical asset allocation strategy. Offering participants access to such diversifying strategies within a well-managed, daily-valued global portfolio may help reduce volatility and render such investments appropriate, even for a core lineup.

Yet some plan sponsors may want to seek diversification beyond global tactical strategies. For instance, they may be interested in adding absolute return, private real estate, private equity, or even hedge funds to their DC plan. As plan sponsors consider these diversifying strategies, they are likely to conclude that making such investments available as stand-alone core investment options may be problematic. Volatility, liquidity, and other risks as well as the difficulties associated with communicating the makeup of these strategies to plan participants may preclude their inclusion as core investments. However, adding a small allocation to alternatives within custom target-date strategies may make a lot of sense.

Mark Ruloff, director of asset allocation at Towers Watson, agrees that diversifying target date asset classes can strengthen a plan sponsor's investment strategy but cautions against "including them as straight options in a DC plan core investment lineup" to keep plan participants from investing exclusively in higher-risk alternatives. "With custom target-date strategies you can add higher-risk alternatives to the blended offerings, yet not offer them within the core lineup."[21]

Ross Bremen and Rob Fishman of NEPC also agree that exposure to nontraditional or alternative investments should occur only within the blended strategies because that approach helps reduce "the amount of danger into which participants can get themselves." In terms of core investments, they advocate letting the fund managers make decisions about selecting alternatives. "We could create a diversified portfolio of less-liquid or illiquid strategies using two, three, or even four managers, while trying to get equity-like returns with lower volatility than a traditional equity strategy."[22] Bremen and Fishman describe the optimal diversified portfolio as including

> allocations to global tactical asset allocation, risk parity and absolute return. This structure should provide both equity-like returns as well as broad diversification with the potential for greater inflation protection. We can build fund-of-fund structures for GAA, direct real estate, or long-short equity, for example. Depending on illiquid

security exposure, we may need a heavy allocation to cash to permit
daily liquidity for participant trading and withdrawals.

To create greater diversification, inflation protection, and liquidity, they
also suggest TIPS, commodities, and real estate. Bremen and Fishman state
that adding alternative strategies certainly helps "improve the risk-versus-
return profile. Equity alternatives include many strategies designed to provide equity-like returns with more bond-like risk levels, which is attractive
for a DC plan." However, they stress that they cannot ask participants to
add in these alternatives themselves, since they lack the understanding to do
so, especially since the number of available alternative offerings is limited
and many of these products are expensive. Plan managers can take advantage of strategies that are competitively priced so that liquidity costs do not
outweigh the benefits.

Michael Riak, director of savings and affiliate plans at Verizon, discusses how the company includes alternatives in its global opportunity strategy. While participants can allocate only 15 percent of their assets to this
strategy, it is a significant part of their target-date glide path "because it
really is a diversifying asset. It can go into any market. It can use different
types of strategies, and we expect it to perform well in both up and down
markets."[23]

Verizon also offers a real estate core strategy. The liquid component of
that strategy (about 25 to 30 percent) is comprised of cash and REITs, but
the lion's share of the strategy is invested in what Riak refers to as "hard
real estate assets such as malls, office buildings and apartment complexes."
Verizon sees this as a strong and effective diversification strategy for the
investment lineup. Verizon also gives real estate a key position in its DB
plan lineup.

When we asked Riak why Verizon used private real estate in addition
to REITs, he explained that

REITs are publicly traded companies that invest in real estate. So
they tend to act like the general stock market and tend to correlate
closest to the small cap value assets. By comparison, private real
estate is less correlated to the general stock market. So, again, it can
be a great diversifier relative to the stock market. And we wanted to
give employees the ability to have alternative asset classes, not just
the usual large cap/small cap US equity and international equity.

Looking back at the market downturn of 2008–2009, Mike Henkel,
managing director at Envestnet Asset Management, points out that many
of our "ideas about asset allocation and diversification were challenged."

However, he believes that, overall, diversified strategies offered better performance across the board in portfolios, even those that were balanced at 60/40. "That said, to diversify successfully we must look at asset allocation from different perspectives. For instance, over the past year, adding commodities, real estate, and TIPS to an allocation provided better diversification than just stocks and pure bonds."[24]

When we asked him if he felt the approach to asset allocation taken by professionals has changed, he replied:

> *If you consider the basic tools, there's been some movement in how people are building diversified portfolios. It's still a mean-variance world with most professionals assuming asset-class returns are mean reverting. This leads many to support a buy-and-hold, stay-the-course philosophy. Yet, "buy and hold" is probably one of the more incorrect assumptions about asset allocation. Few good asset-allocation strategies buy into a single set of assets with a given set of weights, then let it ride indefinitely. There's rebalancing, risk overlays, and other strategies that make a difference.*

IN CLOSING

As DC plans continue their evolution, we are likely to see continued simplification yet broader asset diversification. Participants should benefit from a communication, risk management, and return perspective by having access to a limited set of institutional investment offerings that blend investment styles and asset classes. Professional oversight of these strategies should add further value. For instance, more plans may provide participants access to a talented manager who can tactically allocate assets around the globe, seeking opportunities and working to protect participants during market shocks.

CHAPTER 10

Helping Protect DC Assets
from Risk

Do we have a need to help protect our assets as we might our lives? Author Jason Zweig writes that "losing money can ignite the same fundamental fears you would feel if you encountered a charging tiger, got caught in a burning forest, or stood on the crumbling edge of a cliff."[1] Zweig explains the neuroscience behind our financial decision making by describing the function of a small almond-shaped mass of tissue in the brain, known as the amygdala. "When you confront a potential risk, this part of your reflexive brain acts as an alarm system—generating hot, fast emotions like fear and anger that it shoots up to the reflective brain like warning flares." Zweig notes that shocking and inexplicable events such as the financial crash of 1987 are precisely the type of disaster "that sparks the amygdala into flashing fear throughout every investor's brain and body... [acting] like a branding iron that burns the memory of financial loss into your brain. That may help explain why a market crash, which makes stock cheaper, also makes investors less willing to buy them for a long time to come."

No doubt the fear participants have experienced over the last couple of years in managing their defined contribution (DC) assets ignited a neurophysical response. As I write this book, current news supports what Zweig posits. Barrons reported that despite the Dow rising from a March 2009 low of 6,547 to 9,820 in September 2009, investors moved money out of stocks and into bonds. The article noted that investors have grown more cautious, and for good reason. "Following the series of shocks that started nearly two years ago—from a 30 percent decline in the Dow to the collapse of Bear Stearns, Lehman Brothers and AIG to the revelations about Bernard Madoff's $65 billion Ponzi scheme... they want preservation of capital, lower fees and more transparent products."[2]

In this chapter we take a look at the risks that participants face, including behavioral risks that may be driven by neurophysical response. We discuss ways to help preserve DC assets by working to mitigate risk and, with it, participant fear. Market volatility is one type of risk that we need to think about in helping preserve DC assets, yet it is not the only one about which we need to worry. There are other risks against which we must help protect ourselves, including shortfall, time-period, inflation, longevity, and taxation risk.

HOW DO WE EXPERIENCE RISK?

Talking about risk and experiencing it may be two completely different things. In 2008 DC participants experienced a roller coaster of market ups and downs that rivaled "The Demon," Six Flags Great America's legendary roller coaster. Participants experienced the same double corkscrew death-defying ride in the markets. Their stomachs churned as they watched their retirement savings airlift and then freefall to lows they could not have imagined possible. Panic set in and many wanted off the demon, yet the vast majority stayed the course. In October 2008, participants closed their eyes and held on tight as the Standard & Poor's (S&P) 500 rose 11.6 percent, then dropped 9 percent, dropped again by 6 percent, then rose 10.8 percent. By the close of the month, the S&P 500 was down by 16.8 percent.

When the ride stopped at the end of the year, participants on average had an estimated loss of 25 percent of the value of their accounts, and DC assets had declined by over $1 trillion, from roughly $4 trillion at the beginning of the year to $3 trillion by year's end, according to the Employee Benefit Research Institute.[3] Participants of all age groups lost money. Those who were supposedly ready to step out into retirement, the 56- to 65-year-old group, were hit nearly as hard as DC participants on average, losing 22 percent of their account values. If we look at that in terms of actual dollars lost, many people in that age group lost several hundred thousand dollars in account value.

Fear was visceral in 2008 and it was everywhere—just as Zweig described. I know that I personally experienced fear in reaction to the markets in 2008. Like many Americans, I have only my DC plan to rely on in retirement (and perhaps Social Security, but who knows?), and I was one of those who had started saving prudently and consistently when the plans became available in 1981. The personal frisson of fear I experienced reminded me of a trip to Thailand where I had the opportunity of visiting the Tiger Palace. I paid extra to go to a shorter line that promised an opportunity to take pictures of the tigers, not realizing that this meant going in with the tigers! Before I could rethink my choice, I found myself in the pen with a 350-pound tiger in my lap, wondering what I had gotten myself into and how I was going to get myself out of this. I forced a smile for a photo or two while the tiger's heavy head rested in my lap, sound asleep. (Had they drugged it?) It was not exactly the "charging tiger" of which Zweig spoke, yet my heart raced with fear nonetheless. Meanwhile, a crowd of people looked on, probably as entertained by the tigers as by the unthinking Americans who risked getting so close to them—actually touching them, holding one in their laps. Insane! Then as quickly as it had begun, the experience was over and I was back on my feet. Now it was my turn to take pictures of my husband and his tiger.

At this point, my heart was pounding with even more fright. Unlike me, my husband did not sit on the ground with a tiger in his lap. Rather, he stood on his toes behind the tiger, held onto a small tree in a ready-to-tear-out-of-there position, and reached out one hand to tentatively pet the tiger from behind. Unlike mine, his tiger appeared very much awake and apparently hungry as it licked its chops. My husband's ready-to-run stance was justified, given the real danger of his situation, but he too survived the photo session with the tigers. (See Figure 10.1.)

I share this story because the feeling in my heart and stomach when I sat with my tiger was very close to the emotional and physical reaction I had to the wild stock market fluctuations during 2008. I am sure that I am not alone. Suddenly, I found that the amount of risk I was taking in my retirement accounts was more than I was comfortable with taking. It was as if I had been sitting with a sleeping tiger in my lap, which had now awoken. Like many Americans, I experienced the loss in all my assets at once: my

(a)   (b)

FIGURE 10.1 Tiger Encounters
Source: Schaus, 2008.

savings for my children's college education, the value of our home, household savings, and retirement accounts. As we watched the global financial markets sputter and lurch, I was astonished that I could have taken on so much risk. What had I been thinking?

It is not as if I did not understand risk, but somehow I had ended up holding more risk assets than I had ever intended. I vowed that once the storm cleared, I would move more assets to less risky investments and approach risk with the same caution that my husband had displayed with his tiger. Now that the economy is recovering somewhat, I am staying true to my vow and recalibrating my level of risk as I go forward.

As many of us, plan sponsors and participants alike, are now facing similar concerns, let us take a closer look at what happened in 2008 and the risk participants faced. Then we will look at some ways to help protect ourselves from unacceptable levels of risk.

2008 MARKET IMPACT ON DC PARTICIPANT ACCOUNTS

Figure 10.2, based on information gathered by the Employee Benefit Research Institute, shows how much of a decline in account value most participants experienced, based on their age group. While overall participants experienced a 25 percent decline, the percentage differed slightly by group. Those below the age of 35 lost about 22 to 23 percent of their account value, suggesting that the younger participants were taking on a little bit less risk than the rest of the population. On the other end of the spectrum, those closest to retirement age, 56 to 65, also lost 22 to 23 percent of their account value. This point begs these questions: Were the near-retirement participants appropriately invested, and did they understand what they were investing *in*, to have incurred such a dramatic hit to their accounts during that time frame? In other words, were they, like me, taking too much risk and sitting with a tiger in their lap?

What drove those numbers? If we look at the overall asset allocation within DC plans starting at the beginning of 2008, we see that about 70 percent of the money was sitting in equity investments and that the balance was allocated to stable value and fixed income.[4] (See Figure 10.3.) By the end of the year, the asset allocation picture had changed dramatically (see Table 10.1), shifting to nearly a 50/50 balance—with 54 percent invested in equity and the balance in bonds and stable value.

The question is: What moved that money? Was this shift solely due to the market correction, or can it be explained in part by participant-directed transfers? Actually, it was a combination of both markets *and* people moving

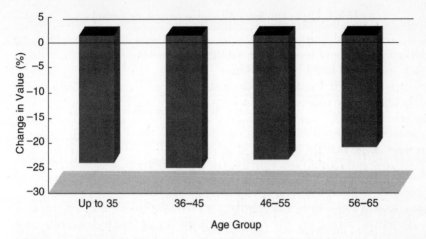

FIGURE 10.2 2008 Change in Average Account Balances among a Consistent Sample of 401(k) Participants, by Age Group
Source: Employee Benefit Research Institute. Change in Average Account Balances Among a consistent Sample of 401(k) Participants by Age and Tenure, Jan 1 – Nov 26, 2008. Tabulations from EBRI/ICI Participant-Directed Retirement Plan Data Collection Project; 2007 and 2008 Account Balances: EBRI estimates. The analysis is based on a consistent sample of 2.2 million participants with account balances at the end of each year from 1999 through 2006 and with tenure of 11 to 20 years.

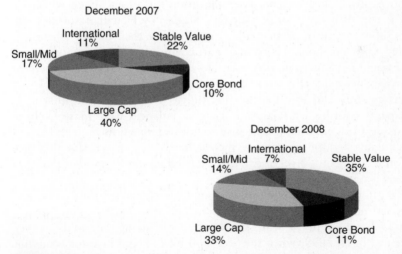

FIGURE 10.3 Market and Participation Action Has Changed Weight of Asset Allocation
Source: Hewitt Associates, 401(k) Index values.

TABLE 10.1 DC Asset Allocation Shift during 2008

2007		2008	
Equity	68%	Equity	54%
Bond	32%	Bond	46%

Source: Hewitt Associates, 401(k) Index values.

their funds. During 2008, according to Hewitt Associates, roughly 5 percent of DC plan assets were reallocated, primarily to stable value and fixed income strategies, at participant direction. The Hewitt 401(k) Index, which was begun in 1997, shows us that there was more movement by participants in 2008 than during any other time in the history of that index. Today, we know that participant trading activity measured by the index correlates with market volatility, which can be tracked by the Volatility Index. Yet even the highly volatile markets in 2008 prompted little transfer activity by participants.

We can only speculate why people moved, but we believe it was out of fear. As the airwaves and news media began to report alarming vacillation in the stock market and the resultant repercussions to the economy, quite a few people likely woke up one morning, opened their retirement statement (or looked at their account values online), and went into shock. Perhaps they had not really looked at their asset allocation for a long time—which we know is true of many plan participants. Studies by Hewitt Associates and others show that most participants generally leave their money where it is invested, with less than 20 percent of participants moving their money each year. Even in 2008, with market volatility at record levels, only 19.6 percent of participants made any sort of fund transfer, according to the Hewitt Associates 2009 Universe Benchmark study.[5] This study notes that male participants with higher salaries and higher balances were more likely to have made a trade. Often people just do not examine how their retirement assets are invested for many years; then suddenly they may realize that they have been taking on a level of risk that they did not understand or that they now feel is unacceptable.

We can only speculate about why some people moved their assets and others did not. All of us may know someone who "just couldn't take it any more" and got out. I heard stories of people saying they sold out even as late as March 2009, when the S&P 500 hit 677 and investor economic confidence measured by the Rasmussen Investor Index reached an all-time low of 52.5. One investor told me that he "didn't want to be the one who kept holding on and lost it all." So he sold—in March. Then he regained

TABLE 10.2 2008 Change in Average Account Balances among a Consistent Sample of 401(k) Participants, by Age Group

Target Date Series	2008 Average Equity Allocation %	2008 Average*	June 30, 2009†
2010	42%	−22%	−10%
2020	56%	−29%	−17%
2030	71%	−34%	−21%
2040	79%	−36%	−23%
2050	79%	−37%	−23%

*2008 average return for target date mutual funds according to the Morningstar database.
†January 1, 2008, through June 30, 2009, average return for target date mutual funds according to the Morningstar database.
Source: Morningstar. No fees or expenses are included in the database.

confidence in September when the S&P 500 hit 1,072 and is now "back in." Ouch!

Thus far, we have looked at how assets were allocated overall in DC plans and how participants faired as most managed their assets on their own. Now let us take a look at the professionals. Perhaps the best way to evaluate how successful professional asset managers were during 2008 is to look at the performance of the most popular asset allocation strategies in DC plans—target date funds. In Table 10.2, we show the average equity allocation and the average returns for target-retirement date funds 2010 to 2050. As you can see, the equity allocation for 2010 was 42 percent and the average return for those people who are supposedly retiring in 2010 was down 22 percent—approximately the same loss as those in the 56- to 65-age group tracked by the Employee Benefit Research Institute. Note that the range in 2008 returns among *all* 2010 target date funds went from a negative 3 percent to a negative 34 percent. Wow!

NO PLACE TO HIDE

Why were participants and even the professionals hit so hard in 2008? Regardless of asset diversification, practically all investors were stung—2008 was a year many described as offering no place to hide for investors. Unless you were invested in government bonds or money market funds, it's likely that you experienced a loss. Notably, the losses were significant enough that on a ten-year performance basis, lower-risk assets such as Treasury Inflation

TABLE 10.3 Few Places to Hide in 2008

Benchmark	2008 Performance (as of 12/31)	10-Year Performance (as of 9/08)
Hueler Stable Value Index	4.58%	5.27%
S&P 500 Index	−37.00%	3.06%
Russell 2000 Index	−33.79%	7.8%
MSCI EAFE Index	−41.7%	1.81%
Barclays Capital U.S. Aggregate Index	5.24%	5.2%
Barclays Capital U.S. TIPS Index	−2.35%	7.11%
Dow Jones UBS Commodity TR Index	−35.65%	9.98%

Source: PIMCO with data from Zephyr StyleADVISOR.

Protected Securities (TIPS) outperformed many of the common offerings in DC plans, including stable value (Hueler Stable Value Index), core bond (Barclays Capital U.S. Aggregate Index), large-cap equity (S&P 500 Index), and international equity (MSCI EAFE Index). (See Table 10.3.)

Was there a way to help reduce the blow participants experienced? A way to mitigate the risk they faced and may face in the future? Let us begin with an evaluation of the asset diversification, both within DC plans and separately within target-date strategies. We noted that at the beginning of 2008, DC plan assets overall were invested at nearly 70 percent equity and 30 percent fixed income (including capital preservation such as stable value funds). Yet if we shift our view from looking at the *asset* allocation to evaluating the *risk* allocation, we see an even greater concentration in equity, as shown in Figure 10.4. Many plan sponsors may be surprised when they look at asset allocation in this risk-allocation framework. I know I was when I first saw this. While on the surface our plans may appear to be diversified, when we evaluate the risks underlying an asset allocation, we may be seeing a distinctly different picture.

Participants likely had no idea how much risk they were facing in 2008. For the remainder of this chapter, we discuss the range of risks we need to consider for DC participants. Then we offer a suggestion about how to mitigate the market risk addressed earlier.

While the experience in 2008 was terrifying for many, it is important to note that by year's end, given the ongoing contributions to DC accounts, the amount of loss was muted and, for many, fully recovered. By adding in contributions during 2008, even participants over 55 years of age, on average, were able to recover over half of their 20 percent-plus loss. In total, this loss declined from $260,000 at the beginning of the year to a closing figure of just $238,382 (a slightly more than 8 percent loss by year's end).[6]

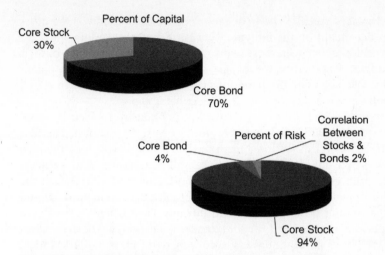

70% / 30% capital allocation to S&P 500 Index and BCAG, respectively.
The basic formula for standard deviation of a two asset portfolio is used to create the figure.
Standard deviation is computed as the square root of three components: (1) [the weight of asset
1 squared multiplied by its variance] plus (2) [the weight of asset 2 squared multiplied by its
variance] and plus (3) [2 multiplied by (the correlation of assets 1 and 2 multiplied by the product
of their weights multiplied by the product of their individual standard deviations]. The time period
is January 2005 to December 2008.

FIGURE 10.4   Asset Allocation is Not Equal to Risk Allocation
Source: PIMCO.

WHAT ARE THE MAIN TYPES OF RISK?

Whether we are talking about DC or defined benefit (DB) plans, we can look
at risk in a number of ways. Classic risks include market risk or volatility
(At which we have been looking so far) as well as shortfall, inflation, and—
for retirees—longevity. However, we should also consider risks that are not
as well recognized, such as tax risk and emotional or behavioral risks. We
begin by discussing emotional risk.

Emotional or Behavioral Risk

There is no doubt that DC plans are managed by human beings who, by
our very nature, are subject to emotions. Moreover, investors seem to be
governed primarily by two emotions: greed and fear. We can imagine investor psychology as being represented by a hypothetical "emotional coin."
On one side it says "GIRF," which stands for "greed inevitably replaces
fear." The other side of the coin says "FIRG," which stands for "fear

inevitably replaces greed." The frequency with which one side or the other turns up is dependent on the individual investor, but we can imagine most investors vacillating between these two emotions through the course of their investment lives. Rationality, for its part, attempts to undermine the potentially destructive behavior that emotions can induce in investors. In effect, rationality tries to prevent the coin from ever being flipped.

For most investors, however, rationality is often overridden by emotions. So it pays to ask which is greater, greed or fear? As mentioned earlier, we can see the answer as we look again to the Hewitt 401(k) Index, which shows how people change their asset allocations in response to movements in the S&P 500. For instance, we saw this on October 9, 2008, when the S&P 500 dropped 7.6 percent: 0.19 percent of assets were moved, and most of this amount transferred to fixed income. Then when the S&P 500 rose 11.6 percent on October 13, 2008, some participants chased this performance, moving 0.15 percent of assets, according to the Hewitt 401(k) Index. While these are small movements, they do prove a point. Historically, participants are more likely to move assets when markets decline versus when they rise, a trading pattern that suggests participants may be motivated more by fear than by greed. Clearly, this behavior is detrimental to participants' ability to meet their retirement-income needs.

From this snapshot of investor behavior, we can infer that emotional risk matters. How do you control emotional or behavioral risk when it comes to your plan? One way is by managing return volatility, or the day-to-day movement in the value of your plan investment options. In essence, if you offer less volatile strategies, participants are less likely to sell out of fear.[7] In Table 10.4, you can see how volatility measured by standard deviation changes, based on the asset mix in portfolios.

Market or Price Volatility Risk

As mentioned, most DC plan sponsors focus on market or price volatility as a DC plan's primary risk consideration. They communicate volatility to participants using basic statistics, such as showing the standard deviations of a strategy's historic returns. As an industry, we have helped manage volatility by blending various asset classes together for participants or by allowing them to allocate on their own across the range of core investment options. As we consider whether to add more investment choices to the core investment menu, our industry typically uses a Markowitz or efficient-frontier model to determine whether the new investment or asset class will help add diversification benefits. We ask: If we add a new investment into a DC plan, will it improve the plan's risk versus return trade-off? As Figure 10.5 shows, adding asset classes can help reduce a plan's volatility. As mentioned, to a

TABLE 10.4 Returns of Blended Portfolios versus Stocks and Bonds Alone (as of June 30, 2009)

Asset Class or Blend	Returns				Volatility
	1 year	3 years	5 years	10 years	10 years
S&P 500 Index	−26.21%	−8.22%	−2.24%	−2.22%	16.03%
Barclays Capital US Aggregate Index (BCAG)	6.06	6.43	5.02	5.98	3.78
Blended 70% S&P 500 Index/30% BCAG	−16.53	−3.83	−0.06	0.24	12.36
Blended 60% S&P 500 Index/40% BCAG	−13.30	−2.36	0.66	1.06	11.13
Blended 50% S&P 500 Index/50% BCAG	−10.08	−0.90	1.39	1.88	9.91
Blended 40% S&P 500 Index/60% BCAG	−6.85	0.57	2.12	2.70	8.68
Blended 30% S&P 500 Index/70% BCAG	−3.62	2.04	2.84	3.52	7.46

Source: PIMCO.

certain extent, we can help manage emotional risk by managing the volatility of a plan's investment options.

Volatility can be reduced by blending investment choices together, such as value and growth equity choices or international and emerging-market equity funds. Optimally, creating asset allocation approaches such as target-risk or target-date strategies will help dampen volatility further as they combine not only equity assets classes but also fixed income and, possibly, other types of assets. These blended strategies are likely to provide a smoother ride for participants, thereby helping reduce emotional or behavioral risk and the attendant urge to sell when markets fall. Target-date strategies also address other behavioral risks, such as the failure to reallocate assets as participants grow older and their ability to withstand risk decreases.

While introducing target-date strategies helps us address emotional and volatility risks, we also need to understand and address shortfall and inflation risks.

Shortfall Risk

Understanding the risk of falling short of your retirement-income goal is critical. When plan participants do experience a shortfall, the culprit is often

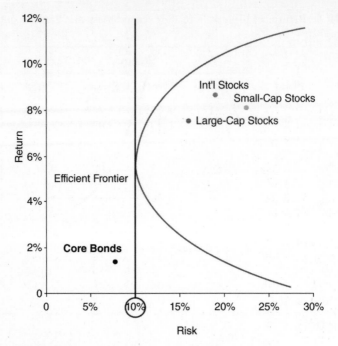

FIGURE 10.5   Return/Risk Frontier: 10% Risk Level
Source: PIMCO. Hypothetical example for illustrative purposes only.

a rare but potentially devastating market shock (a "left-tail" event) that erodes their account values to a level from which they cannot recover by the time they plan to retire. Unfortunately, investment practitioners often fail to accurately model and, consequently, convey the risk of such events occurring. Why is this the case?

Figure 10.6 presents the basic bell curve showing the distribution of various outcomes. In this curve, the first standard deviation is defined by looking at just over two-thirds, or 68 percent, of the data. Next we see, at 2 standard deviations, 95 percent of the outcomes captured. Data beyond this second deviation represent the true tails of the bell curve, totaling 5 percent of possible outcomes.

When investment professionals speak to DC participants about risk, it is customary to show them a volatility measure using the first standard deviation, which in a normal distribution comprises only 68 percent of possible outcomes. For instance, we may tell participants that the risk associated with the S&P 500 Index is 15 percent, which means that in a normal distribution of possible results, 68 percent of observations, the participant should expect

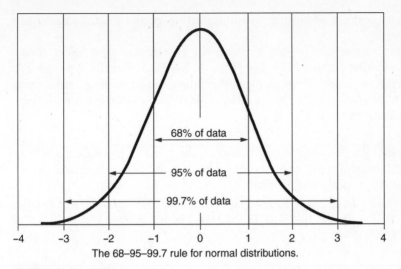

The 68–95–99.7 rule for normal distributions.

FIGURE 10.6 Bell Curve
Source: PIMCO. Hypothetical example for illustrative purposes only.

to receive a return that is within +/− 15 percentage points of the average return of the S&P 500. For example, if the average return over 10 years has been 10 percent, the participant may expect anywhere from a negative 5 percent to a positive 25 percent return. At 95 percent confidence, we might expect the S&P 500 to return from negative 34 percent to a positive 29 percent any given year. But what about the other 5 percent of possible outcomes, especially the lowest 2.5 percent of the curve, which will account for the most devastating outcomes? Are there ways to remedy our current asset allocation and modeling techniques so that they are more sensitive to the possibility and/or probability of left-tail events? Is it even appropriate to

1982	Mexico defaults on bonds leading to international debt crisis
1987	Black Monday, Dow drops 22.6% in one day
1989-91	United States, S&L, and Latin American debt crises
1992-3	European Monetary System crisis
1994-5	Mexican peso crisis, requiring $50 bn US guarantee
1997-8	Asian financial crisis, requiring $40 bn IMF bailout
1998	Russian default and LTCM
2001-2	Argentine default, dot-com bust, Sept 11 terrorist attacks
2007-9	Credit crisis and financial market meltdown

FIGURE 10.7 Major Financial Crises since 1980
Source: PIMCO.

apply the concept of normal distributions to expected volatility or returns on assets?

One author who would question the current use of statistics in the finance field is Nassim Nicholas Taleb. In his book *The Black Swan: The Impact of the Highly Improbable,* Taleb labels rare and unexpected left-tail events "Black Swans."[8] He identifies a Black Swan as an event with these three characteristics.

1. It is an *outlier,* since it occurs outside the realm of regular expectations and nothing in the past can convincingly point to it as a possibility.
2. It carries an extreme impact.
3. In spite of its outlier status, human nature makes us concoct explanations for its occurrence *after* the fact, making it *seem* explainable and predictable.

In managing DC assets, we need to watch out for Black Swans. Such unforeseen, unfortunate events have the ability to derail the best-laid retirement savings plans. One question we might ask is: How rare are Black Swan events in the financial markets? History shows that they may not be as rare as we think. Since 1980, we have had a major financial crisis or Black Swan nearly every three years. (See Figure 10.7.) For instance, at the time of this writing, America and the world are working our way out of the 2007 to 2009 credit crisis and financial market meltdown.

Another way to think of major financial crises is to consider the daily change in the value of the stock market. For instance, what is the likelihood of a daily change in the stock market of more than 7 percent? If we are to look at the Dow Jones Industrial Average (DJIA) as the proxy for the market and a normal or bell-shape distribution of returns, this will tell us to expect a Black Swan or daily change of +/− 7 percent once every 300,000 years. Yet how many have we had? Since 1916 there have been 48 days in which a daily change in the DJIA exceeded 7 percent. (See Table 10.5.)

TABLE 10.5 Left-Tail Events Occur More Often than Normal Expectation

Daily Change (+/−)	Normal Approximation	Actual
> 3.4%	58 days	1001 days
> 4.5%	6 days	366 days
> 7%	1 in 300,000 years	48 days

Source: PIMCO.

These data tell us that we must be careful about using standard deviation when conveying market risk to our participants, especially when considering the probability of market shocks. We need to understand that using normally distributed probabilities can grossly distort the likelihood of experiencing an unfortunate market environment.

While standard deviation is the most commonly used measure of volatility and/or risk in the investment industry, it is by no means the only measure that provides insight into the potential risks that participants may face. Plan sponsors may want to consider other measures of risk such as downside deviation, value at risk (VaR), or maximum drawdown (MaxDD). Downside deviation may be useful as it focuses on downside volatility (i.e., on negative returns), which are the primary concern of most investors (as opposed to positive returns or upside volatility, about which no one complains).[9] VaR estimates the worst expected loss in a normal market environment over a specified time period, given a particular confidence level.[10] Finally, MaxDD is the maximum loss an investment experiences from a peak value to its lowest value during a given time period. This measure is useful because participants may sell at a loss after their investments have experienced a significant drop in value. Structuring glide paths to help minimize the occurrence of large declines is thus likely to also minimize self-destructive behavior on the part of participants.[11]

Yet despite all of these statistical risk measures, we believe that the most valuable may be modeling the probability of loss and evaluating the tail risk (i.e., observations of unacceptable outcomes such as replacement income less than 25 percent of final pay). This analysis can be conducted using a Monte Carlo simulation approach along with conservative capital market assumptions. Zvi Bodie of Boston University, who has run this type of analysis, shared with us his concern that participants are not shown the true level of risk they face. Bodie explained that tail risk typically is "truncated," in other words, the risk of unacceptable outcomes is hidden from the participant.[12]

If more plans auto-enroll people into a default strategy, such as a target-date-type strategy, then what is the risk for participants? As an example, Bodie considers a person earning $50,000 a year who intends to work for 40 years and contributes an increasing percentage of earned income to the plan over time. He asks, "What is the probable, final, real retirement income [this] employee will generate, given today's typical asset-allocation structure in target-date defaults?"

The answer, shown as output from a Monte Carlo simulation model, illustrates 1,500 potential outcomes and their likelihoods. In Figure 10.8, you can see that these outcomes are not distributed normally—the figure is not a standard bell curve. In actuality, the outcomes are skewed significantly.

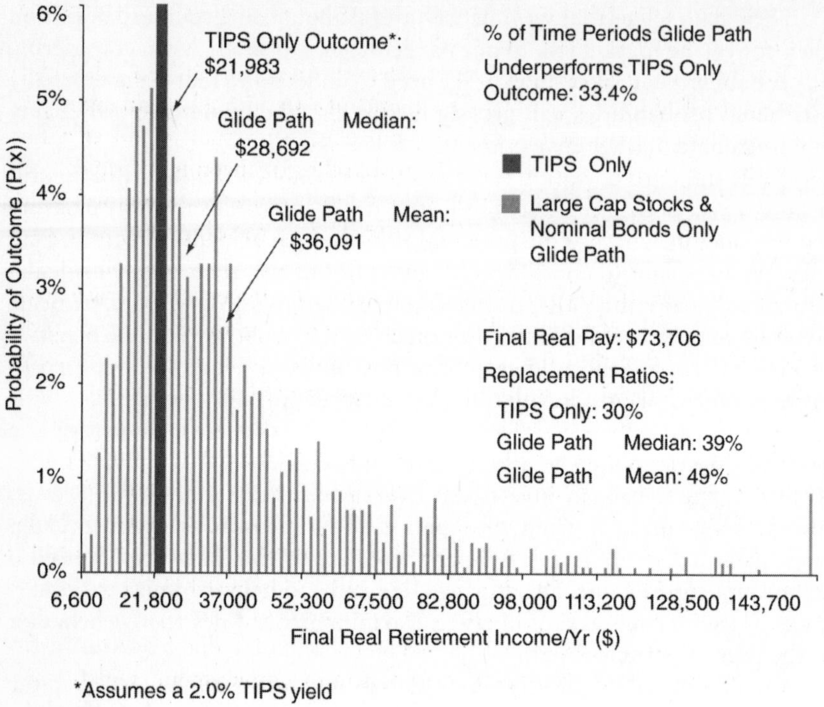
6%
5%
4%
3%
2%
1%
0%
Probability of Outcome (P(x))
TIPS Only Outcome*:
$21,983
Glide Path Median:
$28,692
Glide Path Mean:
$36,091
% of Time Periods Glide Path Underperforms TIPS Only Outcome: 33.4%
TIPS Only
Large Cap Stocks & Nominal Bonds Only Glide Path
Final Real Pay: $73,706
Replacement Ratios:
TIPS Only: 30%
Glide Path Median: 39%
Glide Path Mean: 49%
6,600 21,800 37,000 52,300 67,500 82,800 98,000 113,200 128,500 143,700
Final Real Retirement Income/Yr ($)
*Assumes a 2.0% TIPS yield

FIGURE 10.8 Probability Density of Basic Glide Path Outcomes
Source: PIMCO with assumptions from Zvi Bodie. Hypothetical example for illustrative purposes only.

While many plan participants may receive a very high return, there also is a fat lower tail, or higher probability of lower, less-desirable outcomes.

Bodie's diagram compares an individual who invests in TIPS with someone who invests in a typical target-date strategy. The outcome? The returns on the TIPS actually are higher than a full third of the probable outcomes for the typical glide path (i.e., the typical asset allocation used in the packaged target-date funds available today). So the question becomes: Are we willing to gamble with a typical stock-and-bond allocation that may fall short of meeting our basic income needs for retirement one-third of the time? This is groundbreaking research and of great importance for us as we (1) evaluate risk for participants; (2) select an appropriate default, given a plan's investment objective; and (3) consider how to describe risk to participants. Bodie stresses his concern with financial models and retirement calculators, warning: "You can't separate probabilities from outcomes the way they do. What they're doing in education materials as well as in these models is truncating the tail. So they're throwing out nearly all of the risk."

Mathew Rice, principal and chief research officer at DiMeo Schneider & Associates, LLC, stresses that one significant reason many plan sponsors do not adequately manage left-tail risk is because they try "to put all their eggs in the basket that maximizes the probability of meeting an objective, rather than saying, 'If we fall 1 percent short of the objective, we'll probably be okay. However, if we fall, say, 25 percent short of the objective, we could be in serious trouble.'"[13]

When we asked Rice how DiMeo Schneider manages left-tail risk that seeks to avoid catastrophic underperformance, he explained that the company "create[s] portfolios that blend a broad range of asset classes to help reduce expected volatility, without sacrificing expected median returns compared to many first-generation glide paths."

Whatever risk measures are used, it is imperative that we understand that no one can tell us what the future holds and that no single risk measure or combination will be adequate to show the totality of risk retirees face. One important fact that we must always keep in mind is that the probability and magnitude of participant shortfalls is a function of market performance during the savings life span of each plan participant.

Another reason participants may have a shortfall is due to an unfortunate and unexpected disability or termination of employment, which may reduce their income and possibly force them into early retirement. Disability and terminations can be viewed as additional types of negative left tail events which can leave the participant with insufficient money at the time of retirement as well as possibly higher healthcare costs in retirement. Next we look at time-period sensitivity.

Time-Period Risk

In a DB plan sponsored by a corporation or municipality, individuals pool their resources—and retirement benefits—with others. Since we assume that corporations or municipalities have almost "infinite" lives, they can offset periods of poor performance by future periods of good performance. These organizations generate income from ongoing operations, taxes, and contributions from new people entering the workforce. The overall risk to those fortunate enough to have a DB plan is much lower since they should receive a set payout regardless of market performance. The organization rather than the individual bears the market risk in DB plans.

For DC plans, the story and risk levels are much different. As Seth Ruthen, executive vice president and member of PIMCO's account management group and a pioneer in thought leadership in glide-path design in DC plans, stated:

> *Participants in a DC plan are different from a DB plan. Unlike a corporate DB sponsor, individuals are not perpetuities, do not pool their investment results with others, and do not have large amounts of income from ongoing operations (for example, work) after retirement. As such, it would be inappropriate for DC participants to act exactly like DB plans. DC participants need to be mindful of their effective time frames and the probability and severity of underperformance.[14]*

Unfortunately, in DC plans, participants do not have organizational balance sheets supporting their retirement payouts. As individuals, we end up with outcomes that may or may not be desirable. We do not receive the group's average outcome. Our actual outcome is more likely to be nearer the median expected outcome than the average that takes into account extreme winners and losers.

The one-person-for-oneself nature of DC investing exposes plan participants to the real possibility that if they experience a severe market downturn near their planned retirement dates, they may be forced to prolong their working lives, reduce their standard of living in retirement, or both. Market performance in 2008 has been a stark reminder of this possibility. The year that participants are born as well as when they choose to retire will have a significant impact on the amount of income they likely are able to replace during their retirement years. As shown in Figure 10.9, based on our assumption set, those retiring in 1979 would have had less than half of the income replacement as those retiring in 1997, despite the fact that, in our simulation of past market performance, they saved the same amount and invested in the same asset allocation. Note how rapidly the replacement income level can change, based on the retirement year. The assumptions include a starting salary of $50,000; salary increases of 3 percent; employee contribution of 6 percent, employer contribution of 3 percent, and annuity purchase rate of 7.8 percent.

One way to mitigate the effects of potential market downturns late in the retirement-savings period is to employ a broadly diversified investment strategy and reduce exposure to assets with highly uncertain outcomes—those with greater market risk or volatility. Bodie argued that risk should be minimized until a participant's basic retirement income needs are satisfied. He suggested that "offering TIPS in a DC plan is one way to provide participants with the assurance that people can build a retirement without credit, market or inflationary risks."[15] Others, however, would argue that Bodie's

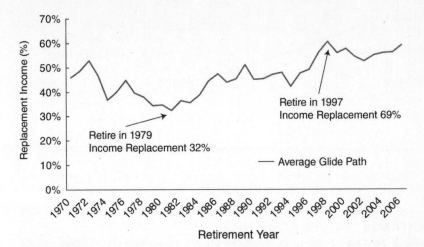

FIGURE 10.9 Real Replacement Income Using Average Lifetime Annuity for Male/Female Participant
Source: PIMCO, 2009.

suggestion is too conservative and that people will likely never reach their goal if they take his advice. Bodie would counter that if they save more, they may reach a respectable income replacement goal and potentially do so in a "worry-free" way. TIPS are particularly valuable in protecting assets from inflation. Let us turn now to inflation risk.

Inflation Risk

Inflation protection is critical in a DC plan, regardless of the economic environment, as inflation is one of the greatest risks participants and retirees face—that is, their money must retain purchasing power as they approach and enter retirement.

As shown in Figure 10.10, with even a modest 3 percent yearly inflation rate, it takes only 10 years to reduce our spending power by 25 percent. If we experience higher inflation, for instance, 6 percent, the outcome is even more devastating, with a 25 percent reduction to our spending power materializing in approximately 5 years.

Some may argue that inflation is not a pressing concern today. In fact, in the current market at the time of writing this book, deflation may be the greater concern. However, while recent U.S. inflation has been mild, we should not expect this low level to continue indefinitely. As PIMCO and other market experts look out over the next three to five years, most

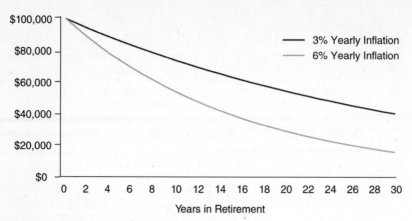

FIGURE 10.10 $100,000 Adjusted by Inflation
Source: PIMCO. Hypothetical example for illustrative purposes only.

anticipate inflation to rise. Experts point to the amount of stimulus money that has been pumped into our economy, coupled with resource demands from emerging markets, as likely catalysts to an inflationary environment in the future.

Anna Rappaport, president of Anna Rappaport Consulting and chairperson of the Society of Actuaries Committee on Post Retirement Needs and Risks, agrees that inflation is a looming threat on the horizon. Citing the Retirement Risk Survey, she reported that 57 percent of respondents are "very or somewhat concerned about inflation . . . 52 percent [are] concerned about having enough money to pay for a long stay in a nursing home, and 51 percent [are] concerned about having enough money to pay for adequate healthcare."[16] She also noted that, while participants were taking this survey during a period when inflation was relatively low, it was also a period where healthcare expenses were rapidly rising.

Whether we will have sufficient retirement income may depend largely on how we manage inflationary risk. Typically, DC plan participants have been told that investing in equities is a sure way to help protect assets against rising inflation. While historically equities have outpaced inflation over the long run, history also shows us that over shorter time frames, equities often do not keep pace with inflation. This was true just prior to the inception of 401(k)s in 1981. From 1965 to 1979, equities failed to keep pace as inflation spiked to the highest levels seen in our lifetimes. In 1979, inflation reached a peak of 13.3 percent. Participants who invested in equities during this time frame would have been in jeopardy of having insufficient real income to sustain their lifestyles during retirement.

Unfortunately, as mere mortals, our lives may not be long enough for us to wait for equities to outpace inflation. Rather, we must consider how to help protect ourselves from inflation over shorter time frames. It is critical to help protect DC participants from inflation, particularly within 10 years of retirement and, more important, once they are in retirement, when they no longer are able to make up for the eroding impact of inflation. Again, those approaching and in retirement may not have enough "long run" to wait it out. Both a market loss and inflation can be devastating, particularly during retirement, when retirees begin drawing down their DC savings.

Let us consider a typical participant earning $50,000 a year who at the beginning of 2008 had an account balance of $60,000. If he lost 25 percent of his account, it would take him less than two years to recoup the loss, given a typical contribution rate of 9.5 percent of an assumed investment return of 6 percent. By comparison, the retiree would fare much worse. Assuming the retiree begins with a $600,000 balance, a 25 percent loss coupled with the drawdown of 50 percent of pay adjusted for 3 percent inflation and a 6 percent return means that the retiree's money would run out after 10 years. Avoiding the 25 percent loss in the first year and receiving a 6 percent return would have made the retiree's money last an additional 5 years. Enduring a market shock in retirement can derail the best-laid plans.

How Do We Help Protect against Inflation?   There is no way to project whether employees will be accumulating most of their retirement assets during a time when the economy is booming or during a downtime, or what the economy will be like when they finally reach retirement. For that reason, Rappaport feels that employers have a responsibility to make sure that the retirement education or software they are using to help plan their glide path takes inflation risk into consideration. "Employers should ensure that any program they recommend handles inflation risk in a way that's reasonable and consistent with the treatment of investment returns. The program should treat investment returns for various asset classes in a sensible way for different inflationary environments."

Timing the market for inflation protection securities is dangerous; plan sponsors should not wait until inflation spikes to add protection, just as participants should not wait until the dam breaks to get flood insurance. Inflation protection securities should be part of DC plans at all times. If a plan does not have assets such as TIPS, now is the time to add this important inflation protection feature. These assets may also add important diversification benefits, helping to reduce volatility and improve potential return even in times of low inflation. As plan sponsors consider TIPS, real asset experts at PIMCO John Cavalieri, senior vice president and product manager, Gang Hu, senior vice president and portfolio manager, and

Mihir Worah, managing director and portfolio manager, suggest that "active management can provide more efficient exposure [to TIPS] for investors."[17] They note that the lower relative liquidity, nontrivial transaction costs, and multiple recurring risk premiums provide opportunity for active managers to add value. They explain:

> *The TIPS market is disproportionally held by passive and buy-and-hold investors, which tends to dilute the efficient market hypothesis and inhibits the recurring price patterns . . . from being arbitraged away. As long as the market is characterized by a large number of passive or risk-averse investors who trade in predictable ways at predictable times, there will likely always be attractive opportunities for active managers to deliver relative outperformance for their clients. . . . "Passive TIPS investing" as it is commonly understood actually involves making active, arbitrary trading deviations from what defines the market. Employing a systematic trading pattern to follow an index that specifies exposures be implemented in the last few minutes of the trading day is not passive in any sense of the word. Worse yet, it can be very costly.*

TIPS offer important inflation protection as well as the credit quality of Treasury securities. As plan sponsors consider inflation protection securities, they may add TIPS to their plans first. In addition, they may add real estate and even commodities, which also can provide inflation protection. Some also may look at infrastructure, timber, energy, or other types of investments. Or they may prefer to add a diversified global tactical asset allocation strategy that may tap into all of these investment types and is managed to outpace inflation.

Roger Williams, managing director and head of defined contribution consulting at Rogerscasey, believes that it is "critical to have inflation protection as a participant approaches and enters retirement. Treasury Inflation Protected Securities (TIPS) should be part of any target-date fund for people approaching or in retirement."[18] As someone who is old enough to have actively experienced the last big inflationary environment, Williams remembers the anecdotes shared by many elderly people who had to survive on fixed incomes during those challenging times. "Investors need to have some inflation protection, whether it is TIPS or some diversified real estate."

Tom Idzorek, chief investment officer at Ibbotson Associates, agrees that while our salaries rise with inflationary levels, participants cannot expect the same guarantees with their portfolios once they have gone into retirement, unless that inflation risk is built directly *into* that portfolio. "All else being equal in retirement, we must think about using asset classes that are more likely to match inflation. We think of Treasury Inflation Protected Securities, real estate, and commodities as real-return asset classes that are more likely to hedge a portfolio against inflation."[19]

Therefore, when designing a glide path for participants, Idzorek advises plan sponsors "to think about all elements of that individual balance sheet—our financial capital, our human capital and the nature of our liabilities." Our goal in retirement should be "an inflation-adjusted, ongoing series of payments or income so that we can maintain our living standard" at a level at which we are comfortable.

While Idzorek believes that, over the long run, equities can help to hedge inflation, he agrees that the asset classes that will perform best year to year inflation hedging over the long term are "TIPS, real estate and commodities" because these "generally are thought to provide a more immediate inflation hedge, even when there are short time periods of high inflation." (See Table 10.6.)

Longevity Risk

Planning for retiree longevity also matters. These days it is not unheard of for people to live into their 100s. No doubt we may need to make our money last for a long time. In terms of longevity, perhaps the three most important variables to consider are:

1. The starting value of the retirement portfolio
2. The actual withdrawal needs, expressed in either real dollars per year or a real rate
3. The investment portfolio's ability to preserve and enhance purchasing power, taking inflation into consideration

Depending on an individual's wealth and health, an annuity (either immediate or deferred [i.e., "longevity insurance"]) or other insurance product may be the best option to address longevity risk. Rather than buying an insurance product, many people may have sufficient assets and risk appetites to remain invested in their DC target-date strategies or other investment structures during their retirement years. We return to a discussion on retirement income and helping preserve assets for longevity in Chapter 13.

Taxation Risk

Taxation of retirement assets is another type of risk. In other words, when we finally begin to draw from our retirement plans, the money that comes

TABLE 10.6 Correlation Matrix (March 1997–June 2009)

	Dow Jones UBS Commodity TR Index	Dow Jones US Select REIT TR Index	Barclays Capital U.S. Treasury Index: U.S. TIPS	Barclays Capital U.S. Aggregate Index	S&P 500 Index	Consumer Price Index, Non-Seasonally Adjusted
Dow Jones UBS Commodity TR Index	1.00					
Dow Jones US Select REIT TR Index	0.22	1.00				
Barclays Capital U.S. Treasury Index: U.S. TIPS	0.34	0.21	1.00			
Barclays Capital U.S. Aggregate Index	0.10	0.14	0.74	1.00		
S&P 500 Index	0.24	0.52	0.04	0.01	1.00	
CPI, NSA	0.29	0.11	0.10	−0.20	0.02	1.00

Source: Zephyr StyleADVISOR.

out will be taxed, typically at ordinary income tax rates. Unfortunately, we cannot accurately project how much tax rates will be in the future, but given the demographic trends with an aging population of Baby Boomers and the increasing national debt, most experts anticipate that taxes will rise.

Deena Katz, author, financial planner, and associate professor at Texas Tech University, addresses this issue. She points out that plan sponsors need to help participants understand that each pocket in their retirement portfolio has a different tax and expense related to it. For example, people might look at their individual retirement accounts (IRAs) and say, "Wow, I've got a half a million dollars in there." Advisers explain, "Yes. But in reality, Uncle Sam gave you a low-cost loan over a period of time. Eventually, you need to pay some tax on it. So, in that case, it's not *all* your money."[20]

For this reason, Katz stresses that financial planning education should include not only advice about how to help protect oneself against the impact of inflation but also against the future impact of taxes. Since most people do not "understand the basic tax benefits or even the rudiments of how DC plans work," she feels that teaching participants the "basics of tax-deferred saving" should be a priority. "We need to be able to manage our taxes and expenses, so that our net gross return is realistic, going forward."

Norman Boone, founder and president of Mosaic Financial Partners, Inc., also believes that advisors and plan sponsors should take their clients through a process where they plan for taxation upon retirement. Boone states that it is important to decide "how you are going to work with retirement accounts that have tax characteristics that are different from taxable accounts. We think it is really important for the advisor and the client to have discussed and reached agreement on all of these issues so that neither side will be surprised by something that comes up later."[21]

Depending on their outlook for inflation, participants should consider tax strategies such as converting tax deferred DC assets into a Roth IRA. Upon conversion, tax on the deferred amount is owed to the government, but then once paid, the Roth assets, including future earnings, are never taxed again. In addition, unlike traditional DC and IRA assets, retirees are not forced to withdraw Roth assets in minimum distributions after age $70^1/_2$.

Increasingly plan sponsors offer Roth accounts within their DC plans; the Profit Sharing/401k Council of America 2008 survey reports that over a third of plans now allow Roth contributions. For those still accumulating assets, investing in a Roth allows participants to put away more money (since this money goes in after tax and up to the same limit as pretax money) and to begin tax diversification as they build their retirement account. This strategy requires more money for investment yet seeks to avoid the risk of higher future taxes.

HELPING PROTECT DC PARTICIPANT ASSETS FROM RISKS

Now that we have discussed the range of risks participants face, let us take a closer look as some of the ways to help reduce the various risks. We have already talked about the value of asset diversification. Increasing diversification by finding assets that have lower correlations to those already provided to participants can help reduce price volatility, which is likely to reduce fear and thus the emotional risk of selling out during a market low. This diversification may also help address other market risks, shortfall, inflation, and, to a certain extent, longevity.

As discussed earlier in Chapters 8 and 9, plan sponsors may consider assets such as TIPS, commodities, and real estate investment trusts (REITs) that may provide not only diversification benefits but also inflation protection. These assets can be considered as individual core options yet may be more appropriate when blended together in a single investment offering, or along with other assets in a broader strategy such as a global tactical portfolio, or even added directly into target-date strategies. Global tactical asset allocation strategies also may add diversification and inflation protection by tapping into stocks and bonds around the world and reallocating assets based on forward-looking assumptions. Tactical asset allocation allows the portfolio manager to move in and out of markets based on expectations of gaining greater potential returns or avoiding possible losses. This approach can be implemented in target-date strategies enabling the manager to allocate more or less to various assets within a band surrounding the glide path. Diversifying assets or tactical asset allocation strategies also may reduce left-tail risk, i.e., the risk of highly unfortunate retirement income replacement levels. Another way to reduce this risk is to add explicit tail-risk hedging in the portfolio.

In actively managed target date strategies, we can think of ways to help reduce this left-hand tail risk. We may want to consider tactical asset allocation as well as tail-risk hedging. Tail-risk hedging may be conducted in addition to the tactical asset allocation. In essence, this tactic invests a small percent of the portfolio (e.g., 25 to 75 basis points) in such a way that it helps reduce the potential negative impact of a market shock on the asset values.

IMPORTANCE OF TAIL-RISK HEDGING

Joseph Simonian, defined contribution analytics leader, and Mark Taborsky, CFA and executive vice president, both of PIMCO, agree that "most investment strategies may not adequately hedge against tail risk" and that in the DC market, "the vast majority of target-date strategies were woefully unprepared for the financial storm that has engulfed the world" during 2008.[22] The reason for this, they believe, is because most actively managed target-date funds have aggressively gone after large returns at the cost of not paying proper attention to the management of risk. In their view, passive strategies present even more of a risk since "by design they are committed to going where the market will take them, even if the destination is ultimately a financial abyss." For this reason:

> *It is no surprise then that most target-date strategies have recently proven to be highly vulnerable to systemic shocks, as most are designed to perform well in equilibrium environments with very little heed, if any, given to unexpected and severe left-tail events and the threat they pose to investors' long-term financial plans. A related source of vulnerability is the traditional asset class framework, which provides an "illusion of diversification" by masking the interconnections that exist between assets.*

Because of this, during unforeseen times of financial downturn, investors who use these riskier assets in their target-date plans have few safe havens to which they can turn. However, Simonian and Taborsky go on to explain that plan sponsors who "preemptively institute a 'tail-risk' hedging strategy can provide their portfolios a measure of downside risk mitigation during a crisis. Such a strategy consists primarily of selectively acquiring options on the various indices (for example, the S&P 500) that broadly track the assets in a portfolio, especially during non-crisis times when the options are relatively inexpensive." They point out that the driving factor behind tail-risk hedging "is not to provide a hedge against frequent small to medium downswings in the market, but to provide a hedge against the rare but catastrophic events that can cause long-lasting damage to portfolios."

IN CLOSING

Risk means more than market price volatility. We need to help protect participants from a wide range of risks, from emotional, to market, to inflation, to longevity—and let us not forget taxes. Diversifying assets will help in reducing many of these risks, namely price volatility, yet a broad asset mix alone may not take us far enough. We also need to consider managers who can look forward in navigating the markets and not only seek opportunities but also seek to avoid market blows. This may mean finding managers who can tactically allocate assets as well as possibly introducing tail-risk hedging into their portfolios. It also may mean finding ways to help minimize the risk of future tax hikes as well as the possibility of outliving your assets. In Chapter 13 we come back to a discussion on risk as we consider retirement income and guarantee products. For now, let us move on to benchmarking the performance of target-date strategies.

CHAPTER 11

Approaches to Benchmarking

The term "benchmarking" has a colorful history. It was first used by cobblers, who placed their customers' feet onto a "bench" to measure them and mark out a pattern for making their shoes. Then, once the leather was cut for the shoe, it would be compared back to the bench mark. In a way, the cobbler's skill in cutting the leather was evaluated relative to the bench mark. In the investment management industry, the same concept applies. We compare investment returns and risk to an appropriate benchmark to measure a manager's skill. For instance, we typically compare an active large-cap equity manager to the Standard & Poor's (S&P) 500 Index and consider whether the manager has outperformed the index or reduced risk; we hope for both outperformance and lower risk measured by volatility in returns. Investment experts also compare performance to a peer group of similar managers, in this example a set of other large-cap equity managers. By comparing to both an index and a peer group, the plan sponsor answers the question: Could we have done better by investing in the index or in a different manager? Organizations such as Morningstar and Lipper provide data and systems to allow plan sponsors or their consultants to compare the investment lineup in a plan to the relevant indices and peer groups. But what about benchmarking target-date strategies?

Benchmarking target-date strategies raise a number of challenges for plan sponsors. Should sponsors compare target dates to an index or to a peer group, or both? Further, should they look at each underlying investment as well as at the glide path? How can they evaluate the glide path structure? Or should they evaluate whether the target-date strategies are likely to meet their defined objective, that is, provide a certain level of income replacement in retirement?

Whether you benchmark packaged or custom target-date strategies, the issues are the same. Yet with custom strategies, if you are dissatisfied with any one of the managers or the glide path, you have the ability to make a change. In this chapter, we take a look at ways that plan sponsors benchmark target-date strategies. We consider indices, peer groups, and retirement-income replacement probabilities as well as other approaches.

INTRODUCTION TO TARGET DATE BENCHMARKING AND THE MEASURE OF SUCCESS

As we consider benchmarking approaches, we would like to share some of the opening remarks offered by Matt Ketchum, a defined contribution (DC) specialist at UBS Global Asset Management, who served as moderator for the benchmarking panel at the April 2008 Pensions & Investments Custom Target Retirement Date-Strategy Conference. Here is what he had to say about benchmarking to monitor the performance of custom target-date funds.

> *The selection and monitoring of target-date strategies is an important fiduciary responsibility for plan sponsors. One of the key elements of any investor product selection for a defined contribution plan is benchmarking the investment strategy. When plan sponsors consider the concept of benchmarking target-date strategies, they must first differentiate between benchmarking and measuring success. This is an important distinction. Benchmarking target-date strategies and measuring the success of a turnkey investment solution are two interrelated but different concepts. At times, the line between both concepts tends to be blurred.*
>
> *Since target-date strategies are viewed as turnkey, single-solution investment approaches, the optimal measure of their success is, in some measure, the strategy's ability to satisfy a specific outcome. In the case of retirement plans, that outcome is the inflation-adjusted income generated by and produced for a participant living in retirement. In effect, the question is: Did the target-date strategy that was provided generate an appropriate level of real replacement income during a participant's retirement years?*
>
> *The characteristics of defined contribution plans and the behavior exhibited by participants may create hurdles for implementing, in a practical way, real income replacement ratios as a benchmark for an initial target-date strategy selection and ongoing monitoring of that plan. The difficulty and complexity should not, however, prevent us as an industry from working towards a thoroughly developed solution.*
>
> *As plan sponsors, record keepers, consultants, and solution providers, we have considerable amounts of data about plan*

participants, and we should use that data to more accurately measure real outcomes for the participants as they approach and live in retirement. Clearly, benchmarking target-date strategies has proven to be difficult, unclear, and certainly non-standardized. While relative return and risk for target-date strategies are important, these measures can be particularly impacted and skewed by the asset allocation characteristics of the strategies.

Benchmarking any investment product should be conducted through the lens of measuring an investment product's success relative to its investment objective. In target-date strategies, the ultimate objective for the vast majority of investors is to accumulate assets sufficient to provide for a targeted level of real income replacement throughout the full life of retirement.

Furthermore, since target-date strategies are generally considered a holistic solution for an individual through their company retirement plan, arguably one of the key focuses for participants is to limit the instances of loss of their principal or the size of the loss of their overall account value. When saving for retirement, downside capture has a material impact on ending wealth value, particularly as one approaches retirement and balances are relatively larger. It is the magnitude and timing of large negative returns that can have a material impact on ending wealth and affecting participant behavior.[1]

At PIMCO, we agree with Ketchum's distinction between measuring success and benchmarking. Our suggested approach also is to start with projecting probable outcomes of the various target-date glide paths. As discussed in Chapter 8 on glide path design, we suggest evaluating the potential glide path structures or products to determine the likely income replacement level as well as the tail risk or unacceptable outcomes. Our glide path analysis software PIMCO Your Optimal DC Allocation (YODcA^{TM}) is designed to aid plan sponsors and consultants in evaluating and comparing glide paths relative to the probable income replacement results. We suggest seeking a glide path that has a high probability of delivering an acceptable median replacement income level coupled with the lowest possible probability of unacceptable outcomes. This approach can help the plan sponsor evaluate the likely success of a strategy, not only at the time of glide path selection but also during ongoing monitoring as the glide path is modified over time.

Of course, every projection is based on a set of assumptions that are entered into the models we build. We will not know for decades whether the models and the assumptions applied were correct or not. Nonetheless, as fiduciaries, we need to do our best to look forward and test the potential scenarios. We need to consider whether our participants are likely to succeed or not in meeting their goals. What is more, we need to recalibrate a glide path if the potential risk participants may face is unacceptable. Monte Carlo analysis provides a valuable approach for us to randomly test thousands of possible scenarios and then make adjustments to improve the overall risk versus return as well as the projected success of a glide path structure. This approach provides a look forward, showing the plan sponsor how target-date strategies *may* perform given a set of assumptions. Now let us look at benchmarking approaches, which look backward rather than forward. They answer the question: How *did* our strategies perform relative to alternative approaches or products?

COMMON APPROACHES TO BENCHMARKING TARGET-DATE STRATEGIES

To evaluate the past performance of a target-date strategy, there are a number of approaches to consider, including proprietary composites, peer group, and indices. One or several of these approaches may be attractive to plan sponsors. In its 2009 Target-Date Fund Manager Survey, Callan Associates asked plan sponsors what benchmarking practices they followed. Figure 11.1 is what Callan found in terms of prevalence.

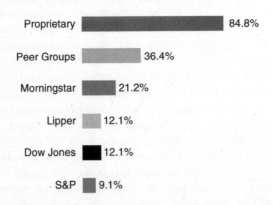

Figures do not add to 100% due to multiple responses allowed.

FIGURE 11.1   Benchmark Prevalence
Source: Callan Associates, 2009.

Let us take a look at each of the benchmarking approaches. Although there are different ways to categorize the approaches, we would group them as shown next.

- **Proprietary or custom composite.** This approach creates a custom composite or hybrid benchmark for each of the target-date strategies. This approach requires construction of a passive benchmark using the beta or underlying index weights of the asset allocation within the glide path to track performance and volatility relative to the strategy. For example, the 2050 strategy may have a 10 percent allocation of bonds, 40 percent to U.S. large-cap equity, 20 percent to international developed equity, and so on. The proprietary benchmark would then be comprised of the weights of the underlying indices, for example, 10 percent to the Barclays Capital U.S. Aggregate Index, 40 percent to the S&P 500 Index, 20 percent to the MSCI EAFE Index, and so on, for the other weights within the glide path.

  A proprietary approach will show plan sponsors how the custom strategy has performed relative to the underlying indices. You will see how your active and passive managers in combination have performed relative to a purely passive benchmark. Further, to the extent that your glide path is modified day to day using a tactical asset allocation approach relative to the benchmark, you may gain a sense of whether that active management has added value. Yet you will likely want to take a closer look than this approach allows. Keep in mind, however, that a proprietary or hybrid benchmark is not a strategy set in which you can invest. In other words, you could not have invested in the hybrid as opposed to the custom strategy since it actually does not exist as an investment alternative mix in the market. But the next two approaches are investible.

- **Peer group.** This benchmarking approach compares how your target-date strategy has fared relative to actual packaged target-date products on the market. For example, you may want to compare the custom strategy that you are managing to a set of target-date mutual funds that have similar risk characteristics or general asset allocation structures. Keep in mind, however, that no set of peer target-date funds is likely to provide a *perfect* match to the philosophy, glide path, and asset mix within your custom strategy. Nonetheless, this approach does help answer the question of how your strategy has performed as well as its risk profile relative to the other investible choices in the market. You may want to select a peer group on your own or use a peer group index approach, such as the one provided by Callan Associates or Standard & Poor's.

Callan offers a series of target-date indices with dates ranging from 1995 to 2055. These indices are constructed as a consensus glide path, given the actual glide paths of mutual fund and collective investment trust managers available in the market. The indices at the time of writing track 38 different providers' glide paths over 80 years (40 years of accumulation and 40 years after retirement) to provide an average asset allocation among this group as well as a summary of the allocation across 17 asset classes. While one may argue that this Callan Target-Date Index is investible, if one buys into all of the underlying target-date funds, such an investment approach is unlikely.

Similar to Callan, Standard & Poor's provides a consensus peer group index. The S&P Target-Date Index establishes an investable benchmark based on a consensus among peer group funds with comparable asset classes. Its index allocations can be comprised of exchange-traded funds, mutual funds, separate accounts, or commingled funds that track and broadly represent each of the nine asset classes: (1) U.S. large cap; (2) U.S. mid cap; (3) U.S. small cap; (4) international equities; (5) emerging markets; (6) U.S. real estate investment trusts (REITs); (7) core fixed income; (8) short-term treasuries; and (9) Treasury Inflation Protected Securities (TIPs). To create the indices, S&P conducts an annual survey of the holdings within target-date funds with assets exceeding $50 million. Then asset class exposures for each fund are calculated by mapping those assets to the applicable asset class category and to the applicable target date. Note that only asset classes which are represented in a significant proportion of target-date funds are included in the S&P's indices.

Again, this approach shows how your target-date strategies have fared relative to the average manager or set of managers in the marketplace. Whether you construct your own peer group or use a consensus index, such as the one managed by Callan or S&P, it is important to evaluate how well that peer group fits with your glide path philosophy, risk parameters, and asset class exposures.

- **Target-date index.** Another benchmarking approach is to compare your target-date strategy to an investible index, such as the Dow Jones Target Date Indexes or the Morningstar Lifetime Allocation Index. Dow Jones offers two sets of indices:

1. Dow Jones Target Date Indexes offers two series of benchmarks (U.S. and global) with target dates set in five-year increments. Asset allocations in this first series are limited to stocks (U.S. and global respectively), bonds (U.S. and global respectively), and cash.

2. Dow Jones Real Return Target Date Indexes was designed to provide the industry with a benchmark representing life cycle portfolios

focused on growing and preserving real (as oppose to nominal) value over time. The index construction methodology incorporates concepts of inflation protection, recognition of TIPS as a conceptual risk-free (all investment carry the possibility of risk.) asset in a DC environment, and the use of real assets as hedges against inflation and as portfolio diversifiers. These asset-allocated indices include global equities, U.S. bonds, TIPS, real estate, and commodities. Just as mutual funds may be managed to a particular index, such as the S&P 500, target-date mutual funds can be managed to track the Dow Jones Target-Date Indexes. In fact, such products exist in the market today.

Morningstar also offers a set of target-date indices called the Morningstar Lifetime Allocation Index. Applying the asset allocation methodologies developed and maintained by Ibbotson Associates (a Morningstar company since 2006), the approach includes a family of 13 indices available in five-year increments across three risk profiles: aggressive, moderate, and conservative. It includes 10 indices for the 2010-to-2055 accumulation period, plus the 2005, 2000, and Income indices, which cover investors' postretirement allocation needs. How does a plan sponsor decide which index may be best for benchmarking? We suggest evaluating the construction of the glide path as well as the array of underlying asset classes to find the best fit. It also might help to run a retirement-income replacement projection of the indices relative to your custom glide path to determine what is the most appropriate benchmarking strategy.

Again, plan sponsors may want to use a combination of the listed approaches as they evaluate their custom target-date strategies. Using a proprietary approach is, not surprisingly, most prevalent. This approach enhances the ability of plan sponsors to evaluate how their active custom-date strategies have fared relative to a passive glide path with passive investment management.

Other providers, such as Russell Investments, are developing ways to take a more complete picture of each target-date series and evaluate the impact it has on wealth generation. The Russell Target-Date Metric is a returns-based metric designed to measure the performance of an entire family of target-date funds relative to any benchmark family of funds. This ratio shows the retirement wealth generated by one family of target-date strategies compared to the potential returns generated by investing in the benchmark.

Mike Henkel, managing director at Envestnet Asset Management, suggests a more comprehensive strategy starting with a comparison of projected outcomes from the various target-date strategy alternatives. This is similar to Ketchum's approach as well as to ours at PIMCO.

Henkel makes it clear that he is "not a fan of combining all target-date funds into a common index then comparing any one fund to the aggregate performance. That's because peer groups must be very specialized in their approaches. It's a tough thing to do."[2] He goes on to explain that "the problem with aggregate groupings is that when markets are poor like they've been [in 2008 and 2009], it forces plan sponsors to gravitate toward conservative strategies. When markets are hot, sponsors move toward more aggressive strategies. It's the tail wagging the dog." When asked what plan sponsors can do to evaluate the actual performance of their target-date strategies, Henkel suggests that "the more correct way to evaluate them is to open up the hood on any given target-date strategy and ask, 'How have the underlying managers performed? Have they done well?'" He warns that plan sponsors should not look at aggregate performance of the target-date fund alone. Rather, they should be disaggregated.

What does he mean by "disaggregate"? Henkel is suggesting the importance of measuring both the glide path performance (i.e., how much value the asset allocation added) as well as the glide path implementation (i.e., how well the individual investment managers performed for the underlying asset classes, including active versus passive). In other words, he stresses that evaluating both the glide path and the implementation is important.

Looking beneath the hood at the implementation of custom target-date strategies is a practice already in place at most organizations, as this approach is similar to the ongoing investment monitoring that goes on for the plan's core investment lineup. As discussed in Chapter 3 on why custom strategies make sense relative to packaged products, the ability to monitor and control the underlying managers is a significant benefit. This type of monitoring also is highly efficient, since you already are monitoring the core strategies, which are likely to be the primary, if not the exclusive, investments used to comprise the target-date strategies. When plan sponsors use many of the same managers in their core and custom strategies as they do in their defined benefit plans, the efficiency in monitoring increases all the more.

Let us take a look at some other suggestions on benchmarking from experts in the field.

Consultant Perspectives on Benchmarking

Steve Charlton and Ross Bremen of NEPC addressed two ways among many to implement benchmarking. First, they suggested that sponsors "create a custom benchmark using the index for each of the underlying assets in the mix. A custom benchmark can help the plan sponsor understand whether the manager has added value through asset allocation or by selecting active managers for some or all asset classes."[3] Second, sponsors should compare fund returns to others with the same target date—that is, look at a peer group. To refine this approach, they suggested that plan sponsors "look closer and create an even more tailored peer group based on the current asset allocation (glide path)," although they acknowledge that this approach can be more challenging. Rather than choosing just one approach, they suggested that plan sponsors might want to evaluate their plans using multiple approaches. Another investment consultant perspective comes from Peter Grant at Towers Watson. Grant concurred with Charlton and Bremen saying that you could benchmark your plan by comparing it to a peer group, but that you had to be selective. "The remarkable thing, if you look at a lot of glide paths out there, is how incredibly similar they are. There are definitely some differences, but if you take a plan participant with a certain savings rate and a certain income, and you run through a lot of these glide paths, you will be amazed at how similar the outcomes are."[4]

However, Grant felt that if plan sponsors kept watch on the glide paths of their peers over the next 5 to 10 years, they would certainly observe that there are "a handful of glide paths that are going to do badly, and another bunch of glide paths that are going to do very well." These observations could help plan sponsors understand why they "made the decision with respect to the fund they ended up with, or the customized solution they ended up with" and help them to see whether they should be modifying that glide path, becoming even more aggressive or cautious, "based upon what is going on in the market environment."

Phil Suess, the DC practice leader at Mercer Investment Consulting in Chicago, also talked to us about how Mercer benchmarks DC plans. As we have seen, typically each plan investment is benchmarked to an index and peer group of similarly managed funds. However, this is more difficult with target-date strategies since the strategies involve many asset classes and asset-allocation decisions must be evaluated. We wanted to hear Suess's views on how plan sponsors could best benchmark blended strategies.

Suess explained that the benchmarking approach of comparing "underlying assets to the respective indices for each" gives plan sponsors a good sense of how well managers, active ones in particular, "are generating a premium over an unmanaged index." However, he felt that these evaluation strategies needed to be taken farther. "We need to evaluate whether the asset allocation is effective versus the alternatives. We need a benchmark that focuses not only on the underlying investments, but also on the appropriateness of the asset allocation at different points in time."[5] What's more, Suess believes that plan sponsors should

> *establish benchmarks for target strategies that address the issues of life expectancy, retirement-income adequacy, and volatility. In essence, this type of benchmark says, "This is what's reasonable and, to the extent you do better than that, that's great." To the extent a glide path falls below the expectation, we can evaluate the reason for its shortfall.*

At PIMCO, we suggest that plan sponsors benchmark their target-date strategies in a number of ways, including projecting retirement-income adequacy as well as comparing to a best-fit peer group or index. In addition, we suggest comparing the strategies to a model that is designed to assess how the participant might fare if he or she invested in TIPS alone. We say this because, given the goal of real income replacement, TIPS may be a more appropriate "risk-free" (all investment carry the possibility of risk.) investment for retirement savers than Treasury bills since TIPS is designed not only to provide government credit but are indexed to inflation as well. We know that if participants save a high enough percentage of their pay, they may reach a respectable retirement income level without taking on credit or inflation risk. If participants buy and hold these bonds rather than investing in a fund, they also may not need to worry about daily bond pricing fluctuations. This can be challenging to achieve within a DC plan. However, by taking a look at how participants would have done with TIPS alone, we can evaluate the potential benefits of adding in these broader asset allocation approaches. The appropriate question in such a case is: What did participants gain for the added risk that they accepted by investing beyond TIPS?

Plan Sponsor Approach to Benchmarking

Charles Claudio, pension manager at Ahold USA, explained that since Ahold's glide path is exclusive to the company, it had to develop a custom benchmark. Instead of benchmarking its customized retirement-date strategies portfolio "against similar funds or a universe of target-date funds," Ahold utilizes a custom composite benchmark approach "with the same asset allocation as the portfolio's target asset allocation."[6] Under this system, the performance of asset classes is represented by index returns.

> *We calculate benchmark returns by weighting the monthly index returns of each asset class according to the portfolio's monthly target allocation for each class. Target allocations adjust quarterly in accordance with the custom retirement strategy's standard glide path. We use the S&P 500 Index to represent the allocation to U.S. large-cap equities, Russell 2500 Index to represent U.S. small-/mid-cap*

equities, MSCI EAFE Index to represent non-U.S. equities, Barclays Capital U.S. High Yield Index (2 percent constrained) to represent high yield, Barclays Capital U.S. Aggregate Index to represent intermediate-duration bonds, Barclays Capital U.S. TIPS Index to represent inflation-protected securities, and Lipper Money Market Fund Average for cash.

Developments in Benchmarking Alternatives for Plan Sponsors

Thomas Idzorek, the chief investment officer at Ibbotson Associates, also addressed how plan sponsors with target-date DC plans should approach benchmarking. "First, when it comes to any kind of target-maturity solution, plan sponsors need to think differently about benchmarking and performance evaluation than they have historically. The traditional approach is, 'Here's a manager and here's a benchmark and then we can evaluate its performance.'"[7] Idzorek went on to make it clear that this is not enough. He cautioned:

If you step back and consider target-date funds or solutions in contrast to the typical investment fund that plan sponsors are comfortable benchmarking, we realize that at some level it's not just an investment option. It's more like a financial plan. To say that one financial plan is better than another is tough and not necessarily a purely quantitative or benchmark-relative endeavor. When comparing financial plans the key metric is the overall appropriateness of the plan based on the best-possible understanding of the investor's overall economic situation and how that situation changes over time—the same is true for target-date strategies.

Idzorek claimed that plan sponsors do much more than simply compare the performance of their target-date strategies to a particular benchmark. He also pointed out that, compared to several years ago, strong benchmarking indices are now available, for example, the Dow Jones families of indices, the S&P 500 Index, and the new target-date indices that Morningstar has launched.

They couldn't do it three years ago, but plan sponsors can now plot on a chart the glide paths of their target-date funds, along with the funds that make up their whole fund families, as well as the glide paths of various benchmarks. Ultimately, we then can pick a target-date benchmark whose risk and return or equity exposure is fairly consistent with the target-date funds we're attempting to benchmark.

Idzorek also pointed out that "as a secondary measure the different target-date benchmark families have different construction methodologies and biases, and use different asset classes. We can obtain these details and try to find a benchmark series that lines up well with our own target-date solution. While not a perfect benchmark, it's a fairly appropriate one."

When asked whether a sponsor should select not only an index but also the peer group that has the closest alignment with its own philosophy and glide-path structure, Idzorek clearly stated that he saw value in peer group comparisons.

> By looking at the stock-versus-bond split of all the different funds— as well as the detailed asset-allocation decisions they make moving forward—it's fairly easy for those who try to evaluate the performance of various target-date funds to both select an appropriate benchmark and build a custom peer group with which to benchmark or make performance comparisons.

We were curious about whether he advocated creating a custom benchmark by taking the underlying passive strategies and looking at how those had performed. Idzorek stated that this was a "critical element" and that he assumed that everyone was doing that. "One way to decide whether a tactical program, or using active managers to implement a glide path, adds value is to construct for comparison a passive version of your glide path. Then use a composite of different indices weighted according to your glide path."

BENCHMARKING MANAGED ACCOUNTS

What if you have decided to use a managed account approach instead of target-date strategy? Can managed accounts be benchmarked? Absolutely. Mike Henkel of Envestnet explained that

> we can benchmark managed accounts in much the same way [as target-date strategies]. We have to disaggregate the components. Plan sponsors should ask the same questions: "What drives the glide path? Is it just age? What price do we pay for the custom glide path?" We can ask the managed account provider to show how participants' accounts are defaulted based on age, then run an analysis of risk and retirement-income replacement just as we would with target-date strategies.[8]

Henkel went on to encourage plan sponsors to "dig in and ask: 'What are we buying? If everyone who retires in 2020 has the same asset allocation regardless of circumstance, do we really need to purchase this managed account program?' What triggers the differences in allocations? Is it what the plan sponsor likes and what it thinks will work?"

IN CLOSING

When it comes to benchmarking, there is not a single best approach for plan sponsors to pursue. Rather, taking a look at target strategies from a number of perspectives is important. Starting with the likely success of the strategies using a retirement-income replacement model such as PIMCO YODcA may provide insight and allow comparisons among various glide-path structures. It also is useful to look at the actual performance of the target-date strategies from one or a few angles, including a proprietary composite of the glide-path asset allocation, peer group, and target-date index comparison. As discussed, we also suggest comparing the strategies to an investment in TIPS alone. Finally, an important advantage offered by custom strategies is that you can evaluate each of the underlying or core investments that make up each of the strategies. At the end of the day, you need to select a target-date glide path and investment managers that together are most likely to help meet the specific objectives for your plan. Fortunately, consultants are well versed in these issues and alternative approaches so that they can work with you to structure a benchmarking approach for your plan.

PART Four

Looking to the Future

CHAPTER 12

Financial Education, Advice, and Retirement Planning

Can financial stress actually make you sick? Research says that yes, it can. Researchers Jinhee Kim and E. Thomas Garman "determined that financial stress was negatively related to organizational commitment and was positively associated with absenteeism."[1]

What are people worried sick about? Many people today are fearful that they will not be able to save enough money to last them through retirement. A joint report, assembled by leading academics and business experts in finance, which brought together the decades-long research of 11 major business-sponsored surveys, demonstrated just how widespread this anxiety is.[2] Here are some of the significant findings in that report. One financial literacy study in this compilation, taken from a Bankrate.com study, found that almost half of respondents (45 percent) "were concerned about being able to put away enough for their retirement" and that 78 percent "are very concerned about their long-term financial future." This paper quoted a CIGNA survey that reported that 39 percent of employees felt that they could hardly keep up with their bills, resulting in their having "little discretionary income to save for college or retirement," and that "more than two-thirds (68 percent) of parents with children under age 18 are extremely or very concerned about having enough money for their children's education."

Fear of not having enough money to live comfortably during retirement, not having enough resources to weather health or economic crisis, or outliving one's retirement benefits are concerns being expressed across all economic strata of American society. A National Survey on Financial Stress and Retirement Savings conducted by the American Express Retirement Services found that 44 percent of respondents, overall, were stressed about retirement. This study showed that "the stress levels by income groups were: 30 percent up to $30,000; 22 percent $30,000–$50,000; 22 percent

$50,000–$75,000; 17 percent $75,000–$100,000; and 9 percent $100,000 or more."

Furthermore, a significant number of employees said that they did not feel that they understood enough about their retirement plans; some even said that they feared they would not be able to retire at all. A MetLife study reported that 25 percent of employees "have not done any specific retirement planning, and only 31 percent believe that they are 'on track' for reaching retirement goals." What is more, almost half of respondents "believe they will have to work full- or part-time in retirement." Of those employees aged 41 to 60, "only 4 percent have reached their retirement goals," and 48 percent of that group report that "outliving their savings" is their "greatest retirement fear."

Sadly, a Putnam Investments poll reports that 46 percent of current employees "are resigned to accepting that they will struggle financially in retirement," and that 13 percent "believe they cannot amass enough to retire so they are not going to save for retirement at all." In other words, they feel powerless to secure their financial future.

Overall, these statistics strongly indicate that many of today's plan participants sorely need some kind of financial education, including retirement-planning support. In fact, the Kim and Garman study referred to earlier shows that effective financial education programs can not only help employees experience relief from financial stress but improve productivity as well: "employers might reduce employee absenteeism and improve organizational commitment by helping employees reduce financial stress through effective workplace financial education programs."[3] Kim and Garman also show that financial education gives participants more confidence that they are making the right investments:

> *Workplace financial education programs have been found to increase the participants' confidence in their investment decisions, change their attitudes in positive directions ... and improve their financial management, such as saving more money.... Workers who attended financial education seminars and workshops reported less financial stress, and greater financial well-being than those who did not.*

In this chapter we look at financial education, advice, and retirement planning, including the types of programs offered by employers today. We also discuss managed account programs.

WHY PLAN SPONSORS PROVIDE EDUCATION AND ADVICE

Plan sponsors may offer education and advice for many reasons. For instance, they may offer it out of altruism, knowing that their employees need this type of support. Or they may provide it understanding that this help may reduce absenteeism and therefore produce a cost savings for their organization. Others perhaps are interested in reducing the phone calls and questions they receive from their workers. Surveys point to other primary reasons for offering such programs. For instance, according to a Profit Sharing/401k Council of America (PSCA) survey, 33 percent of plan sponsors said that their desire to increase plan participation is the primary purpose of providing education.[4] This may be for the benefit of the worker; however, often it is to make sure the plan meets the discrimination testing, thus allowing higher-paid workers to contribute the maximum amount. If lower-paid workers are not participating, government rules require that higher-paid workers' contributions to the plan be reduced.

PSCA's survey shows the second most common purpose for providing education is the plan sponsors' desire to "increase appreciation for the plan" among its workers. Notably, for the largest plans (those with 5,000+ participants), increasing participation was the number-one goal; for the smallest plans (those with fewer than 50 people), increasing participation was most important. Other reasons PSCA shows for offering education are to improve asset allocation, reduce fiduciary liability, introduce plan changes, and increase deferral rates.

IS ADVICE NEEDED WHEN A PLAN HAS AUTO-ENROLLMENT AND TARGET-DATE STRATEGIES?

Plan sponsors may wonder whether education and advice are needed once both auto-enrollment and target-date strategies are in place. By automatically enrolling participants, the plan sponsor does not need to spend endless time and money trying to convince the employee to participate. Plus, don't target-date strategies replace advice? Don't they answer the question "How should I allocate my money?" In some ways they do, since so many asset allocation decisions are already made for the participant under this system. Yet is that enough? Don't participants need advice beyond asset allocation?

Most of us would argue that yes, participants do need additional education and advice. While auto-enrollment, contribution escalation, and target-date strategies contribute notably to addressing the need to educate workers about participation, contribution levels, and asset allocation, they fall short in a number of key areas. For instance, they do not help employees understand how to manage credit card debt, ways to go about buying a first home, or how to finance a child's education. Employees who are in debt or who are wondering how to buy a home or cover a child's education may see these as reasons to not participate in their plan. Or they may take out loans or even cash out their savings when they change jobs, thus undermining their retirement savings.

More relevant perhaps is helping employees understand *how much* they need to save in their plans and what their savings may translate into in terms of monthly income during retirement. Further, educating them on types of risk and providing advice on how to manage those risks is critical. For instance, education can help participants understand the impact of saving at a higher rate versus taking on a higher level of market risk. Programs also may help them understand the need for health and disability insurance.

EDUCATION AND ADVICE OFFERED BY PLAN SPONSORS

Employees tend to receive a wealth of materials in print, online, or both that describe the plan and its investment offerings. Such materials typically include enrollment kits, fund performance sheets, and seminars or workshops. They may also include retirement gap calculators to help employees determine how much more they may need to save or other modeling software. In addition to these education programs, PSCA reports that just over half of plan sponsors offer advice. This might take the form of one-on-one counseling sessions (most prevalent for the smallest employers) or via an Internet provider (most common for the largest employers), or, less typically, via a telephone hotline. While advice programs are offered by half of plan sponsors, PSCA reports that less than a third of plan participants utilize these services when they are made available. These numbers may appear disappointing. Yet many participants, especially those closer to retirement with larger balances and higher incomes, may seek advice outside of the plan. Unfortunately, for younger and lower-paid workers, the cost of outside advice often is too expensive for them to pursue. As a result, these workers are the ones who are likely to benefit most from plan sponsor-provided programs.

Hewitt Associates offers a look at how education and advice programs have grown over time. As shown in Table 12.1, education, advice, and financial counseling have all grown in prevalence. Of note, Hewitt considers target-date strategies as a type of guidance or advice. Asset-allocation advice

TABLE 12.1 Forms of Help Provided to Plan Participants

	2005	2007	2009
Target-date funds	28%	52%	79%
Seminars/workshops	19%	20%	33%
Advice	15%	20%	31%
One-on-one financial counseling*	19%	22%	29%
Online guidance	16%	18%	28%
Managed accounts	6%	11%	25%

Source: Hewitt Associates, 2009. *Includes in-person and via phone.

offered within the target-date strategies is the most dominant form of support put forth by plan sponsors today. Perhaps this is not surprising, given the statistics provided earlier, which show that so few participants utilize other forms of advice, when offered.

However, even with the preponderance of target-date strategies, plan sponsors have not backed away from offering other types of education and advice. In fact, these programs have increased across the board. Seminars or workshops, as well as online advice and guidance, are being offered by nearly a third of plan sponsors. One-on-one financial counseling, whether over the phone or in person, also is provided by close to a third of companies. This type of individual counseling tends to go beyond asset-allocation and retirement-gap issues to address the breadth of financial planning concerns, such as debt management, college savings, home financing, insurance needs, and other personal matters. Finally, managed account programs have increased as well and are now available at close to 25 percent of companies.

Plan sponsors often ask whether managed accounts make sense in a plan if target-date strategies are offered. I believe they can exist in harmony, as different participants will prefer one type of program over another. Let us look at how plan sponsor thinking has evolved from simply offering basic education, to guidance, to online advice, to managed accounts.

EVOLUTION FROM EDUCATION TO MANAGED ACCOUNTS

As mentioned, the majority of plans provide basic education on how the plan works and the investments provided within it. In the early days, this material may have included a sample of asset-allocation pie charts using the asset categories offered in the plan. For decades, plan sponsors tried to steer clear of offering "advice" and held firmly to the idea of providing guidance only. The delineation between the two may be challenging, but a line can be drawn between suggesting an allocation at the asset-class level versus suggesting a specific fund. For instance, telling participants they may want to have 20 percent of their assets in small-cap equity is different from telling them to invest 20 percent in the XYZ Small Company mutual fund.

Clearly, plan participants wanted much more than guidance. They wanted someone not only to direct them to the asset class but also to tell them exactly what investment to select. Most plan sponsors were not willing to offer that level of direction, and, unfortunately, the cost of going to an investment advisor was prohibitive for most workers. In the 1990s, with the advent of Internet-delivered investment advice, many in the industry thought that we had found the silver bullet to providing advice to the masses at a reasonable cost.

At long last, online advice providers came onto the scene, offering to answer plan participants' number-one question: How should I invest my money? Early entrants included 401(k) Forum (which later became mPower and then was bought by Morningstar Associates), Financial Engines, Ibbotson Associates, and Morningstar Associates. All of these firms offered Internet-based advice models that could be integrated into a benefits platform, and all of these models showed participants a projected value for their account based on three key variables: savings rate, risk tolerance, and retirement age. Participants could change any one of these variables to improve their projected retirement results. Each model would show their current investment portfolio and suggest an improved portfolio requiring a reallocation of assets. These models provided a clear advance relative to the early static asset-allocation pies and risk quizzes, which were all that many plans provided.

Unfortunately, despite the low cost, ease of use, and integration of these models with their benefit sites, the vast majority of workers did not use them. Advice providers came up with an ingenious solution: If participants would not use the advice on their own, then they would do it for them. This was the start of "managed accounts." Applying the same advice that participants would receive if they ran a model on their own, advice firms could structure individual asset allocations among the core investment options in the plan. Not only could they provide this managed account service to those electing to use it, they also could provide it as a default investment option instead of a target-date or other balanced strategy. In fact, as you may recall, the Department of Labor identified this investment approach as one of the three qualified default investment alternatives along with balanced (risk-based) funds and target-date strategies (age-based funds).

Managed accounts allow plan participants to hand over the reins of managing their defined contribution (DC) assets to a professional investment manager, typically for a fee. The managed account provider then connects electronically with the record keeper to take over the quarterly evaluation and rebalancing of the accounts of those who sign up for these services. Managed account providers have a range of philosophies about how to manage asset allocations. On one end of the spectrum, a provider may use the simple heuristic of 100 minus the participant's age to determine the equity allocation. On the other end of the spectrum, providers utilize far more sophisticated models.

Some plan sponsors have found that using managed accounts as a default for their DC plan makes sense. For instance, McDonald's Corporation has selected managed accounts as the default for its plan. Participants who fail to make an investment selection are automatically defaulted into a managed account based on their age. Karen Barnes, ERISA counsel at McDonald's, discusses how it has incorporated managed accounts into its DC plan, offering investment guidance to participants, including an "online-advice firm and a full-service financial planning/investment organization."[5] McDonald's manages its plan "conservatively in terms of the number and the types of investment choices" and "also offer[s] investment advice to encourage participants to contribute at an appropriate level and to allocate assets based on their preferences." When asked how the DC plan is evolving over time, Barnes replied that McDonald's is "constantly redesigning the plan and the menu of choices to adapt to changes in our workforce, the business environment, and the DC environment. We seek out employees' opinions to gain insight into their needs and perceived value of plan changes."

Barnes emphasized that the services added in the DC plan, including managed accounts, are set up to attract talented employees to the company and to provide them with the best retirement guidance possible. "Our founder Ray Kroc used to say, 'Take good care of those who work for you, and you will float to greatness on their achievements.' It's a wonderful quote because it reflects what corporate benefits are all about."

According to the PSCA survey, only 2.9 percent of sponsors offer managed accounts as their *default* investment option within their plan, rather they typically default new hires into the target-date strategies based on their age.

Managed accounts provide a step forward for DC plans, yet as with target-date and other balanced strategies, they also require scrutiny. Plan sponsors should take a look at the default asset allocation in particular and evaluate it in the same way they would a target-date or other asset allocation strategy. Managed account providers may argue that their advice cannot be evaluated or benchmarked, since it is individualized. However, if participants can be defaulted based on their age, these defaults create a glide path that can be evaluated side by side with other default alternatives.

Ask managed account providers to show you the default for 20-year-olds, 25-year-olds, 30-year-olds, and so on. Use this set of defaults to compare the asset allocation relative to the target date or other alternatives that you may consider for your plan. Then look at the projected income replacement when you take into account all of the costs of each approach. This analysis should help you determine the appropriate direction for your plan. This is particularly important if you are considering managed accounts as the default because it is possible that those participants who are defaulted into these accounts may not take advantage of the individual tailoring offered by the provider; for instance, they may not change the assumed retirement date, risk level, or add in outside assets. Most participants may not have outside assets to add into the model. Further, they may have no understanding of their individual risk preference. As a result, the main variable used to determine the risk category into which they will be defaulted will be their age, which means the managed account has the same default basis as target-date strategies.

COMPARISON OF MANAGED ACCOUNTS AND CUSTOM TARGET-DATE STRATEGIES

As you consider the advice underlying managed accounts or their implied glide path, we at PIMCO encourage you to compare this glide path to the one embedded within your custom target-date strategies. Some advice providers can work with you to integrate your custom glide path into the advice models. This will help enable plan participants either to go with the default glide path or to be redirected to a mix of core funds that use the same asset allocation philosophy yet may be modified, based on their desired retirement age, outside funding, or risk preferences.

As with target-date strategies, it is advisable to set up an ongoing benchmarking methodology for managed accounts and other advice models. Look at how well your participants have fared under the advice provided by these programs. Also determine how the models deal with inflation-protection assets such as Treasury Inflation Protected Securities to confirm whether the provider can allocate to these diversifying, inflation-protecting strategies.

As we have seen, a plan *can* offer *both* target-date strategies and managed accounts. You may find that one part of your population is attracted to target-date strategies while another is interested in managed accounts. Again, offering an asset-allocation philosophy that remains in sync across the choices provided in the two offerings is important.

A 2009 Hewitt Associates and Financial Engines study of seven large plans found that on average 25 percent of participants use asset allocation help provided by their employer. Three forms of "help" were included: target-date strategies, online investment advice, and discretionary managed accounts. The study counted participants who were invested in managed accounts, held allocations of 95 percent or more in target-date strategies, or had received specific investment advice recommendations in the past year. The research found that age was more predictive than balances in determining what type of help is used: "older participants were 50 percent more likely to use managed accounts" while "younger participants were twice as likely to use online advice."[6]

ADVICE BEYOND ASSET ALLOCATION

Managed accounts and advice models can be particularly attractive because they not only provide asset allocation for participants but also provide a projection of each participant's retirement income needs and identify whether a savings gap may exist. Once participants see this savings gap, the hope is that they will increase their savings rate to help close it. According to Paul Solman, business and economics correspondent for the *PBS NewsHour with Jim Lehrer*, one reason it is important for participants to have models to help them understand adequate retirement savings is because most employees are confused about what it means to save: "Everyone knows Ben Franklin's misquoted aphorism, 'A penny saved is a penny earned.' Actually, he wrote that a penny saved" is two pence dear. "Franklin's point: savings, if invested, will grow with time. But as Andy Tobias puts it in his *The Only Investment Guide You'll Ever Need*, 'a penny saved is two pennies earned'... because of taxes. That is, you have to earn two pennies (at a 50 percent tax rate) for every one you save." Since both men are right, Solman says a penny saved could be worth millions—eventually.[7]

Solman went on to state that most participants do not understand that saving and investing are two distinct and separate processes. He quipped that instead of stuffing your money into your mattress or letting it languish in your bank account, "you can do any number of other things with those savings, and many of those things are forms of investment—doing something with the money so that it (hopefully) generates a greater potential return in the future."

Helping participants understand that they may need to save more (which will likely be true for most people) is invaluable. Ideally, the models translate their savings rates into a monthly income that will help employees to understand the value of their projected savings in today's dollars. In other words, models show participants, based on their savings rate and asset allocation, what they may have in monthly income at retirement after accounting for the likely erosion of inflation. Here it is important for plan sponsors to look at the assumptions underlying the provider's models. For example, if the capital market assumptions, such as investment returns, appear high (e.g., 10 percent for large-cap equity), the model may be offering overly optimistic projections for participants. Further, asking how a model deals with inflation is important because showing participants what they need in nominal dollars (before inflation) may lead to undersaving.

Anna Rappaport, president of Anna Rappaport Consulting and chair of the Society of Actuaries Committee on Post Retirement Needs and Risks, addressed the importance of having good models for how much participants should save. Even though the 2009 Retirement Risk Survey conducted by the SOA indicates that many people hope to retire later than originally planned, many people will likely end up retiring earlier than they wish, for various reasons, such as health problems and outdated skills. Therefore, having a realistic model of what adequate retirement savings levels would be—and actually saving that money every month—is important.

To help participants achieve this goal, Rappaport felt that plan sponsors need to look for software models that include assumptions about inflation and rising healthcare costs. "One of the challenges in DC planning and in determining how much to save, is that you don't know what investment returns or inflation will be. If you consider results over a long time, the state of the economy, inflation and the particular point in time at which people retire influence success in building assets."

As discussed in Chapter 6 on communications, showing participants what their retirement life may be like based on their current savings rate may be enough to change their behavior. That is well and good; however, do they need more help than this?

ADVICE BEYOND ADVICE MODELS

While many, if not most, participants will be well served with advice models that answer their top questions—How should I invest my money? How much do I need to save for retirement?—others will be seeking answers to other very critical questions, such as:

- Should I take a loan from my plan to pay off credit card debt or for my child's education?
- Should I keep my money in the plan or roll to an individual retirement account (IRA)?
- How can I manage my money to meet my retirement-income needs?

Barbara Kontje, director of retirement plan investments at American Express, discussed the need for plan sponsors to create greater financial literacy in their workforce. "Employees come to work. They're concerned about paying their mortgages, paying for their cars, saving for retirement, saving for their children's educations, taking vacations. They have so many concerns. Some don't all have the necessary skills to balance those needs. So they worry about it. It's important to master the basics of life."[8] She emphasized helping people learn how to invest for the future now, in the present, so that they feel financially empowered rather than helpless and confused.

> *We need to help people understand the ways to invest for the future, do all the right things today, and still have enough money remaining to live and do what they want. We don't want people to feel as if they're saving for retirement but retirement may never come because they can't afford to retire. Given the market volatility, people need to see that it's still important to save now, even with all that's going on.*

Models and Internet tools may not always be adequate at answering these more personal questions. Certainly online education and modeling can help, yet at some point, providing a participant access to a knowledgeable advisor makes sense. Identifying objective advisors who can provide comprehensive financial planning to your participants is certainly something plan sponsors should consider.

WHAT IS FINANCIAL PLANNING?

Self-help books, finance software packages, and magazines help individuals with financial planning, but it is challenging to be one's own financial planner for a number of reasons. To create a successful financial plan, people have to understand levels of risk in their portfolio as well as their personal risk tolerance. They need to understand how to adjust savings and investments not only to provide for retirement but also to accommodate changing family circumstances, such as the birth of a new baby, saving for children's college education, or unexpected expenses, such as health challenges or taking care of aging parents. Most of the time, an expert can do a better job of helping with long-term planning and setting up a strong investment portfolio. Yet beyond all of these reasons, another critical factor in using an advisor is to be motivated to address the tough issues and to take action. Just as with a personal trainer, a good planner can offer encouragement and support for participants to set up a healthy financial program.

Participants often do not understand what financial planning is. They may think it is only about investing, or that such services are restricted to the wealthy or elderly. The Financial Planning Association explains that financial planning "is about helping individuals and families, regardless of age and financial circumstances, envision and realize their dreams and goals by marshaling and managing their financial resources."[9] A good part of an advisor's time is spent on retirement-planning issues. Just as you would with managed accounts and target-date glide paths, if you plan to select an advisor or advisory firm to provide retirement-income planning for your participants, take a look at its process, approach, and models. Is the firm's advice in sync with your philosophies? Are the models reasonable? What capital market assumptions is it using? Does it account for issues such as inflation or longevity in planning models?

Participants and plan sponsors also need to make sure that providers are making comprehensive financial planning available rather than just investment management. If you are considering offering financial planning to your participants, ask the providers about their credentials and planning process as well as how they are compensated. Unfortunately, anyone can call him- or herself a financial planner without even a single credential. Perhaps someone has filled out a form or taken a securities exam; this is not enough. Look for relevant experience as well as financial planning credentials.

Perhaps the most respected credential among financial planners is the CFP mark, the Certified Financial Planner™ designation. Professionals with this credential typically have completed a comprehensive course of study at a college or a university that offers a financial planning curriculum approved by the CFP Board. Plus, they have passed the comprehensive two-day, 10-hour CFP® Certification Examination, which covers the financial planning process, tax planning, employee benefits and retirement planning, estate planning, investment management, and insurance. In addition, they must have three years' minimum experience in the financial planning process prior to earning the right to use the mark. Finally, these practitioners agree to abide by a strict code of professional conduct and must pass a background check by the CFP Board.

FINANCIAL PLANNING PROCESS

The Certified Financial Planner Board of Standards, Inc., describes the six-step process of financial planning:[10]

1. **Establishing and defining the client-planner relationship.** The financial planner should clearly explain or document the services to be provided to you and define both his and your responsibilities. The planner should

explain fully how he will be paid and by whom. You and the planner should agree on how long the professional relationship should last and on how decisions will be made.

2. **Gathering client data, including goals.** The financial planner should ask for information about your financial situation. You and the planner should mutually define your personal and financial goals, understand your time frame for results, and discuss, if relevant, how you feel about risk. The financial planner should gather all the necessary documents before giving you the advice you need.

3. **Analyzing and evaluating your financial status.** The financial planner should analyze your information to assess your current situation and determine what you must do to meet your goals. Depending on what services you have asked for, this could include analyzing your assets, liabilities and cash flow, current insurance coverage, investments, or tax strategies.

4. **Developing and presenting financial planning recommendations and/or alternatives.** The financial planner should offer financial planning recommendations that address your goals, based on the information you provide. The planner should go over the recommendations with you to help you understand them so that you can make informed decisions. The planner should also listen to your concerns and revise the recommendations as appropriate.

5. **Implementing the financial planning recommendations.** You and the planner should agree on how the recommendations will be carried out. The planner may carry out the recommendations or serve as your "coach," coordinating the whole process with you and other professionals such as attorneys or stockbrokers.

6. **Monitoring the financial planning recommendations.** You and the planner should agree on who will monitor your progress towards your goals. If the planner is in charge of the process, she should report to you periodically to review your situation and adjust the recommendations, if needed, as your life changes.

Again, planners without certification and those who fail to follow a planning process may not be planners at all. Take a look at their training, plus how they are paid.

FINANCIAL PLANNING FEES

Plan participants often have trouble understanding how financial planners get paid, and sometimes they are afraid to ask. Financial planners can be paid in a number of different ways, and each has its merits.

Depending on the participant's financial situation, one payment method may be superior to the next. What is important is that the participant should have a clear understanding of an advisor's fees prior to entering into a relationship.

The Financial Planning Association explains the ways planners may charge.[11]

Fee-only
All of the financial planner's compensation from his or her client work comes exclusively from the clients in the form of fixed, flat, hourly, percentage, or performance-based fees.

Commission-only
There is no charge for the planner's advice or preparation of a financial plan. Compensation is received solely from the sale of financial products you agree to purchase in order to implement financial planning recommendations.

Combination Fee/Commission
A fee is charged for consultation, advice, and financial plan preparation on an hourly, project, or percentage basis. In addition, the planner may receive commissions from the sale of recommended products used to implement your plan.

Salary
Some planners work on a salary and bonus basis for financial services firms.

The association warns: "In all of the above categories of compensation, you should request information on any real or potential conflicts of interest. In addition to commissions received from any financial product sales, you should ask whether there are outside incentives or bonuses to be gained by the planner for certain recommendations."

Plan sponsors can help DC plan participants understand what financial planning is, how to find a certified planner, and how they charge fees. Yet sponsors may want to go a step further in offering these services directly to their participants. Doing this may include hiring salaried professionals as staff members or providing access to them on-site, at their offices, or via a call center.

Georgette Gestely, director of the New York City Deferred Compensation Program, commented that even though the Pension Protection Act states "that advice is now going to be protected," the city's board of directors was still uncomfortable about giving advice.[12]

But it allowed us to think about how far we could go with our employee education without moving into the realm of advice. Since then, we started a financial-planning component. We hired a company with Certified Financial Planner™ practitioners to sit in our office and give free financial planning seminars to participants, to help people see the deferred compensation plan as just a piece of a larger financial picture, and to help them understand how it fits into a complete financial world. The seminars are by invitation only, but we're slowly making our way through the population.

Here are some ways a plan sponsor may offer access to financial planners:

- **Integrated call center services.** Your DC provider may offer services from a salaried financial advisory team. This could be an excellent solution, especially when the advisors are able to see into participants' DC accounts and help them with many of the questions posed earlier. These professionals may help participants with debt management, college savings, retirement planning, and more. As salaried professionals, they can help participants with questions such as: Should I stay in the plan, roll over, or take an annuity? They are likely to provide advice or guidance without bias to winning a retiree's account or selling a product.

- **Third-party advice call centers.** You may be able to hire an independent advice provider via an accounting or financial firm. While such a firm may not have access to participants' benefits information, they may have extensive information on the plan. This guidance or advice may be paid for by the employer or through an annual fee charged to participants, much like a flexible benefit. These professionals can provide many of the benefits of unbiased advice, such as helping participants understand why they may want to remain in the plan.

- **In-person advice.** Advisors who work through a broker/dealer, insurance company, or other financial services firm may offer to work with your participants. It is critical to understand the breadth of their offerings and how the firms are paid for their time. While some may offer "free" financial planning, be careful to understand the ultimate cost of these services. This is not to say that such offers should be turned down. Often the support provided is very attractive and may be one of the only alternatives for participants who cannot afford the cost of a fee-only financial planner. Again, make sure that these providers have professional credentials, such as the CFP mark. Also, be careful if you want to retain retiree assets in your DC plan, as many of these planners may encourage participants to roll out of your plan to an IRA, which allows them to actively manage the retirees' assets and to establish ongoing compensation for their services. Again, this is not necessarily bad, you simply need to be aware of a potential conflict of interest.

Employees should be encouraged to create a comprehensive financial plan. However, we know from experience that many participants generally begin to plan only when there is an urgent need to do so. This often happens when a life-changing event occurs, such as getting married (and needing to set up a good retirement plan in case you outlive your spouse), having a child (and realizing you must plan for his or her college education), or the death of a loved one (realizing that you are not immortal and also that health challenges can cause a catastrophic drain on inadequate retirement funds). Providing benefit Web sites and support to help plan for significant life changes can be invaluable. While we regularly purchase items such as a new car, a television set, or a new wardrobe, most people do not stop to consider that "the most expensive thing that you will likely ever buy in your lifetime is ... your retirement."[13] No doubt, comprehensive financial planning may be an aspiration for many, yet anything a sponsor can do to encourage participants to take action—even if it is just a small piece of planning—is a step in the right direction.

IN CLOSING

As Dallas Salisbury, president and chief executive of the Employee Benefit Research Institute, said, the Baby Boomer generation is facing a lot of tough decisions as they approach retirement age, especially in this challenging economy. Can they retire as early as they planned? Since they will likely be living longer, how will they make sure they can afford good health care? Will Social Security still be strong? "Those may be family conversations, since boomers tend to talk to their kids more about finances than their parents did, and as more boomers come up against the line."[14]

Along with these concerns, Salisbury stated, employees are going to need and are going to be seeking more financial guidance and advice not only from employers but from policy makers as well.

I'm optimistic that financial literacy, investor behavior, and personal preparation are going to improve. And employers will likely be there to help because it's how they may convince people to come work for them in an increasingly tight labor market. The data says we know what we need to do. The probability is that we'll do more of it—and a better job of it—in the future. And the results should be better.

Offering adequate retirement advice involves more than just helping participants allocate their assets. In many ways, target-date strategies have already addressed that pressing question. Participants also need help with other critical financial management questions related to financing a home, providing a college education for their children, and various issues that will likely arise in retirement. Plan sponsors can bring significant value to participants by screening services in the market and offering access to programs that will help reduce the cost of financial advice and help participants plan at a reasonable cost. Encouraging participants to produce a comprehensive financial plan may help reduce stress about the future.

In the next chapter we take a closer look at retirement-income strategies and approaches.

CHAPTER 13

Retirement Income
and Guarantees

Plan sponsors increasingly ponder whether they should help participants manage their retirement income. Some may argue that it is not their place to help retirees; rather their focus should be on current workers. In addition, retirees can find endless help for their retirement needs in the retail market. Others, however, may argue that the cost and confusion in the retail market are too great for retirees to manage on their own and that there may be advantages to the plan in helping retirees.

As custom target retirement-date strategies come of age, plan sponsors are seriously considering whether to offer participants guidance about managing their assets beyond retirement. Georgette Gestely, director of the New York City Deferred Compensation Program, encourages retirees to retain their assets in the plan after retirement. She shared her philosophy on managing the plan for both current participants and retirees:

> Whereas a DB plan's investments are the employer's responsibility, a DC plan's financial implications, in the end, fall on the employee. We adhere to a good-faith contract that says, "I'm offering you a plan and I'll do my best to offer you the best plan and to give you the best information about how to create the best outcome. And that's why you should be comfortable investing here."[1]

Today, more plan sponsors are interested in helping participants not only accumulate assets *for* retirement but also convert those assets into monthly income *at* retirement. As sponsors consider the markets and retirement-income needs of retirees, they may be looking for payout alternatives that possibly offer participants a guarantee. For instance, Barbara Kontje, director of retirement plan investments at American Express, pointed out that, following the economic downturn of 2008 and 2009, plan participants would like to know that there are some guarantees or insurance built into their retirement plan:

Everybody's gotten shaken up by this. But participants are starting to look for more help. Eventually, plan sponsors may begin to look at annuity-types of payments again. Alternatively, participants may start looking for annuity products to purchase on their own.[2]

So, if we want to extend the responsibility for our defined contribution (DC) plans into retirement by offering participants payout options and possibly guarantees, along with support and professional oversight that will help make their retirement investments last a lifetime, how best can we do that? In this chapter we take a look at the ways that plan sponsors can help participants with retirement income. To start off the discussion, let us consider the ways participants can convert retirement assets into retirement income. There are three basic approaches to consider:

1. **Income-only plan.** Those with sufficient wealth may manage their assets so that they can live off the income from those assets without spending the principal. This plan may include income from bonds, such as Treasury Inflation Protected Securities (TIPS) or nominal bonds in pretax accounts (such as DC plans or individual retirement accounts [IRAs]). It may also include municipal bonds in after-tax brokerage or savings accounts. In addition, participants might consider laddering certificates of deposit (CDs) or look to stock holdings for dividend income. Purchasing real estate can also provide rental or other income. If income from these possible sources is insufficient, however, the retiree may need to dip into principal.
2. **Systematic/partial withdrawal plans (SWPs).** Most retirees lack sufficient assets to live solely off the income generated by those assets. Rather, they will need to begin drawing down principal in addition to investment income. There are several ways to set up a SWP, such as withdrawing a fixed-dollar amount adjusted for inflation, taking a required minimum distribution amount that increases the percentage of assets withdrawn as the participant ages, or setting up a retirement bucket approach that earmarks certain assets to meet specific expenses. Many advisors who advocate a SWP approach suggest that retirees draw down no more than 4 to 5 percent of their retirement assets each year. Yet even at this withdrawal rate, participants risk running out of money too quickly. As discussed in earlier chapters, if a participant hits a prolonged bear market (particularly in the early years of retirement), a market shock, or a high inflationary period, a SWP approach may fail. Later in this

chapter we take a closer look at the probability of this strategy lasting through retirement.

3. **Guaranteed income/annuitization.** Those with a lower risk tolerance or a greater expectation of longevity may want to convert a portion of their DC or other retirement assets into an immediate or other type of income-producing annuity. In essence, by annuitizing, retirees create an income stream that provides a monthly payout for the remainder of their lives. This income stream is typically paid nominally (i.e., not adjusted for inflation); however, several insurance companies offer the ability to increase the payouts by a set percent each year or even index the payout to inflation. Further, annuities may also be variable, meaning that they are tied to investment returns (e.g., if the investment market values increase, the annuity payouts may rise). Many types of annuities are being introduced within DC plans, including immediate, deferred fixed income, living benefit, and longevity insurance. In the next discussion, we consider a few of the product types offered in the DC market today.

Concerns raised with annuities often include the possible loss of control over your money, the cost of the products, the inability to leave money for bequests, and, overall, the feeling of being comfortable having a sizable account value one day and then becoming a pensioner and feeling less secure as the retiree converts a percentage of retirement assets into a far-less-impressive monthly paycheck. Insurance companies have worked to address some of these concerns within some of the newer products in the market.

Retirees may decide to pursue a combination of some or all of the listed approaches as they structure what they consider to be an appropriate retirement-income stream. For instance, they may create one account, perhaps income only or SWP, to cover certain types of expenses and then may use another pool of assets to buy a single annuity or even several annuities over time. Laddering income annuities may provide retirees with the benefit of buying only when annuity purchase rates or interest rates or the value of their invested assets may be higher. In addition, buying annuities as a person grows older causes the payout to increase since the expected number of years the insurance company will need to pay decreases with life expectancy. Similarly, if the annuity is purchased on a deferred basis, the cost of purchasing the annuity will be lower, because of the mortality and interest discounting.

Susan Bradley, financial planner and author of *Sudden Money*, suggests that retirees look over their retirement assets and then divide them into "buckets" of money, each one tagged to cover a particular type of living expense—and even allow for some further investment if possible.

The first bucket is discretionary cash to cover food, clothing, enter-tainment, transportation and travel—expenses over which you have some control. It's the most obvious category. We have to account for inflation. So if we target, say, $80,000 of expenditures a year today, we need to make sure the lifestyle that costs $80,000 today is still affordable in 20 or 30 years when it costs $150,000. The sec-ond bucket is for relatively fixed and generally mandatory expenses such as mortgage payments, property taxes, and maybe insurance. The third bucket is for emergency funding to cover unexpected costs such as roof repair. Finally, the last bucket is for investing.[3]

Bradley points out that if the first three buckets are well designed to cover "variable, fixed and unexpected expenses, the final investment bucket may drop in value for periods of time, yet the retiree's basic lifestyle isn't in jeopardy." She also suggests ways to match each retirement asset with the perfect bucket; for example, she suggests covering cash-flow needs with the 401(k) and using "Social Security income to cover fixed expenses such as property taxes." Others may suggest matching retirement income with built-in inflationary adjustments to expenses most likely to be sensitive to price rises, thus ensuring that the income source tagged to cover a particular expense keeps pace with that cost as it increases with inflation. In a way, this bucket approach, or income-to-expense matching, is similar to the liability matching conducted in the defined benefit world. That is, many pension managers mitigate risk by matching assets to liabilities in a liability-driven investment framework. Individuals can do the same.

Now that we have considered the many ways that retirees may structure income in retirement, the next question we ponder is whether any or all of these goals can be achieved within a DC plan. Much of the answer to that question will depend on the interest of a plan sponsor in retaining retiree assets in the plan and willingness to offer investment solutions as well as distribution flexibility to support retiree needs. From an operational perspective, a DC plan may offer retirees access to any one of the three income approaches outlined earlier. However, it is up to the plan sponsor to make the necessary products available and then to provide the distribution flexibility to allow retirees to structure the desired income stream.

As we consider ways to create retirement income, the first question plan sponsors should answer is whether they want to encourage plan participants to retain their assets in the plan. Next, they will want to consider whether they should offer their participants in-plan guaranteed retirement-income options or income payout options at retirement. Let us start with a look at whether plan sponsors should encourage former participants to retain their assets in the plan.

ENCOURAGE PARTICIPANTS TO STAY IN THE PLAN OR GO?

Recent retirement trends, such as higher plan costs, increases in job turnover, and concern with retirement-income adequacy, have encouraged employers to examine more closely the impact past employees' DC rollover decisions have on them and their current plan participants. Today, employers are beginning to ask themselves whether former employees should stay in the plan or go. In other words, should former employees retain their assets in the employer's plan or take their assets with them, roll them into an IRA or into a new employer's plan, or cash out?

Increasingly, employers are interested in retaining past employees' (particularly retirees') DC plan balances within the plan rather than encouraging them to roll their balances over to an IRA or new plan. The Profit Sharing/ 401k Council of America (PSCA) reports that over 21 percent of plan participants are no longer actively employed by the plan-sponsoring company.[4] Given the larger retiree balances, the percentage of assets from past employees in an employer's DC plan is often as high as 50 to 60 percent of total plan assets. Retiree assets are likely to make up the majority of that percentage. According to PSCA, by the time average retirees leave an organization, they have worked 16.8 years. That is a long time to accumulate a healthy DC account balance. In many cases, whether a company wants a past employee to stay with the plan or move assets out of the plan depends on one major factor: cost.[5]

Why Encourage Them to Stay?

Given the expected outflow of assets with the upcoming baby boomer retirements, many employers see the retention of assets as a tool to positively and significantly reduce DC plan costs for all participants. Retaining the accounts of retirees may be the most effective way of keeping plan costs low for all participants. According to the PSCA 2008 survey data as plotted in Table 13.1, 75 percent of plans allow terminated vested participants ages 65 and older to remain in their plan. This percent is up from two-thirds of plans in 1998. Notably, the largest plans, with over 5,000 participants, are far more interested in retaining retiree accounts; the vast majority (87 percent) allow those 65 or older to stay. In contrast, in small plans with fewer than 50 participants, a smaller majority (66 percent) of sponsors allows retirees to remain.

Employers may encourage former employees and retirees to stay in the plan as long as possible, as the former employees typically can enjoy a lower cost of investment management by remaining in their past employer's plan versus rolling to an IRA. Yet former employees are not the only ones

TABLE 13.1 Percent of Plans Allowing
Retirees to Retain Assets after Age 65

No. Participants	1998	2008
1–49	42.2	65.7
50–199	57.7	67.9
200–999	77.9	75.8
1000–4999	75.4	76.0
5000	84.9	87.3
Total	66.4	74.6

Source: Profit Sharing/401k Council of America. Hypothetical example for illustrative purposes only.

who may benefit. By retaining their assets in the plan (especially retirees' larger balances), economies of scale may reduce the effective cost of asset management as well as the average participant record-keeping charge. Some companies also are taking steps to encourage younger employees, who are more likely to change jobs multiple times throughout their careers, to keep their assets in their DC plans to achieve this additional cost savings.

More specifically, by retaining assets of past employees in the plan, a company's plan participants may benefit in these ways:

- **Lower the cost of investment management for all participants.** When more employees stay in the plan and as assets rise, the cost of these funds may decline as a percentage of assets. There is a greater potential for this to be true for plans that use nonmutual funds, such as separately managed accounts and collective trusts.
- **Spread the cost of administration to a larger base.** Many companies pass the administration fees of the DC plan back to participants by paying them from plan assets (and charging the fees to participants' accounts). A larger number of DC participants, and thus a larger base of plan assets, often reduces the per-participant administration cost. This is especially true if companies retain larger account balances in their DC plans rather than small accounts that could drive up administrative costs.
- **Increase revenue sharing from mutual fund companies.** For plans that invest in mutual funds, often revenue sharing is paid by the fund companies to help support plan administration. For instance, a fund company may pay 25 to 35 basis points (bps) on the assets invested via the plan in its mutual funds. Naturally, this revenue sharing will increase as assets increase; thus, retaining large balances from retirees may benefit the plan. Yet from a total cost perspective, the plan may be better served

by moving to lower-cost investment vehicles that do not offer revenue sharing at all. This is an issue we addressed in Chapter 5 on plan costs.

- **Provide a lower-cost savings program to retirees and other past employees.** Relative to the retail market, retaining assets in the DC plan may save a retiree a considerable amount of money. It would not be surprising to have the total investment cost within the plan to be over 100 bps lower than investing via an IRA in the retail market. That 100 bps savings can make a significant difference in the life of DC assets during retirement years, perhaps extending the drawdown on the assets by several years.

Why Encourage Them to Leave?

A small percentage of plan sponsors would prefer to make a clean break with former employees upon termination of employment, encouraging them to take their DC plan balances with them when they leave. Such companies tend to be influenced by a number of factors, including:

- **Investment cost reduction appears unattainable.** Many DC plans use mutual funds that do not enable cost savings as assets in the plan rise. These funds could be moved to lower-cost funds as assets increase, but in some cases, it may not be worthwhile to do so. The decision is typically driven by plan size and investable assets per fund.
- **Administrative costs may rise as former employees retain assets in the plan.** Companies with an unusually large number of small account balances recognize that total DC plan costs will rise if exiting employees leave their small accounts in the plan. In such cases, cost savings, whether from revenue offsets from mutual funds or economic gain via spreading the plan costs across a wider asset base, may be unachievable.
- **Continued connection with past employees may be undesirable as it may create a potential liability.** Given the increasing number of lawsuits by employees who voice dissatisfaction with the plan, some companies are concerned that retaining the accounts of terminated employees may subject the organization or trustees to heightened fiduciary liability.

How to Encourage Participants to Stay in the Plan

If you wish to encourage participants to stay in the plan, you should consider:

- Structuring the plan to manage the types of risk retirees face
- Increasing distribution flexibility
- Adding retirement-income products
- Allowing consolidation of outside assets into the plan

Structuring the Plan to Manage Risks Faced in Retirement   Much of what we discussed in the prior sections on risk management applies directly to helping retirees who decide to remain in the plan. This includes working to reduce volatility, market risk, and inflation risk by:

- Blending asset classes and styles
- Adding diversifying assets, such as emerging markets
- Offering inflation protection via TIPS, commodities, and real estate

As you design your custom target-date strategies, you will want to consider how they may work for retirees who decide to remain within the strategies during retirement. Increasing diversification and helping reduce exposure to assets that produce highly uncertain outcomes are critical for retirees, particularly as they no longer have the ability to earn back what may be lost in an unfortunate market. At PIMCO, we suggest running a stochastic model to determine the probability of financial ruin in retirement.

In addition to diversification and reducing exposure to more volatile assets, plan sponsors also need to be vigilant in protecting the spending power of retirees' assets. Inflation can be particularly devastating in retirement since retirees no longer have wages that rise with inflation. Even 3 percent inflation can create a 50 percent reduction in retirement income over a 25-year period. A 5 percent inflation rate can produce a 70 percent reduction in one's standard of living. As we discussed in Chapter 10, while inflation rates have averaged 2.8 percent over the last two decades, most experts anticipate that inflation will rise in the future due to the amount of stimulus money that has been pumped into our economy and resource demands from emerging markets. An inflationary surprise would certainly adversely affect a retiree's standard of living. Even variable inflation averaging only 2.8 percent can be a tremendous risk, making it difficult for retirees to make ends meet.

As discussed in Chapter 10 on helping protect DC assets, equities are not the best inflation hedge for those close to or in retirement. Table 13.2 demonstrates why. Over longer time frames of 30 to 50 years, equities correlate with inflation or move with it, but over shorter time frames, such as a decade, there is little correlation. As a result, participants are better served if plan sponsors identify securities that have a tighter correlation to inflation over shorter time frames. These securities include TIPS, commodities, real estate investment trusts (REITS), and to a certain extent equities.

Increasing Distribution Flexibility   Offering participants the ability to gain access to their money is a very important incentive to encourage them to stay in the plan. Often plans do not offer this flexibility. In fact, according to the Hewitt Associates survey, only 41 percent of companies allow participants

TABLE 13.2 Correlation Matrix (September 1999–August 2009)

	Dow Jones UBS Commodity Total Return Index	Dow Jones US Select REIT Total Return Index	Barclays Capital U.S. TIPS Index	Dow Jones U.S. Total Stock Market Index	Consumer Price Index, Non-Seasonally Adjusted
Dow Jones UBS Commodity Total Return Index	1				
Dow Jones US Select REIT Total Return Index	0.21	1			
Barclays Capital U.S. TIPS Index	0.35	0.21	1		
Dow Jones U.S. Total Stock Market Index	0.29	0.57	0.04	1	
Consumer Price Index, Non-Seasonally Adjusted	0.28	0.09	0.09	0.04	1

Source: PIMCO. Hypothetical example for illustrative purposes only.

to access their money when they need it via partial withdrawals.[6] Further, just over half (51 percent) support participants by providing installment payments from their plan. What is more, often when partial payments or installments are made available, the money is distributed by drawing down the investments within the plan pro rata (e.g., an equal percent from each of the investments in the plan), which may be undesirable to the participant. The bottom line is that most participants are faced with an all-or-nothing choice, which leads to most deciding they need to take out all of their money at retirement. (See Table 13.3.)

Adding Retirement-Income Products According to the 2009 PIMCO DC Consultant Survey, 78 percent of the 32 consulting firms responding to the survey reported that their clients are "somewhat to highly likely" to add guaranteed income investment options to their plan.[7] (See Table 13.4.)

TABLE 13.3 DC Distribution Options and Usage

Type of Payment Form	Percent of Plans Offering Payment Form	Average Percent of Participants Electing Payment Form*
Lump sum	100%	84%
Installment payments	55%	10%
Partial distributions	54%	17%
Annuity	14%	1%

*When form of payment is available.
Source: Hewitt Associates Trends and Experience in 401(k) Plans, 2009.

Table 13.5 shows the interest in the various products.

Yet consultants identified many concerns expressed by plan sponsors who consider offering access to these products. The issues they raised are listed in Table 13.6.

Let us discuss the types of retirement-income options plan sponsors may want to consider. First, we discuss systematic withdrawal plans, including depleting-principal bond ladder approaches, which do not carry a guarantee. Then we address the guaranteed income products that can be offered either within or outside of the plan.

Systematic Withdrawal Plan Rather than buying an annuity or other insurance, participants may decide to set up an income stream to flow from their DC plan or other investments. Unlike a guarantee, this type of approach lacks insurance that the assets will last a lifetime. Whether you offer packaged or custom target-date strategies, this approach can be accommodated by offering installment payments that tap into the desired assets in the plan (e.g., 100 percent of the installment payment may come from the target-date strategy). With this approach, however, retirees face the

TABLE 13.4 How Likely Are Your Clients to Add Guaranteed Income Investment Options into Their Plan?

Likelihood of Adding Guarantee	Total	Percentage
Highly likely. Some have added already.	2	6%
Likely. Discussions are underway.	6	19%
Somewhat likely. Discussions are slow but moving.	17	53%
Unlikely in the next two years.	7	22%

Source: PIMCO. DC Consulting Support and Trends Survey 2009.

TABLE 13.5 How Attractive Are the Following Guaranteed Income Products?

Guaranteed Income Product	Total	Percentage
Lifetime income (guaranteed minimum withdrawal benefit)	26	84%
Fixed annuity	20	65%
Payment-stream product that pays out earnings and/or principal (3–7 percent, without income or longevity insurance)	11	35%
Longevity insurance	10	32%
Variable annuity	8	26%
Other (e.g., laddered TIPS, target date funds with insurance wrapper, immediate variable annuities)	3	10%
Capital-market derivative or noninsured principal-preservation strategy	2	6%

Source: PIMCO. DC Consulting Support and Trends Survey 2009.

possibility that they may deplete their savings too rapidly, especially if their assets lack sufficient downside risk hedges. This risk may be decreased by investing in a more conservative portfolio or by managers adding tail-risk hedging to the strategy.

Let us look at the probability of running out of money too soon by examining three different glide paths in Table 13.7. How might retirees fare

TABLE 13.6 What Are the Primary Concerns that Would Stop Your Clients from Offering Guaranteed Income Products?

Primary Concerns	Total	Percentage
Insurance company default risk	27	84%
Cost	23	72%
Transparency	21	66%
Fiduciary oversight	19	59%
Insufficient government support (e.g., safe harbor, regulatory clarity)	13	41%
Lack of participant demand	9	28%
Monitoring/benchmarking concerns	6	19%
Other (e.g., liquidity, portability, administrative issues, product immaturity, communication difficulties)	5	16%
Selection criteria	3	9%

Source: PIMCO. DC Consulting Support and Trends Survey 2009.

by investing in each of the glide paths? The next analysis demonstrates that at the median of the 10,000 scenarios, a participant is likely to run out of money after 18 years in retirement by continuing to invest in a typical stock and bond glide path, compared to 23 years for a diversified glide path, assuming that he or she is drawing down 50 percent of final pay adjusted for inflation. Note that at the 25th percentile of retirement, the income drawdown of the typical stock and bond glide path runs out at 13 years, while the diversified glide path continues to 18 years. Also take a look at TIPS, which surpass the typical stock and bond at the 25th percentile by two years.

TABLE 13.7 Using a 50 Percent Drawdown

| Years in Retirement | 25% Percentile | | | 50% Percentile | | |
	Diversified Glide Path	Typical Stock & Bond	100% TIPS	Diversified Glide Path	Typical Stock & Bond	100% TIPS
1	$647,843	$473,420	$517,455	$808,840	$651,649	$599,380
2	$611,355	$436,932	$480,967	$772,352	$615,161	$562,892
3	$574,867	$400,444	$444,479	$735,863	$578,673	$526,404
4	$538,378	$363,956	$407,991	$699,375	$542,185	$489,916
5	$501,890	$327,467	$371,503	$662,887	$505,697	$453,427
6	$465,402	$290,979	$335,015	$626,399	$469,208	$416,939
7	$428,914	$254,491	$298,526	$589,911	$432,720	$380,451
8	$392,426	$218,003	$262,038	$553,423	$396,232	$343,963
9	$355,938	$181,515	$225,550	$516,934	$359,744	$307,475
10	$319,449	$145,026	$189,062	$480,446	$323,256	$270,986
11	$282,961	$108,538	$152,574	$443,958	$286,767	$234,498
12	$246,473	$ 72,050	$116,085	$407,470	$250,279	$198,010
13	$209,985	$ 35,562	$ 79,597	$370,982	$213,791	$161,522
14	$173,497	$0	$ 43,109	$334,493	$177,303	$125,034
15	$137,008	$0	$ 6,621	$298,005	$140,815	$ 88,546
16	$100,520	$0	$0	$261,517	$104,327	$ 52,057
17	$ 64,032	$0	$0	$225,029	$ 67,838	$ 15,569
18	$ 27,544	$0	$0	$188,541	$ 31,350	$0
19	$0	$0	$0	$152,053	$0	$0
20	$0	$0	$0	$115,564	$0	$0
21	$0	$0	$0	$ 79,076	$0	$0
22	$0	$0	$0	$ 42,588	$0	$0
23	$0	$0	$0	$ 6,100	$0	$0
24	$0	$0	$0	$0	$0	$0
25	$0	$0	$0	$0	$0	$0

Source: PIMCO YODcA™. Hypothetical example for illustrative purposes only.

For many, the risk of depleting retirement funds too early is simply unacceptable. In that case, they may want to consider an insurance or annuity product.

Retirement-Income Guaranteed Solutions   For participants who seek assurance that they will not run out of money, guaranteed income solutions such as annuities may make sense. Typically, they offer a guarantee of income for life, which is not true of the other retirement-income solutions we have discussed. What is more, annuities tend to pay out a higher monthly income than that which a participant would feel comfortable withdrawing from managed assets; for instance, participants may receive a lifetime payout of 6 to 8 percent from an annuity yet would draw down only 4 percent from managed assets due to the fear that they might run out of money too soon. The reason they can receive more from the annuity is because they receive a "mortality credit," that is, added income from the insurance company, which recognizes that not all those receiving annuity payments will live as long as the statistics on average indicate. In essence, these earlier deaths increase the payout to annuitants overall—that is the mortality credit. Many types of annuities can be offered to participants, either within or outside the plan. They also may be offered for either distribution or accumulation.

When we asked Roger Williams, managing director and head of defined contribution consulting at Rogerscasey, if he agreed that plan sponsors should look seriously at guaranteed income products, he strongly concurred:

> There is no doubt that we need them. Getting people to the finish line with enough assets is step one. The next challenge is helping them determine budgets and manage longevity risk. We have not focused on this enough. We can't just encourage employees to take a rollover and wish them well. Our sponsoring organization may not pick up the tab for their failure, but society surely will.[8]

Williams pointed out that it made more sense for plan sponsors to try to solve this problem within the plan rather than by utilizing retail markets, which could get very expensive. Yet he raised several concerns with insurance products. First, he stated that it is a real concern that plan sponsors feel secure signing on with an organization, since who knows whether that organization will be in business many years down the road? Williams felt that some type of federal government protection was called for before some sponsors would feel confident enough to make guaranteed income products available to participants. "In addition, the industry needs to solve the portability problem at the employee and plan level. At the plan level, what do you do if your vendor loses its credit rating; can you shift to another firm? Plan sponsors are reluctant to sign up for something that's vulnerable."

Ultimately, Williams felt that a big issue sponsors are facing with these types of products is education: getting employees not only to "understand the value of the guaranteed income product" but also to be willing to "change their mind-set" enough to sign up for it.

Let us take a look at how guaranteed income solutions have been offered within DC plans historically. Then we take a closer look at out-of-plan solutions, and finally we look at the in-plan solutions that are emerging in the market.

Some Historical Background on Annuities in DC Plans[9]   Annuities have been offered as a distribution option within plans since the inception of 401(k) plans. Yet other than money purchase plans, only a minority of plans have offered annuities as a distribution option. Since most companies offered a defined benefit plan that included an annuity income option, plan sponsors generally did not believe supporting such a distribution option in the DC plan was necessary. Besides, DC plans were viewed more as supplemental savings than as retirement-income programs. Today, only 14 percent of plans offer annuities as a distribution choice.[10] According to Hewitt Associates, the percentage of 401(k) plans that offered annuities as a distribution option peaked at 30 percent in 2001 but fell to 17 percent in 2003 with the introduction of the Economic Growth and Tax Relief Reconciliation Act of 2001. Under the act, employers could eliminate annuity distribution options (and others) from profit-sharing, stock bonus, and 401(k) plans, as long as a lump-sum distribution, payable at the same time and under the same conditions as the eliminated form, was available to the participant.

A 2005 Hewitt survey showed that about one-third of affected plans chose to eliminate the non–lump-sum options, primarily because annuities were an unpopular choice among participants and cumbersome to administer. In particular, employers cited these reasons for eliminating annuity distribution options:

1. **Lack of interest.** Sixty-two percent said employees were not interested in annuity options.
2. **Administrative cost.** Forty-seven percent of respondents said it cost too much to offer an annuity option.
3. **Communication challenges.** Thirty-eight percent of plan sponsors said annuity options were complex, difficult to understand, and could not be properly explained to retirees in a simple written communication.

4. **Liability/fiduciary responsibility.** Thirty-two percent of respondents said liability and fiduciary risk were concerns. To satisfy their fiduciary responsibility requirements related to offering an annuity distribution option, plan sponsors had to follow some stringent guidelines established by the Department of Labor. Many were not willing to take on this added responsibility and the potential liability associated with these types of options.
5. **Provider selection and monitoring.** Twenty-seven percent said selecting and monitoring the insurance company provider puts further onus on the plan sponsor to manage additional relationships and/or update more documents.

However, beginning in 2005, the number of employees who selected annuity distribution options when offered began to increase once more. Here are some reasons why annuities are becoming popular among some plan participants:

1. **Guaranteed lifetime income.** Annuities provide a set or minimum payment that lasts for a retiree's lifetime. An employee with a sufficient 401(k) balance could replace his or her paycheck, providing a familiar stream of income for life. Even if the account balance is not sufficient to represent full replacement income, retirees tend to find comfort in knowing that the level of income provided will not change and that they do not have to fear depleting retirement income before death.
2. **Increased asset diversification.** Annuities can be treated as an asset class within the retiree's overall investment portfolio, providing a base-fixed return and enabling retirees to invest the remainder of their assets more aggressively for the long term. Even retirees should diversify their investments, and an annuity can take the place of the more conservative portion of the portfolio.
3. **Elimination of reinvestment risk.** Historically, retirees with significant capital may have considered investing in bonds or dividend-paying stocks as a better way to create income than purchasing an annuity. In an environment of rising interest rates, even the well-to-do are considering annuities to lock in higher payouts and eliminate reinvestment risk in the future (i.e., if future rates decline, they may no longer be able to capture a desirable yield on bonds).
4. **Reduction of dependence on investment management skill or markets.** Many retirees do not have the management skills or desire to oversee their investments. The cost of mismanagement or misfortune can result in the retiree being forced back to work. A retiree who can reasonably estimate the amount of money needed to cover fixed and daily living

costs can purchase an annuity to cover these expenses. For protection from the effects of inflation, he or she may even purchase an annuity with an inflation-indexed payout.

5. **Reduction of the cost of retirement income.** Purchasing an annuity via a company plan typically reduces its cost, which results in a higher payout than is achievable via the retail market. Costs typically are lower via the employer because insurance companies provide group rates or institutional pricing when annuities are offered in this way.

Out-of-Plan Income Solutions   Out-of-plan income solutions offer institutionally priced annuities for retirees at the point of or following retirement. It's important to note that annuities sold outside of the plan are priced based on the participant's gender, whereas those offered within a plan require "unisex" pricing (i.e., while women tend to live longer than men, unisex pricing requires that they receive the same annuity benefit or price as men of the same age). DC platform providers, such as Hewitt Associates, may provide access to competitive-bidding Web sites that allow participants or retirees to purchase fixed or variable immediate annuities and may in the future provide access in the same way to deferred-income annuities (i.e., longevity insurance).

When I was at Hewitt, we set up a Personal Finance Center through which participants could access an annuity-buying platform called Income Solutions® from the program's innovative provider, Hueler Companies. This competitive-bidding Web site was structured as an out-of-plan option for participants (although it is also possible to use the platform for in-plan distribution options). It gave retirees the opportunity to learn about immediate fixed annuities, to request bids from up to 10 insurance companies, and then to buy an annuity by initiating a rollover from their plan to the insurance company.

Employers liked this out-of-plan solution, as it provided institutional pricing to the retirees, yet the cost, oversight, and administrative hassle for the plan sponsors was typically zero. Unlike in-plan annuities, the out-of-plan annuity platform did not require fiduciary oversight of the annuity provider. From the plan sponsor's perspective, this platform functioned much like an IRA rollover offering. Sponsors made it available yet did not endorse the program. Further, they appreciated that it offered choice among the insurance providers and that they were not required to select or monitor those providers. Many plan sponsors considered the decision to add access to an out-of-plan annuity bidding program to be a "no brainer." Employers understood that those using the annuity program would gain value relative to the retail market, including institutional pricing of annuities. Pricing studies conducted in 2005 at Hewitt showed increased retirement income by 3 to

TABLE 13.8 Estimated Income from Single-Premium Immediate Annuity

Terms	Male	Female
Single life age 65	$666	$614
Single life age 70	$764	$695
Single life age 75	$899	$816
Joint life age 65 (100% of joint)	$584	$584
Joint life age 70 (100% of joint)	$606	$606
Joint life age 75 (100% of joint)	$690	$690

Source: Hueler Investment Services, Inc. Income Solutions® 2009.

9 percent.[11] Plus, retirees received help from salaried (versus commissioned) retirement specialists who helped them understand the issues involved in staying in the plan, rolling over to an IRA, or annuitizing. Some employers viewed the out-of-plan annuity program in the same way as they would discount movie tickets or on-site pickup of dry cleaning. Like these other convenience and discount services, employers made annuities available with the clear disclosure that they were not endorsing the platform or providers in any way, nor were they limiting employee access to other providers in the market.

Purchasing an annuity addresses longevity concerns, providing an additional assurance that the retiree will not run out of money. Monthly income from an annuity varies, based on age, gender, and terms. Table 13.8 is an example of some of the nominal monthly payouts a participant may anticipate, based on 2009 insurance company estimates from Income Solutions and a $100,000 investment.

If a participant desires an uncapped inflation-adjusted payout, the monthly amount paid may be reduced at the time of writing by 30 percent or more to account for the higher payouts over time. Several insurance providers offer retirees the ability to add inflation protection to their immediate annuity. Even when this feature is offered, however, typically few retirees take the reduction in income to hedge inflation. How many years would a participant need to live in retirement for the reduction in monthly income to break even? Assuming 3 percent inflation, and a 30 percent reduction in the initial inflation-adjusted payout, it would take 13 years for the inflation-adjusted payment to catch up with the nominal annuity payment and an additional 11 years to pay out the same amount on a cumulative basis. (See Table 13.9.)

Given the lower payout in early years, perhaps it is not surprising that few retirees purchase an inflation-adjusted annuity. However, if retirees anticipate inflation to rise in the future, such a purchase may be a wise

TABLE 13.9 Years to Breakeven on CPI Adjusted Annuity
Payout

Inflation rate	2%	3%	4%	5%
Cash flow	19	13	10	8
Cumulative	>30	20	18	14

Source: PIMCO.

decision. Since no one can predict future inflation, adding inflation protection would be the most prudent path for a retiree, even despite the reduction in the annuity payout in early retirement. Another way to help protect against inflation is to purchase cost-of-living adjustments, in which the annual payment would increase by a specified percentage, say 1, 2 or 3 percent each year.

Variable annuities may help protect from inflation in a less direct way. The value of the assets will increase with the markets and thus may help keep up with inflation. However, the fees and other expenses within these products may reduce the positive impact of the market returns. Plus, as we have seen, equity markets may fail to keep ahead of inflation, especially over shorter time frames. With that consideration, a participant may prefer the explicit CPI adjustment.

Longevity Insurance Coupled with Systematic Withdrawal

Longevity insurance is another guaranteed income solution to consider. This type of insurance is relatively inexpensive, as it only pays out when a retiree reaches a certain age. For instance, at the cost of $15,000 in today's dollars, 65-year-old retirees can buy $1,000 a month in retirement income that begins paying when they reach 85 years of age and continues for the remainder of their lives. For a modest cost, the use of longevity insurance can help protect the individual's risk of outliving his or her savings. Typically, this cost is covered with after-tax dollars.[12] So a participant could use assets outside the DC plan or withdraw money from a retirement plan, pay the taxes due on that amount, and then use the proceeds to buy this type of insurance. In the future, we anticipate that more retirees may buy this type of insurance using pretax dollars within their deferred accounts.

Longevity insurance may be more attractive to participants who then can invest more aggressively in a systematic withdrawal program or a bond ladder that pays out both interest and principal over a set number of years. Retirees may look to their target-date strategies for the SWP or perhaps to

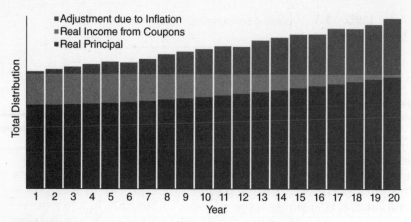

FIGURE 13.1   Sources of Income in TIPS Bond Ladder Strategies
Source: PIMCO.

an alternative product that pays out for a defined period of time, say, over 10 or 20 years. For example, you may find TIPS bond ladder strategies that provide retirees with systematic, income distributions for up to 10 or 20 years. These strategies may provide a real distribution rate that is calculated daily, providing new investors with an indication of the annual payouts they might expect. Unlike the real interest rates seen in the TIPS markets, this rate would likely also include principal returned to investors over the life of the strategies. As a result, new investors typically would see the rate increase as the maturity date approaches; the shorter time horizon means that a larger portion of the initial investment is returned each year. (See Figure 13.1.)

PIMCO retirement product manager Tom Streiff explains this concept (shown in Figure 13.1), which

> *illustrates the various components of the total distributions for a strategy with a 20-year term. Starting on the left in the first year you'll see that the distribution consists of both coupons and principal. As you move to the right into year 20, the distribution consists of more principal than coupon because you only receive coupons from the small amount of the remaining TIPS that haven't already matured. The medium gray bars on top represent the adjustments for inflation. Notice how the dark and light gray bars combined together form equal sized bars in each year. This represents the stable real distribution, or the amount that would be distributed if inflation were zero over the 20-year period. This is equivalent to the real distribution rate that may be calculated daily to give an*

indication of the payment level above inflation that an investor will likely receive.[13]

As an example, this strategy may allow retirees to receive a real distribution rate or payout of 11 percent of the initial investment over 10 years or 6 percent over 20 years. Since these strategies are invested primarily in TIPS, the payout is designed to keep pace with inflation. Additionally, they may be designed to offer a relatively stable monthly income to retirees.

You can compare buying longevity insurance plus a depleting TIPS bond ladder with the single life annuity payouts. As shown in Figure 13.2, this approach may provide the relative stability of payments that retirees would receive from an annuity, plus the inflation protection they could achieve with a CPI-adjusted annuity.

However, the payout from the TIPS ladder generally will be lower than an annuity as it lacks the mortality credit—the added money an insurance company will pay to an annuitant knowing the odds that a certain percentage of annuitants will not reach average life expectancy. On the other hand, with the TIPS bond ladder approach, retirees retain control of their investments, including the ability to bequeath these assets to heirs in the event of death prior to the ladder's maturity date. Once money has been invested in an annuity, however, in general, the money has been permanently released to the insurance company. (Note: Some insurance companies offer longevity insurance with a "pre-commencement death benefit" allowing the retiree to tap into the money earlier than age 85, for instance.)

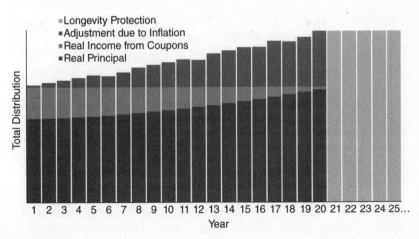

FIGURE 13.2 Sources of Income in TIPS Bond Ladder Strategies Plus Longevity Insurance
Source: PIMCO.

IN-PLAN GUARANTEED INCOME SOLUTIONS

In-plan solutions often are designed not only for retirees but also for active participants during the accumulation phase, with the objective of building predictable future retirement income. These guaranteed income solutions may be connected to an investment option within the plan, including a target-date strategy. Contributions generally may be made to the guaranteed income solution in the same way the participant invests in any other choice in the plan; the investment may include both participant and plan sponsor contributions. As with out-of-plan solutions, in-plan solutions may include fixed or variable annuities, or a variation of one of those product types. While these annuity products are within the DC plan, they are tax deferred, as with other DC assets. Once the payout begins, just as with regular DC withdrawals, the annuity payout will be taxed as ordinary income. Here is a brief overview of each type of annuity that you may see offered within a DC plan:

- **Immediate fixed-income annuities.** These are typically used at the time of distribution as a payout option. These products are designed to provide for a certain term, that is, a set number of years, such as 10 or 20, or for life. They may pay out in nominal dollars or provide an inflation-adjusted or percentage-increase payout. These products can be bought for single life or jointly for oneself and one's spouse, plus they may offer a number of riders, or special features, such as return of premium or a withdrawal option that provide a lump sum upon the early death of the participant or liquidity during the first few years of the annuity. Of course, initiating such features will likely impact the cost of the annuity, or the level of future payments, or both.
- **Fixed-income deferred annuities.** These annuities commence payout either at a specific age or at a deferred point in time initiated by the participant or retiree. This structure can be used within a DC plan during the accumulation years to build a guaranteed future retirement income stream. In essence, each contribution by the employee or employer to the DC plan buys a series of small annuities, the cumulative payout of which may not begin until retirement. These may be offered on a stand-alone basis or integrated into a managed fund, such as target date or target risk. Some of these products have been positioned in the market as a replacement for a defined benefit plan. For example, a plan sponsor may contribute to this type of annuity; however, the participant may not be able to cash it out. (It depends on the product.) Rather, the participant holds onto it until retirement, knowing the set amount that the accumulated value of the annuities will pay to him or her during retirement years. As with fixed-immediate annuities,

fixed-income deferred annuities may pay out nominally; a few providers offer a CPI-adjusted or percentage increasing payout.

- **Longevity insurance.** This is another label for fixed-deferred annuities. For example, a retiree may buy longevity insurance at age 65 designed to begin payout at, say, 85 years of age. However, as discussed, this type of insurance cannot be held easily within a tax-deferred account after age $70^1/_2$ due to required minimum distribution rules.
- **Variable annuity.** Similar to fixed-income annuities, variable annuities may provide a monthly guaranteed payout, depending on whether there is a guaranteed lifetime withdrawal benefit, guaranteed minimum income benefit, or immediate variable annuity. Similar to immediate or deferred fixed-income annuities, variable annuities are a contract between the participant and an insurance company under which the insurer agrees to make periodic payments to the participant either immediately or at some future date. This product can be bought with a lump sum or, as with deferred annuities, with a series of purchase payments (i.e., employee or employer contributions to a DC plan). Unlike a fixed annuity, variable annuity payouts are tied to the performance of the investment options within them (e.g., stocks, bonds, and money markets). In a DC plan, the plan sponsor may tie the variable annuity to a single balanced separate account rather than allow the participant to select from a range of investments within the annuity.
- **Living benefits** (e.g., lifetime withdrawal benefits, such as guaranteed minimum withdrawal benefits or guaranteed minimum income benefits). This type of guarantee allows the participant to make contributions into the fund while knowing that a certain percentage of those accumulated contributions—for instance, 5 percent (Note: This number may be lower, given insurance underwriting risk and market rates)—is guaranteed as a lifetime payment. Living benefits may include periodic step-ups in the guaranteed payment as a result of good investment performance, whereas poor investment performance will not reduce the payment amount. These step-ups are designed to offer protection to participant accounts. Even when the account climbs and then falls dramatically in response to the markets, the payout will be protected at the prefall value. Therefore, this structure is designed to offer the participant some degree of sufficient downside risk hedges as well as guaranteed lifetime income. Living benefits may be attached to a variable annuity in the plan, or they may be stand-alone, tracking the value of a specific account or fund in the plan.

Let us take a look at how these products are being used and perceived in the DC marketplace.

PLAN SPONSORS EXPLORING GUARANTEES

Chris Raham, senior actuarial advisor at Ernst & Young and its retirement income practice leader, addressed the fact that, currently, more DC plan sponsors are beginning to shift their focus toward creating increasingly reliable retirement-income replacement rates. Raham stated that "product structures that help address timing and volatility in conjunction with inflation and longevity ultimately should prove to be most successful at improving participant outcomes."[14] Special attention should be paid to the five years directly preceding and following retirement, when market volatility could significantly impact retirement income.

Raham pointed out that "accumulation-oriented products, such as asset-allocation structures—whether balanced funds, target-date funds, actively or passively managed . . . are designed to get you to the point of retirement and not necessarily take you beyond it in a manner that helps mitigate the four risks." By "the four risks," he means the timing of retirement (whether you retire during a good market or a depressed one), how volatile your investments will be during the five years before and after your retirement, the rate of inflation during retirement, and your longevity.

While additional diversification, making guaranteed income or insurance products available to plan participants, and favorably changing asset allocations can improve the retirement outcome for participants, these strategies still do not address the problem of longevity. To solve this problem, Raham suggested that sponsors add "insurance or another type of risk mitigation option" to their plan. He discussed other options to "help people generate a stable retirement-income stream," including "variable, end-of-plan annuities that allow you to roll money into a variable annuity structure with a guaranteed living benefit payout. As end-of-plan options, none actually helps to manage transition risk, but they may help manage CPI-adjusted inflation and longevity risks as people move through retirement."

When we asked Raham what types of investment structures were gaining the most attention, he mentioned in-plan annuities.

The insurance industry calls this particular class of annuities "insured DC vehicles." A number of products on the market allow participants to direct their contributions into a fixed or variable annuity contract. In return, the annuity contract converts these contributions into an income figure. Typically, there's a commuted value related to the contract so people can, if needed, surrender it for cash. Theoretically, these products generate a lot of attention because they accept contributions, they manage timing and volatility

*risk, maximize the leverage related to mortality and they remove a
lot of the investment-oriented risks from the individual and place
them on the insurer.*

On the downside, Raham pointed out that the newness of these products and the challenges they might present to plan administrators and record
keepers were making some plan sponsors cautious about using them, anal-
ogous to the old joke in the *Dilbert* comic strip: "Change is good. You go
first."

Raham stated that plan sponsors are more likely to utilize "wrapper-
type products, like the guaranteed minimum withdrawal-benefit products
we see emerging with multiple providers" because they do not seem like
such a huge leap forward since "people understand the guaranteed-income
aspect." In addition, these products look "an awful lot like mutual funds."

We asked Raham to evaluate the flexibility of some of the different
products we see on the market in terms of their cash-out options. For most
of these products, participants do have "access options during the accumulation phase of the Insured DC Vehicles (IDC) products," including death
benefits that range from a simple return of premiums to a commuted value-
type calculation.

*But once you commence payout, options may be limited in situa-
tions where you need liquidity.... For in-plan [immediate income]
annuity products, once you begin the payout phase, your annuitiza-
tion is based on the contract value at that time. At that point, you're
typically generating an income stream at an 8-percent payout rate,
albeit nominal.*

The downside is that, since these assets are now owned by the insurance company, liquid assets are unavailable typically. Some products may
allow access to the assets during the payout phase, yet this flexibility results
in payouts that may be significantly reduced. Then, of course, there is always a chance that the plan participant may die prematurely, leaving the
insurance company holding the assets, unless the product purchased has a
pre-commencement death benefit.

Guaranteed minimum withdrawal benefit products are designed to allow
participants to keep assets invested in the plan. "Once you begin the payout
phase, a minimum payout percentage is guaranteed for life, based on the final
account value, even if you deplete your assets. Unlike the annuity products,
you retain control of the assets until they are exhausted. If you need to take
more than the guaranteed drawdown amount, you reduce the future payout,
however."

While Raham pointed out that many plan sponsors are "waiting for a clear winner to emerge" before they head down a path with any of the guaranteed income products, it is important that sponsors begin to "consider an option that helps people manage plan outcomes and generates income in a fashion other than systematic withdrawal." Raham also advised plan sponsors to seek the help of an expert when selecting these guaranteed income solutions, someone who is qualified to benchmark these options.

ALLOWING CONSOLIDATION OF OUTSIDE ASSETS INTO THE PLAN

Another way to get participants to stay within the plan is to enable them to consolidate their outside assets into the plan. A good way to accomplish this may be to add a "deemed IRA" to the plan. "Deemed IRAs" are defined as "an account or annuity under an employer's tax-qualified retirement plan that is treated as an employee's traditional IRA or Roth IRA" and are subject to the same tax rules that govern all IRAs.[15] However, unlike rollover IRA accounts, an employee may contribute savings to a deemed IRA on an ongoing basis. "The advantages of including the Deemed IRA in the employer's plan are that it allows the employee to consolidate the investment of his retirement savings, facilitates additions to those savings and may give the employee access to more advantageous investment alternatives than are possible in a stand-alone IRA." The retirement plans of governmental organizations, not-for-profit organizations, and private employers all have access to deem IRAs.

Georgette Gestely talked about the advantages of offering a deemed IRA in the retirement plan for the New York City Deferred Compensation Program; the plan added this type of IRA to the program after the passage of the Economic Growth and Tax Relief Reconciliation Act of 2001. Gestely pointed out that this type of IRA had advantages over retail IRAs in terms of institutional investments and lower fees. "We thought that if we put an IRA into our program, then the people who wanted to roll into an IRA would simply roll into this one, which we call the New York City Employee IRA—or, NYCE ('nice') IRA. Our NYCE IRA also has pre- and post-tax, traditional IRA, and Roth IRA components."[16]

While there are earnings limitations on contributions to this type of IRA, as there are with traditional IRAs, most of the city's employees can gain access to the deemed IRA by aggregating all of the money they have in their former DC plans and rolling it into the City of New York's more cost-effective deemed IRA. Those who "leave city service and take another job can continue to invest their earned income into our Deemed IRA, just as they would any IRA program." Employee and retiree spouses can also link their own IRAs to this program.

Gestely states that the City of New York actively encourages retirees to stay in its $9 billion plan because

> *for everybody, the more assets the plan retains, the greater the benefit to people in the plan. For those who've retired from city service, staying in this program and in our investment structure lineup is the most cost-effective move. We created a program that is, essentially, on a weighted average, fewer than 30 basis points in total plan fees—including both administrative and investment fees.*

No doubt, allowing both retirees and their spouses to consolidate assets into your plan's DC and deemed IRA program may materially lower their cost of investment management and thus lengthen the life of those assets in retirement. Plus, providing access to institutionally priced retirement-income options may give retirees the benefit of your buying power, resulting in a higher standard of living in retirement or stretching their money over a longer time frame.

IN CLOSING

Helping participants accumulate sufficient savings for retirement is just the beginning. Increasingly, plan sponsors are looking to help participants as they move into retirement and begin to draw down their assets. Plan sponsors may help retirees by providing income only, systematic withdrawal, or guaranteed income programs. DC plans can be modified to support these types of payout strategies. Plans also may be enhanced by adding either in-plan or out-of-plan guaranteed income programs. More development of solutions and plan integration is needed before plan sponsors can feel confident in offering guaranteed income solutions within their plans. We anticipate more direction from Washington over the coming years to help address some plan sponsor concerns, such as insurer default risk. Plan sponsor involvement in the delivery of retirement income may make a significant difference for retirees since the product pricing, fiduciary oversight, and unbiased sponsor-provided education all can potentially contribute to the successful use of these programs.

Conclusion

Target-date strategies coupled with automatic enrollment and contribution escalation in many ways have revolutionized defined contribution (DC) plan investing. No longer are we stuck in first gear, pleading with employees to participate in their DC plan, nor are we chained to the idea of offering only simple investment choices that the majority of people can understand. What is more, custom target-date strategies have propelled us to a new level of possibility: DC plans have at last entered the world of institutional investment management. They have finally crossed the threshold into the "DB-ization" for which we have longed. Designing target-date strategies by tapping into a broad array of core and additional institutional best-in-class investments helps elevate our DC plans to the plane of investment sophistication and improved risk-versus-return trade-offs once beyond the reach of DC participants. No doubt we have entered a new era for DC and for retirement. Getting DC investing right has never been so important—nor have we seen it moving so rapidly in the right direction. Despite criticism of the first generation of target dates and the challenges presented by the economic downturn of 2008–2009, these strategies are here to stay.

At long last, custom strategies have handed over the investment reins to the plan sponsor who provides professional oversight directly or by hiring experts. As more plan sponsors move to take those reins and design best-in-class strategies, we hope this book provides them with the support they need. There are many considerations involved in creating target-date strategies that will help ensure a successful retirement outcome for participants, one where the money will be designed to last and outpace inflation and unexpected bumps in the road. This book has attempted to address most of those considerations by looking at target-date strategies from all angles, taking a close look at the current relevant trends in plan design as well as the ways in which DC plans might continue to evolve. To present all of these viewpoints, we have not only shared our own thoughts and experiences on the important issues in plan design, we have also gathered and synthesized the expertise of many of our nation's leading consultants, legal experts, plan sponsors, academics, and others. By bringing together the opinions and experiences of these talented individuals, we have done our best to present many different perspectives and innovative approaches to designing optimal DC plans.

This book has included a detailed look at the history of the development and restructuring of retirement plans in America, especially in light of the impact that the Pension Protection Act and recent regulations have had on the evolution of DC plans. It has presented a wide variety of plan designs as well as a symposium where experts can discuss the pros and cons of each.

The opening chapters presented the evolution of DC plans, including the development of target-date strategies, adapting core offerings to a DC environment, and the benefits of designing custom strategies versus buying a prepackaged product. As we have seen, a custom approach is designed to offer plan sponsors maximum control over their investment choices along with the ability to seek out best-in-class managers. Legislation such as government identification of qualified default investment alternatives has sped the prevalence of target-date strategies in DC plans. We anticipate that the ongoing scrutiny by Washington of DC plans and target-date approaches will help contribute to the future evolution of these programs.

This book has also presented leading-edge views of consultants and sponsors about plan design and creating effective glide paths for target-date strategies. These days, more and more consultants are using Monte Carlo simulations and analytic approaches such as PIMCO's YODcA™ to project likely retirement income results from various asset allocation or glide-path structures. These modeling techniques have become even more effective as they incorporate inflationary scenarios as one of their variables, helping plan sponsors to design a glide path that has a higher probability of meeting a retirement income goal as well as helping participants' money to last longer into retirement. The core lineup of plans has also been evolving over the past decade. Offering a synthesis of many opinions, we suggested that an ideal core lineup should include capital preservation (stable value or money market), global fixed income, inflation protection, global tactical asset allocation, and global equity strategies. While caution is warranted, plan sponsors also may want to consider alternative investments, such as absolute return and private real estate, as diversifiers to blend within their target-date strategies.

However, it is not enough to design an effective DC plan. Sponsors must communicate these strategies to employees effectively. In this book we have presented a detailed conversation about the important questions surrounding communication and education of plan participants, who often find retirement investment a daunting and confusing task. Not only do employees need to be educated about target-date strategies, they also need to understand their personal risk tolerances. Communication should be clear and simple, making effective use of the many different types of media and tools available, including Web sites, phone or in-person communication, online statements, written material, and various types of innovative approaches, such as visual representations of how one might live in retirement given a person's savings level. Lowering plan costs has been another primary motivation in the development of target-date strategies and DC plans in a climate where reducing plan costs by even a single basis point can result in meaningful increased retirement income for participants. Tapping into institutional pricing, including sliding-fee schedules, can help lower target-date as well as overall plan fees.

Ultimately, helping protect assets from risk has become a major concern for plan sponsors and participants alike in the wake of the economic downturn of 2008–2009, in which employees saw an average decline of 25 percent of their retirement savings and investments. While no one can do away with risk, we can certainly mitigate it by understanding the categories of risk that participants face, helping them to understand their risk tolerance, and then helping them reduce their exposure to risk by encouraging increased savings and asset diversification and adding tail-risk hedging and other risk-management approaches. As consultants and plan sponsors continue to have conversations about where DC plans and target-date strategies will likely evolve in the future, significant focus is on the years prior to and entering retirement. At the time of this writing, experts are debating how aggressive a target date should be as it approaches the retirement age—should it be managed "to" a retirement date or "through" this date to a mortality target perhaps 30 years beyond retirement? Add to this the evolving market for retirement-income guarantee products that are designed to offer participants ways not only to accumulate assets *for* retirement but also to convert those assets into monthly income *at* retirement. Over the coming years, we anticipate more clarity on the "to" versus "through" as well as direction and support of plan sponsors from Washington on retirement income solutions that ease the process of converting DC assets into a lifetime income stream.

While so much has been shared in this book from an extraordinary range of our nation's experts, we know you may still have questions. We encourage you to reach out to many of the consultants and other experts mentioned in this book or to us at PIMCO for help as you develop optimal target-date solutions. We will continue writing and sharing dialogues with the hope of shedding light on and encouraging further advancements in DC plan design. This will include broader support of institutional best-in-class custom strategies as well as more comprehensive financial planning for participants. Our ultimate goal is to help foster a dignified and secure financial future for employees of corporations, not-for-profits, governments, and other organizations.

Notes

CHAPTER 1: DC Plans in the American Retirement System

1. "Financial Plan That Comes with Mug Shots," *New York Times*, January 7, 2007.
2. This and the next quotes are from Stacy Schaus, "Patience Is a Virtue," *PIMCO DC Dialogue* 2, no. 8 (2007).
3. This and the next quotes are from Stacy Schaus, "Fear Before Greed," *PIMCO DC Dialogue* 3, no. 11 (2008).
4. Stacy Schaus, "Diversify, Diversify, Diversity," *PIMCO DC Dialogue* 4, no. 2 (2009).
5. Stacy Schaus, "Your Best Shot," *PIMCO DC Dialogue* 3, no. 12 (2008).
6. This and the next quotes are from Schaus, "Patience Is a Virtue."
7. This and the next quote are from Stacy Schaus, "Two Thin on Models," *PIMCO DC Dialogue* 3, no. 5 (2008).
8. Bureau of Labor Statistics, 2007. Hewitt Associates, ILC, "A Decade of Trends and Experience in 401(k) Plans," (September 2005).
9. This and the next quote are from Stacy Schaus, "Enough Is Enough?" *PIMCO DC Dialogue* 1, no. 2 (2006).
10. Stacy Schaus, "Teach Your Children Well," *PIMCO DC Dialogue* 3, no. 1 (2008).
11. This and the next quote are from Schaus, "Enough Is Enough?"
12. Stacy Schaus, "The Times They Are a-Changin'," *PIMCO DC Dialogue* 1, no. 3 (2006).
13. Profit Sharing/401k Council of America, 52nd Annual Survey Reflecting 2008 Plan Experience.
14. Stacy Schaus, "Where's the Beef?" *PIMCO DC Dialogue* 2, no. 3 (2007).
15. James J. Choi, David Laibson, Brigitte Madrian, and Andrew Metrick, "Saving for Retirement on the Path of Least Resistance," originally prepared for *Tax Policy and the Economy*, November 9, 2001, updated draft, July 19, 2004: 18. Available at: www.hks.harvard.edu/fs/bmadria/Documents/Madrian%20Papers/Saving%20for%20Retirement%20on%20the%20Path%20of%20Least%20Resistance.pdf.
16. This and the next quotes are from Stacy Schaus, "I'd Gladly Pay You Tomorrow," *PIMCO DC Dialogue* 2, no. 6 (2007).

17. Stacy Schaus, "Look, Ma! No Hands," *PIMCO DC Dialogue* 2, no. 7 (2006).
18. Schaus, "I'd Gladly Pay You Tomorrow."
19. This and the next quotes are from Stacy Schaus, "Take the Money and Run!" *PIMCO DC Dialogue* 3, no. 8 (2008).
20. This and the next quotes are from Stacy Schaus, "Don't Give Up," *PIMCO DC Dialogue* 4, no. 6 (2009).
21. This and the next quotes are from Stacy Schaus, "Raising the Bar," *PIMCO DC Dialogue* 3, no. 9 (2008).

CHAPTER 2:   Evolving DC Plan Design

1. Stacy Schaus, "Are We There Yet?" *PIMCO DC Dialogue* 3, no. 2 (2008).
2. 2007 survey conducted by Hewitt Associates.
3. Stacy Schaus, "Look, Ma! No Hands!" *PIMCO DC Dialogue* 2, no. 7 (2006).
4. 2009 survey conducted by Hewitt Associates.
5. This and the next quotes are from Stacy Schaus, "Something for Everybody," *PIMCO DC Dialogue* 1, no. 4 (2006).
6. Schaus, "Are We There Yet?"
7. Hewitt Associates, ILC, "A Decade of Trends and Experiences in 401(k) Plans" (September 2005): 11.
8. Hewitt Associates. "Trends and Experience in 401(k) Plans (2009)."
9. This and the next quotes are from Hewitt Associates, "How Well Are Employees Saving and Investing in 401(k) Plans?" Hewitt Universe Benchmarks (2009).
10. This and the next quote are from Stacy Schaus, "A Complete Flight Plan," PIMCO DC Dialogue 4, no. 7 (2009).
11. Hewitt Associates, "Trends and Experience in 401(k) Plans."
12. This and the next quotes are from Stacy Schaus, "Stay the Course or Not?" *PIMCO DC Dialogue* 4, no. 3 (2009) .
13. This and the next quote are from Schaus, "Complete Flight Plan."
14. Ross Bremen, "Beyond Stocks and Bonds," presented at the Custom Target-Date Strategies Summit, April 23, 2009.
15. This and the next quote are from Stuart Odell, "Beyond Stocks and Bonds," presented at the Custom Target-Date Strategies Summit, April 23, 2009.
16. This and the next quotes are from Stacy Schaus, "Smooth Ride Ahead," *PIMCO DC Dialogue* 3, no. 10 (2008).
17. This and the next quotes are from Stacy Schaus, "Keep the Baby. Lost the Bath Water," *PIMCO DC Dialogue* 3, no. 7 (2008).
18. PIMCO DC Consulting Service Highlights (2009).

CHAPTER 3:   Target-Date Strategies: Packaged
versus Custom

1. Hewitt Associates, "How Well Are Employees Saving and Investing in 401(k) Plans?" Hewitt Universe Benchmarks (2009): 7.

2. PSCA Target-Date Funds Survey (2009).
3. Stacy Schaus, "Simplify, Simplify, Simplify," *PIMCO DC Dialogue* 4, no. 9 (2009).
4. Hewitt Associates shared this data with the author.
5. Stacy Schaus, "Tailored to Fit," *PIMCO DC Dialogue* 2, no. 10 (2007).
6. Stacy Schaus, "Check It Out!" *PIMCO DC Dialogue* 3, no. 6 (2008).
7. Stacy Schaus, "A Good-Faith Contract," *PIMCO DC Dialogue* (2008).
8. Schaus, "Tailored to Fit."
9. This and the next quotes are from Schaus, "Simplify, Simplify, Simplify."
10. Schaus, "Tailored to Fit."
11. Schaus, "A Good-Faith Contract."
12. This and the next quotes are from Stacy Schaus, "To Build or to Buy: That Is the Question," *PIMCO DC Dialogue* 2, no. 2 (2007).
13. This and the next quotes are from Stacy Schaus, "No Pain, No Gain," *PIMCO DC Dialogue* 2, no. 7 (2007).

CHAPTER 4: Legal and Fiduciary Considerations

1. Marla Kreindler, "Off to the Right Start," presented at the Custom Target-Date Strategies Summit, April 23, 2009.
2. Ibid.
3. All of these questions are taken from Stacy Schaus, "A Sensible Approach to Custom Target Retirement-Date Strategies," *PIMCO Practice DC Research* 1, no. 1 (November 2006).
4. Stacy Schaus, "A Good-Faith Contract." *PIMCO DC Dialogue* 3, no. 4 (2008).
5. Stacy Schaus, "Are We There Yet?" *PIMCO DC Dialogue* 3, no. 2 (2008).
6. Stacy Schaus, "Begin with the End in Mind." *PIMCO DC Dialogue* 2, no. 5 (2007).
7. U.S. Securities and Exchange Commission, "SEC Proposes Mandatory Redemption Fees for Mutual Fund Securities" (2004); available at: www.sec.gov/news/press/2004-23.htm.
8. This and the next quotes are from Schaus, "Begin with the End in Mind."
9. Profit Sharing/401k Council of America, 52nd Annual Survey of Profit Sharing and 401(k) Plans Reflecting 2008 Plan Experience.
10. This and the next discussions are from Stacy Schaus, "Target Date Strategies: On the Hot Seat," *PIMCO DC Dialogue* 4, no. 8 (2009).
11. Dechert Financial Services Group, "Joint DOL and SEC Hearing on Target-Date Funds," *Dechert on Point,* no. 17 (August 2009): 1.
12. Ibid., 2.
13. This and the next quotes are from PLANSPONSOR, "Promises They Can't Keep: Misconceptions about Target-Date Funds," May 5, 2009; available at: www.plansponsor.com/NewsStory.aspx?Id=4294981790.
14. Majority Staff of the Special Committee on Aging, United States Senate, "Target Date Retirement Funds: Lack of Clarity among Structures and Fees Raises

Concerns," Summary of Committee Research (October 2009); available at: www.aging.senate.gov/letters/targetdatecommitteeprint.pdf.

CHAPTER 5: Record Keeping and Trust

1. This and the next quotes are from Stacy Schaus, "Keep the Baby. Lose the Bathwater" *PIMCO DC Dialogue* 3, no. 7 (2008).
2. This and the next quotes are from Tom Eichenberger, "Tackling the Operational Challenges," presented at the Custom Target-Date Strategies Summit, April 23, 2009.
3. This and the next quotes are from Stacy Schaus, "Check It Out!" *PIMCO DC Dialogue* 3, no. 6 (2008).

CHAPTER 6: Communication Challenges and How to Meet Them

1. Hewitt Associates, ILC, "A Decade of Trends and Experience in 401(k) Plans" (September 2005).
2. This and the next quotes are from Barbara J. Hogg, "Communication Issues," presented at the Custom Target-Date Strategies Summit, April 22, 2008.
3. Profit Sharing/401(k) Council of America, 51st Annual Survey Reflecting 2008 Plan Experience.
4. Stacy Schaus, "Your Best Shot," *PIMCO DC Dialogue* 3, no. 12 (2009).
5. May Beth Glotzbach, "Communication Issues," presented at the Custom Target-Date Strategies Summit, April 22, 2008.
6. This and the next quote are from Stacy Schaus, "Basics of Life," *PIMCO DC Dialogue* 4, no. 5 (2009).
7. Stacy Schaus, "A Complete Flight Plan," *PIMCO DC Dialogue* 4, no. 7 (2009).
8. Stacy Schaus, "I'll Gladly Pay You Tomorrow," *PIMCO DC Dialogue* 2, no. 6 (2007).
9. Stacy Schaus, "Into the Future," *PIMCO DC Dialogue* 2, no. 4 (2007).
10. This and the next quotes are from Stacy Schaus, "Check It Out!" *PIMCO DC Dialogue* 3, no. 6 (2008).
11. This and the next quotes are from Stacy Schaus, "Tailored to Fit," *PIMCO DC Dialogue* 2, no. 10 (2007).
12. This and the next quotes are from Stacy Schaus, "Stay the Course...or Not," *PIMCO DC Dialogue* 4, no. 3 (2009).
13. This and the next quote are from Schaus, "Basics of Life."

CHAPTER 7: Evaluating Costs in Custom Strategies

1. Stacy Schaus, "Just Tell Me, 'How Much?'" *PIMCO DC Dialogue* 2, no. 1 (2007).

2. This and the next quote are from Stacy Schaus, "Diversity, Diversify, Diversify," *PIMCO DC Dialogue* 4, no. 2 (2009).
3. This and the next quote are from Schaus, "Just Tell Me, 'How Much?'"
4. Stacy Schaus, "A Good-Faith Contract," *PIMCO DC Dialogue* 3, no. 4 (2008).
5. This and the next quote are from Stacy Schaus, "Smooth Ride Ahead," *PIMCO DC Dialogue* 3, no. 10 (2008).
6. Stacy Schaus, "Check It Out!" *PIMCO DC Dialogue* 3, no. 6 (2008).
7. Schaus, "Just Tell Me, 'How Much?'"
8. This and the next quotes are from Lori Lucas, "Is It Important for 401(k) Fees to Be Equitable?" *Workforce Management* (September 2009): 2.
9. This and the next quote are from Stacy Schaus, "No Pain, No Gain," *PIMCO DC Dialogue* 2, no. 7 (2007).
10. This and the next quote are from Schaus, "Just Tell Me, 'How Much?'"
11. Stacy Schaus, "I'll Gladly Pay You Tomorrow," *PIMCO DC Dialogue* 2, no. 6 (2007).
12. This and the next quotes are from Stacy Schaus, "Are We There Yet?" *PIMCO DC Dialogue* 3, no. 2 (2008).
13. This and the next quotes are from Schaus, "Just Tell Me, 'How Much?'"

CHAPTER 8:   Glide-Path Design

1. Stacy Schaus, "A Complete Flight Plan." *PIMCO DC Dialogue* 4, no. 7 (2009).
2. Roger G. Ibbotson and Paul D. Kaplan, *Financial Analysts Journal* 56, no. 1 (2000): 26–33.
3. Markowitz (1952) and then expanded by Sharpe et al. (1964).
4. 2008 PIMCO survey. Highlights: Defined Contribution Consulting Support and Trends 2008 p. 4–5.
5. Based on similar assumptions of the Capital Asset Pricing Model (CAPM) risk perspective. The risk-free asset represents a reference point of a generally less risky asset in a DC asset allocation and is used to hedge inflation risk. All investments carry risk.
6. This and the next quotes are from Stacy Schaus, "Change Is Good. You Go First," *PIMCO DC Dialogue* 3, no. 3 (2008).
7. This and the next quotes are from Stacy Schaus, "Simplify, Simplify, Simplify," *PIMCO DC Dialogue* 4, no. 9 (2009).
8. This and the next quotes are from Stacy Schaus, "Diversify, Diversify, Diversify," *PIMCO DC Dialogue* 4, no. 2 (2009).
9. This and the next quotes are from Stacy Schaus, "Basics of Life," *PIMCO DC Dialogue* 4, no. 5 (2009).
10. This and the next quote are from Stacy Schaus, "Your Best Shot," *PIMCO DC Dialogue* 3, no. 12 (2008).
11. This and the next quotes are from Stacy Schaus, "Check It Out!" *PIMCO DC Dialogue* 3, no. 6 (2008).

CHAPTER 9:   Asset Classes and Alternatives

1. This and the next quote are from Richard H. Thaler and Cass R. Sunstein, *Nudge: Improving Decisions about Health, Wealth, and Happiness* (New York: Penguin, 2009), 131.
2. Schlomo Bernartzi and Richard H. Thaler, "Naive Diversification Strategies in Retirement Saving Plans," *American Economic Review* 91, no. 1 (2001): 79–98.
3. This and the next quote are from Stacy Schaus, "Simplify, Simplify, Simplify," *PIMCO DC Dialogue* 4, no. 9 (2009).
4. S. S. Iyengar and M. Lepper, "When Choice Is Demotivating: Can One Desire Too Much of a Good Thing?" *Journal of Personality and Social Psychology* 79 (2000): 995–1006.
5. Sheena S. Iyengar, Wei Jiang, Gur Huberman. "How Much Choice is Too Much?: Contributions to 401(k) Retirement Plans," Pension Research Council Working Paper, 9.
6. George A. Miller, "The Magical Number Seven, Plus or Minus Two: Some Limits on Our Capacity for Processing Information," *Psychological Review* (Princeton, NJ: Princeton University Department of Psychology, 1956).
7. Stacy Schaus, "Basics of Life," *PIMCO DC Dialogue* 4, no. 5 (2009).
8. This and the next quotes are from Stacy Schaus, "Fear before Greed," *PIMCO DC Dialogue* 3, no. 11 (2008).
9. This and the next quote are from Steve Ferber and Bret Estep, "Look Behind the Curtain: Does your Stable Value Fund Stack Up?" *PIMCO Viewpoints* (2009).
10. Schaus, "Simplify, Simplify, Simplify."
11. Stacy Schaus, "And the Beat Goes On," *PIMCO DC Dialogue* 4, no. 11 (2009).
12. David Fisher, "The Case for Global Bonds." (2009).
13. Stacy Schaus, "A Penny Saved Is a Penny Earned," *PIMCO DC Dialogue* 4, no. 1 (2009).
14. Robert Greer, "PIMCO Q&A" (2006).
15. Lori Lucas, James Veneruso,. Callan Investments Institute Research 2009 Callan Target Date Fund Manager Survey. Defined Contribution Trends Survey, 2.
16. Stacy Schaus, "Shoot the Messenger," *PIMCO DC Dialogue* 4, no. 4 (2009).
17. Stacy Schaus, "Plan for the Worst, Hope for the Best," *PIMCO DC Dialogue* 4, no. 12 (2009).
18. Mohammed El-Erian, October 2008 interview.
19. This and the next quote are from Stacy Schaus, "A Complete Flight Plan," *PIMCO DC Dialogue* 4, no. 7 (2009).
20. This and the next quote are from Ross Bremen, "Beyond Stocks and Bonds," presented at the Custom Target-Date Strategies Summit, April 23, 2009.
21. Schaus, "Too Thin on Models."
22. This and the next quotes are from Schaus, "Smooth Ride Ahead."
23. This and the next quotes are from Stacy Schaus, "No Pain, No Gain," *PIMCO DC Dialogue* 2, no. 7 (2007).
24. This and the next quotes are from Stacy Schaus, "Wishful Thinking," *PIMCO DC Dialogue* 4, no. 10 (2009).

CHAPTER 10: Helping Protect DC Assets from Risk

1. This and the next quote are from Jason Zweig, *Your Money & Your Brain: How the New Science of Neuroeconomics Can Help Make You Rich* (New York: Simon & Schuster, 2008), 159, 163.
2. Leslie P. Norton, "The New Investor Has Different Priorities," *Barron's*, September 23, 2009; available at: www.smartmoney.com/investing/economy/the-new-investor-has-different-priorities/?cid=1122.
3. Prepared by the Employee Benefit Research Institute using 2007 Account Balances: Tabulations from The Employee Benefit Research Institute/ICI Participant-Directed Retirement PlanData Collection Project; 2008 and 2009 Account Balances: The Employee Benefit Research Institute Estimates. The analysis is based on all participants with account balances at the end of 2007 and contribution information for that year.
4. This data comes from the Hewitt 401(k) Index^{TM}, which looks at 2.2 million participants and measures their relative DC trading activity.
5. "How Well Are Employees Saving and Investing in 401(k) Plans" 2009 Hewitt Universe Benchmarks.
6. EBRI 2009.
7. A. Shleifer, *Inefficient Markets: An Introduction to Behavioral Finance* (New York: Oxford University Press, 1999); H. Shefrin, *Beyond Greed and Fear: Understanding Behavioral Finance and the Psychology of Investing* (New York: Oxford University Press, 2002).
8. Nassim Nicholas Taleb, *The Black Swan: The Impact of the Highly Improbable* (New York: Random House, 2007).
9. Downside deviation is particularly informative for distributions that are asymmetrically skewed to the downside. In such cases, standard deviation is likely to mask the true risk inherent in an investment strategy. For more on downside risk, see W. V. Harlow, "Asset Allocation in a Downside-Risk Framework," *Financial Analysts Journal* 47 (1991): 28–40; F. A. Sortino and R. Van Der Meer, "Downside Risk," 17 (1991): 27–32; and F. A. Sortino and L. N. Price, "Performance Measurement in a Downside Risk Framework," *Journal of Investing* 3 (1994): 59–64.
10. A risk measure related to VaR is CVaR, which remedies some of the weaknesses that VaR has in adequately evaluating the rarest and/or most catastrophic events A technical explication of VaR and CVaR is beyond the scope of this book. For details on VaR and CVaR, see P. Artzner, F. Delbaen, J. Elber, and D. Heath, "Coherent Measures of Risk," *Mathematical Finance* 9 (1999): 203–228; T. Rockafellar and S. Uryasev, "Optimization of Conditional Value-at-Risk," *Journal of Risk* 2 (2000): 21–41; A. Gaivoronski and G. Pflug, "Value-at-Risk in Portfolio Optimization: Properties and Computational Approach," *Journal of Risk* 7 (2005): 1–31; P. Jorion, *Value at Risk: The New Benchmark for Managing Risk,* 3rd ed. (New York: McGraw-Hill, 2007).
11. E. Acar and S. James, "Maximum Loss and Maximum Drawdown in Financial Markets," *Proceedings of International Conference on Forecasting Financial*

Markets (London: (1997); D. Sornette, *Why Stock Markets Crash: Critical Events in Complex Financial Systems* (Princeton, NJ: Princeton University Press, 2003); D. Harding, G. Nakou, and A. Nejjar, "The Pros and Cons of Drawdown as a Statistical Measure for Risk in Investments," *AIMA Journal* (April 2003): 16–17; M. Magdon-Ismail, A. Atiya, A. Pratap, and Y. Abu-Mostafa, "On the Maximum Drawdown of a Brownian Motion," *Journal of Applied Probability* 41 (2004): 147–161.

12. This and the next quotes are from Stacy Schaus, "Out of the Laboratory: Seven Essential PIMCO DC Dialogues™ for Plan Sponsors."

13. This and the next quote are from Stacy Schaus, "Keep the Baby. Lose the Bathwater," *PIMCO DC Dialogue* 3, no. 7 (2007).

14. Seth Ruthen, "Creating the Next-Generation Glidepaths for Defined Contribution Plans," PIMCO (2005).

15. Stacy Schaus, "Where's the Beef?" *PIMCO DC Dialogue* 2, no. 3 (2007).

16. This and the next quote are from Stacy Schaus, "Don't Give Up," *PIMCO DC Dialogue* 4, no. 6 (2009).

17. This and the next quote are from John Cavalieri, Gang Hu, and Mihir Worah, "Passive versus Active Management of TIPS: Helping Investors Obtain the Best Exposure." PIMCO (2009).

18. This and the next quote are from Stacy Schaus, "Stay the Course . . . or Not?" *PIMCO DC Dialogue* 4, no. 3 (2009).

19. This and the next quotes are from Stacy Schaus, "Diversity, Diversity, Diversify," *PIMCO DC Dialogue* 4, no. 2 (2009).

20. This and the next quote are from Stacy Schaus, "Fear before Greed," *PIMCO DC Dialogue* 3, no. 11 (2008).

21. Stacy Schaus, "Shoot the Messenger?" *PIMCO DC Dialogue* 4, no. 4 (2009).

22. This and the next quotes are from Joseph Simonian and Mark Taborsky, "Asset Allocation for a Changing World," *PIMCO DC Practice Analytics* 1, no. 2 (2009).

CHAPTER 11:   Approaches to Benchmarking

1. Matt Ketchum, "Benchmarking," presented at the Custom Target-Date Strategies Summit, April 22, 2008.

2. This and the next quote are from Stacy Schaus, "Wishful Thinking." *PIMCO DC Dialogue* 4, no. 10 (2009).

3. This and the next quote are from Stacy Schaus, "Something for Everybody," *PIMCO DC Dialogue* 1, no. 4 (2006).

4. This and the next quote are from Peter Grant, "Benchmarking," presented at the Custom Target-Date Strategies Summit, April 22, 2008.

5. This and the next quote are from Stacy Schaus, "Begin with the End in Mind," *PIMCO DC Dialogue* 2, no. 5 (2007).

6. This and the next quote are from Stacy Schaus, "Simplify, Simplify, Simplify," *PIMCO DC Dialogue* 4, no. 9 (2009).

7. This and the next quotes are from Stacy Schaus, "Diversify, Diversify, Diversify," *PIMCO DC Dialogue* 4, no. 2 (2009).
8. This and the next quote are from Schaus, "Wishful Thinking."

CHAPTER 12: Financial Education, Advice, and Retirement Planning

1. J. Kim and E. T. Garman, "Financial Stress and Absenteeism: An Empirically-Derived Research Model, *Financial Counseling and Planning* 14, no. 1 (2003): 31–42.
2. This and the next quotes are from E. T. Garman et al., "Financial Stress among American Workers, Final Report: 30 Million Workers in America—One in Four—Are Seriously Financially Distressed and Dissatisfied Causing Negative Impacts on Individuals, Families and Employers" (2005). (Independent report from the authors is available at www.EthomasGarman.net.)
3. This and the next quote are from Kim and Garman. "Financial Stress and Absenteeism."
4. This and the next quote are from PSCA 52nd Annual Survey of Profit Sharing and 401(k) Plans, "Reflecting 2008 Plan Experience" (2008).
5. This and the next quotes are from Stacy Schaus, *PIMCO DC Dialogue* (2007).
6. Hewitt Associates and Financial Engines, "Help in 401(k) Plans: Is It Working and for Whom?" September 29, 2009.
7. This and the next quotes are from Stacy Schaus, "A Penny Saved Is a Penny Earned." *PIMCO DC Dialogue* 4, no. 1 (2009).
8. This and the next quote are from Stacy Schaus, "Don't Give Up," *PIMCO DC Dialogue* 4, no. 6 (2009).
9. Financial Planning Association, "Financial Planning: The Purpose and Benefits," October 5, 2009; available at: www.fpaforfinancialplanning.org/ToolsResources/Articles/FinancialPlanning/FinancialPlanningThePurposeandBenefits/.
10. Certified Financial Planners Board of Standards, "Financial Planning Process"; available at: www.cfp.net/learn/knowledgebase.asp?id=2.
11. Financial Planning Association, "How Planners Charge"; available at: www.fpaforfinancialplanning.org/FindaPlanner/HowPlannersCharge/.
12. This and the next quote are from Stacy Schaus, "A Good-Faith Contract," *PIMCO DC Dialogue* 3, no. 4 (2008).
13. Financial Planning Association Web site, www.fpaforfinancialplanning.org.
14. This and the next quote are from Stacy Schaus, "Teach Your Children Well," *PIMCO DC Dialogue* 3, no. 1 (2008).

CHAPTER 13: Retirement Income and Guarantees

1. Stacy Schaus, "A Good-Faith Contract," *PIMCO DC Dialogue* 3, no. 4 (2008).
2. Stacy Schaus, "Basics of Life," *PIMCO DC Dialogue* 4, no. 5 (2009).

3. This and the next quote are from Stacy Schaus, "Into the Future," *PIMCO DC Dialogue* 2, no. 4 (2007).
4. Profit Sharing/401k Council of America, 52nd Annual Survey Reflecting 2008 Plan Experience (2008).
5. The source for this and the following facts is Stacy Schaus, *Journal of Pension Benefits* 13, no. 1 (2005).
6. Survey conducted by Hewitt Associates.
7. Tables created by PIMCO are based on the information gathered in the "Survey Highlights: Defined Contribution Consulting Support and Trends," PIMCO DC Practice (2009).
8. This and the next quotes are from Stacy Schaus, "Stay the Course . . . or Not?" *PIMCO DC Dialogue* 4, no. 3 (2009).
9. The text in this section is taken from the Stacy Schaus, *Journal of Pension Benefits* 12, no. 4 (2005).
10. Hewitt Trends and Experience in 401(k) Plans (2009).
11. Pricing studies conducted in 2005 at Hewitt.
12. As of this writing, longevity insurance is complicated to purchase within a tax-deferred program, such as a DC plan or an IRA, given issues with required minimum distributions. However, Congressman Earl Pomeroy has proposed legislation that would change those rules.
13. Tom Streiff, "Preparing Your Participants and Retirees for an Inflationary Environment: PIMCO Introduces New Inflation Hedging Strategies including Real Income," *PIMCO Issues and Answers* (October 2009).
14. This and the next quotes are from Stacy Schaus, "Change Is Good. You Go First," *PIMCO DC Dialogue* 3, no. 3 (2008).
15. Louis Kravitz & Associates Inc., "IRS Finalizes Rules on Deemed IRAs, but Drawbacks Remain" (October 2004); available at: www.kravitzinc.com/pubsarticles/pdf/deemed_iras.pdf.
16. This and the next quotes are from Stacy Schaus, "A Good-Faith Contract," *PIMCO DC Dialogue* 3, no. 4 (2008).

Index